CE

13+

Latin

Exam Practice Questions and Answers

GALORE PARK

AN HACHETTE UK COMPANY

About the author

Nicholas Oulton taught Latin and Greek for ten years before writing the *So you really want to learn Latin* course and founding Galore Park in 1998. He is also the author of *Latin for Common Entrance Books 1–3* and the *Latin Revision Guide*. He runs the *So you really want to learn Latin* YouTube channel and believes Latin to be the most important subject in the school curriculum.

This book is dedicated to the memory of Herodotus, the manuscript-munching cocker spaniel who never had a chance to get his paws on this one.

Acknowledgements

The publishers would like to thank the Independent Schools Examinations Board for permission to use extracts, both adapted and unadapted, from recent Common Entrance papers. Thanks are also due to Stephen Anderson, Rodewald Lector in Classical Languages at New College, Oxford, for his scrupulous work in reading the proofs and suggesting numerous improvements.

Although every effort has been made to ensure that website addresses are correct at time of going to press, Galore Park cannot be held responsible for the content of any website mentioned in this book. It is sometimes possible to find a relocated web page by typing in the address of the home page for a website in the URL window of your browser. Hachette UK's policy is to use papers that are natural, renewable and recyclable products and made from wood grown in well-managed forests and other controlled sources. The logging and manufacturing processes are expected to conform to the environmental regulations of the country of origin.

Orders: **Teachers** please contact Hachette UK Distribution, Hely Hutchinson Centre, Milton Road, Didcot, Oxfordshire, OX11 7HH. Telephone: (44) 01235 400555. Email: primary@hachette.co.uk. Lines are open from 9 a.m. to 5 p.m., Monday to Friday.

Parents, Tutors please call: (44) 02031 226405 (Monday to Friday, 9:30 a.m. to 4:30 p.m.).

Email: parentenquiries@galorepark.co.uk

Visit our website at www.galorepark.co.uk for details of revision guides for Common Entrance, examination papers and Galore Park publications.

ISBN: 978 1 3983 5199 8

Typeset in India

Printed and bound by CPI Group (UK) Ltd, Croydon, CR0 4YY

A catalogue record for this title is available from the British Library

Contents

Introduction

This collection of practice exercises is designed to provide material for pupils in the early stages of learning Latin, particularly those preparing for the ISEB Common Entrance examination at Level 1, 2 or 3.

It provides extensive material for translation, both into and out of Latin, giving pupils the opportunity to revise or consolidate skills they have learnt in those courses. Much of the material, particularly the passages for translation, will be familiar to those who have used Bob Bass's excellent collection of *Practice Exercises for Levels 1/2/3*, previously published by Galore Park.

The vocabulary, grammar and syntax are deliberately geared to the CE revised syllabus. The format of the exercises often, but not always, matches that of the examination, and where appropriate the allocation of marks is the same. Obviously, where particular topics are being revised, it has not always been possible (or useful) to stick to the format and mark scheme of the examination.

In some exercises, pupils are invited to go beyond the requirements of the examination, particularly in the area of English to Latin translation. It is felt that the best way to reinforce some grammatical or syntactical topics is to translate into Latin, and this often requires the use of vocabulary (or grammar) that will not be tested in the examination.

A full set of answers to the exercises is included at the back of the book. As one would expect, these are not intended to be prescriptive, and pupils should not be penalised where their answer does not precisely match the one given, particularly in areas such as the precise form of a tense used. The verb **amabat**, for example, can regularly be translated as 'he loved', 'he was loving', or 'he used to love'; it would be wrong to penalise a pupil who selected a meaning that differed from the one given as the 'answer'. Please note also that in the answers where a verb is 3rd person singular without a nominative, 'He' has been used where of course the answer could be 'He/She/It'.

The syllabus and your exams

For CE Latin, you will sit an exam lasting one hour. You will choose one of the three levels, Level 1, Level 2 or Level 3, as agreed with your teacher.

The format of each level is the same, but the material gets harder. In each level, there are four questions worth a total of 75 marks, as follows:

Question 1 (15 marks)

A short passage of Latin will be set, on which you will be asked questions, testing your understanding of the passage. You will not be expected to write a translation of the passage, but clearly you need to have translated it in your head, in order to answer the questions.

Question 2 (30 marks)

Another, slightly longer passage will be set, continuing the story from the passage in Question 1. You will be asked to translate this passage, writing your translation on alternate lines.

Question 3 (10 marks)

Another short passage of Latin will be set, continuing the story from the earlier two passages. Questions will be set, testing your knowledge of Latin grammar and how the language works. You will be asked about the derivation of English words, and will be expected to do some simple manipulation of Latin, for example changing the tense of a verb. You will not be asked to translate this passage, but again you will find it difficult to answer the questions unless you have translated it for yourself.

Question 4 (20 marks)

You will be set four sentences to translate into Latin, using words from the English into Latin section of the prescribed vocabulary list.

A note on slavery

There are multiple references to masters and slaves in this book. These are key words for students to learn in Latin – they are in the ISEB's specification, so could appear in examination papers. However, slavery is a challenging topic, and it is important that it is approached with sensitivity. Students should be taught about the prevalence of slavery in the Roman world alongside the impact slavery has had (and still has) upon today's world.

Tips on revising

Get the best out of your brain

- Give your brain plenty of oxygen: get fresh air and exercise if you can. This will help you revise more effectively.
- Eat healthy food while you are revising. Your brain works better when you give it good fuel.
- Think positively. Give your brain positive messages so that it will want to study.
- Keep as calm as possible. Your brain operates more effectively when it is less stressed.
- Take regular breaks during your study time.
- Try to get enough sleep. Your brain will carry on sorting out what you have revised while you sleep.

Get the most from your revision

- Don't work for hours without a break. Revise for 20–30 minutes, then take a five-minute break.
- Do good things in your breaks: listen to your favourite music, eat healthy food, drink some water, do some exercise or juggle. Don't read a book, watch TV or play on the computer; it will conflict with what your brain is trying to learn.
- When you go back to your revision, review what you have just learnt.
- Regularly review the material you have learnt.

Get motivated

- Set yourself some goals and promise yourself a treat when the exams are over.
- Make the most of all the expertise and talent available to you at school and at home. If you don't understand something, ask your teacher to explain.
- Get organised. Find a quiet place to revise and make sure you have all the equipment you need.
- Use year and weekly planners to help you organise your time so that you revise all subjects equally. (Available for download from www.galorepark.co.uk.)
- Use topic and subject checklists to help you keep on top of what you are revising. (Available for download from www.galorepark.co.uk.)

Know what to expect in the exam

- Use past papers to familiarise yourself with the format of the exam.
- Make sure you understand the language examiners use.

Before the exam

- Have all your equipment and pens ready the night before.
- Make sure you are at your best by getting a good night's sleep before the exam.
- Have a good breakfast in the morning.
- Take some water into the exam if you are allowed.
- Think positively and try to keep calm.

During the exam

- Have a watch on your desk. Work out how much time you need to allocate to each question and try to stick to it.
- Make sure you read and understand the instructions on the front of the exam paper.
- Allow some time at the start to read and consider the questions carefully before writing anything.
- Read every question at least twice. Don't rush into answering before you have a chance to think about it.
- Leave yourself a little time at the end to check over your work.

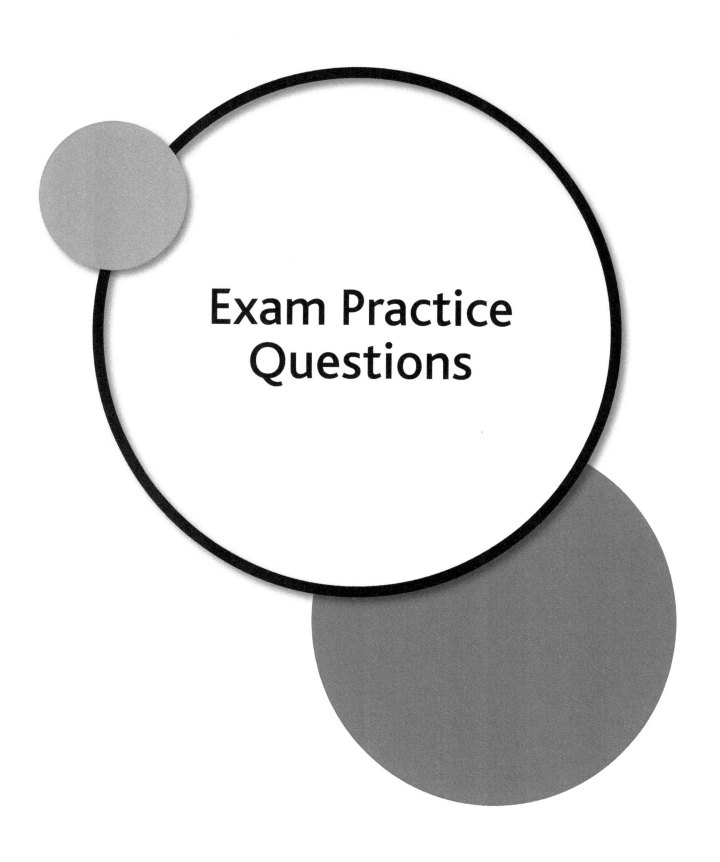

Exam Practice
Questions

Level 1

Chapter 1: 1st conjugation verbs and **sum**, present tense; 1st declension nouns, nominative and accusative

Exercise 1.1

Translate the following Latin sentences into English.

1	femina filias non spectat.	(5)
2	poeta agricolam superat.	(4)
3	nauta insulam amat.	(4)
4	regina poetas et agricolas spectat.	(6)
5	sagittas et pecuniam paras.	(5)
6	puellas et agricolas non vocatis.	(6)

Total: 30

Exercise 1.2

Translate the following English sentences into Latin.

1	We do not love the woman.	(4)
2	The sailor watches the queen.	(4)
3	The girl and the woman are preparing a letter.	(6)
4	The sailors do not call the girl.	(5)
5	Girls love spears.	(4)
6	The girl and the woman do not love the sailor.	(7)

Total: 30

Exercise 1.3

Translate the following Latin sentences into English.

1	nautae insulas amant.	(4)
2	poetae agricolam superant.	(4)
3	regina poetam et agricolam spectat.	(6)
4	puellae et agricolae aquam parant.	(6)
5	feminae filiam non spectant.	(5)
6	aquam et pecuniam paramus.	(5)

Total: 30

Exercise 1.4

Translate the following English sentences into Latin.

1	The queen does not prepare the dinner.	(5)
2	The sailor looks at the money.	(4)
3	The girl is not preparing dinner.	(5)
4	The sailors do not love spears.	(5)
5	We do not look at the queen.	(4)
6	The queens and the sailors do not love the woman.	(7)

Total: 30

Exercise 1.5

Translate the following Latin sentences into English.

1 feminae et agricola festinant. (5)
2 regina poetas et agricolas amat. (6)
3 nos insulam spectamus. (4)
4 incolae viam parant. (4)
5 ego patriam incolarum amo. (5)
6 Flavia et agricola nautam vocant. (6)

Total: 30

Exercise 1.6

Translate the following English sentences into Latin.

1 Sailors love the money and the dinners. (6)
2 The girls do not look at the money. (5)
3 The sailors are preparing the street. (4)
4 The queen does not love the sailor. (5)
5 You (sing.) do not call the woman. (4)
6 The queen and the woman love the sailors. (6)

Total: 30

Exercise 1.7

Study the passage below (do not write a translation) and answer the questions which follow. Complete sentences are not required.

A sailor takes a fancy to Flavia; Flavia takes a fancy to him, too.

1   Flavia ambulat. Flavia ambulat et cantat. Flavia non laborat. nauta ambulat. nauta ambulat et cantat. nauta non navigat. nauta Flaviam spectat. nauta Flaviam amat. Flavia nautam spectat. Flavia nautam amat.

5   Flavia clamat. Flavia nautam vocat. nauta clamat. nauta Flaviam vocat. Flavia et nauta cenam parant. Flavia et nauta cantant. Flavia et nauta non pugnant. nauta Flaviam amat et Flavia nautam amat.

1 Flavia ambulat et cantat. (line 1)
   What is Flavia doing? (2)
2 nauta ambulat et cantat. (lines 1–2)
   What is the sailor doing? (2)
3 nauta non navigat (line 2)
   What else do we know about the sailor? (1)
4 nauta Flaviam spectat. nauta Flaviam amat. (line 2)
   What does the sailor think when he sees Flavia? (2)
5 Flavia nautam spectat. Flavia nautam amat. (lines 2–3)
   Does Flavia think the same of the sailor? (1)
6 Flavia clamat. Flavia nautam vocat. nauta clamat. nauta Flaviam vocat. (line 4)
   How do Flavia and the sailor communicate with each other? (3)
7 Flavia et nauta cenam parant. Flavia et nauta cantant. Flavia et nauta non pugnant. nauta Flaviam amat et Flavia nautam amat. (lines 4–6)
   Describe in your own words what happens at the end of the story. (4)

Total: 15

Exercise 1.8

Translate the passage below into good English.

A goddess interrupts a romantic meal.

1 Marcus est agricola. agricola laborat. Flavia est puella. Flavia agricolam amat.

Marcus Flaviam spectat. Flaviam amat. Flavia cenam parat. agricola cenas amat.

5 Flavia agricolam spectat. agricola cantat et laborat. agricola terram parat et villam aedificat. villam aedificat et viam parat. Flavia villas amat. Flavia agricolas amat.

Minerva dea est. dea agricolam et puellam spectat.
10 dea agricolam non amat. dea patriam non amat. incolas non amat. incolae deam non amant. dea puellam et agricolam vocat. 'dea sum,' inquit.   inquit = she says
'dea Minerva sum.'

Marcus et Flavia non cantant. non laborant. Flavia
15 cenam non parat. Marcus aquam non parat. agricola deam non amat. puella deam non amat. deam Minervam non amant.

Total: 100

Exercise 1.9

Study the passage below and answer the questions which follow. Complete sentences are not required.

Marcus and Flavia get their dinner together after all.

1 Marcus est agricola. Flavia est puella. ancilla est. Marcus et Flaviam deam Minervam non amant.

Minerva est dea. Minerva agricolas non amat. ancillas non amat. incolas non amat. dea agriolam et puellam spectat. Marcus et Flavia laborant. Marcus Flaviam vocat. 'agricola sum' inquit. 'agricola sum et cenam amo.'

5 Flavia agricolam spectat. deam non amat sed cenam amat. Flavia agricolam vocat. 'laboras sed cenam amas. aquam amas. deam non amas. deam non amo. sed cenam amamus.' agricola et puella villam intrant. cenam amant. dea agricolam non spectat. puellam non spectat. cenam non spectat.

1 This question tests your knowledge of the origins of English words. Complete the table below. One example has been completed for you.   (4)

Latin word from passage	Meaning of the Latin word	An English word which comes from the Latin word
spectat (line 3)	watches	spectator
vocat (line 3)		
aquam (line 6)		

→

2 **deam** (line 1) What is the case of this noun?
    A nominative
    B accusative
    C genitive
    D ablative   (1)

3 **spectat** (line 3) This means *she watches*. How would you say in Latin *they watch*?
    A spectatis
    B spectas
    C spectamus
    D spectant   (1)

4 **laboras** (line 5)
    a) Give the person of this verb.
        A 1st
        B 2nd
        C 3rd   (1)
    b) Give the number of this verb.
        A singular
        B plural   (1)

5 **intrant** (line 7) What is the object of this verb?
    A agricola
    B ancilla
    C et
    D villam   (1)

6 **non spectat** (line 7) What is the subject of this verb?
    A dea
    B agricolam
    C non   (1)

Total: 10

Exercise 1.10

Translate the following English sentences into Latin.

1 The sailors are building a street.   (4)
2 The women look at the letter.   (4)
3 The girl does not love the queen.   (5)
4 The girl and the woman prepare the dinner.   (6)
5 You (pl.) call the woman and the sailor.   (5)
6 The queen loves the girl and the woman.   (6)

Total: 30

Chapter 2: 1st conjugation verbs and sum, imperfect tense; 1st declension nouns, all cases; prepositions

Exercise 2.1

Translate the following Latin sentences into English.

1	femina patriam laudabat.	(4)
2	poeta agricolam necabat.	(4)
3	nauta aquam non portabat.	(5)
4	regina pecuniam feminae dabat.	(5)
5	agricola in via stabat.	(5)
6	feminae et agricola in villa habitabant.	(7)

Total: 30

Exercise 2.2

Translate the following English sentences into Latin.

1	The women were carrying money.	(4)
2	The sailor was not praising the queen.	(5)
3	The girl was entering the street.	(4)
4	The sailors and women do not carry spears.	(6)
5	We were not killing girls.	(4)
6	The girl and the woman were not praising the sailors.	(7)

Total: 30

Exercise 2.3

Give the case and number of the underlined words and then translate the following sentences into English.

1	<u>nautae</u> ad insulam navigabant.	(1 + 6)
2	poetae contra <u>agricolas</u> pugnabant.	(1 + 5)
3	cum <u>poeta</u> et agricola ambulabas.	(1 + 6)
4	ad agricolam <u>aquam</u> portabant.	(1 + 5)
5	<u>feminae</u> filia cantabat.	(1 + 4)
6	pecuniam <u>reginae</u> dabamus.	(1 + 4)

Total: 36

Exercise 2.4

Give the case and number of the underlined words and then translate the following sentences into Latin.

1	<u>Flavia</u> was preparing the dinner.	(1 + 4)
2	The sailor was looking at the <u>money</u>.	(1 + 4)
3	The girls and the <u>woman</u> were preparing dinner.	(1 + 6)
4	Sailors and <u>queens</u> do not praise spears.	(1 + 6)
5	We were not watching the <u>queen</u>.	(1 + 4)
6	The girls and the <u>sailors</u> were carrying money.	(1 + 6)

Total: 36

Exercise 2.5

Give the person and number of the underlined verbs and then translate the following Latin sentences into English.

1. feminae in villam <u>festinabant</u>. (1 + 5)
2. incolae prope villam <u>laborabant</u>. (1 + 5)
3. nautae ex insula <u>navigabant</u>. (1 + 5)
4. incolae per vias <u>festinabant</u>. (1 + 5)
5. agricola trans insulam <u>festinabat</u>. (1 + 5)
6. pecuniam et sagittas <u>portabat</u>. (1 + 5)

Total: 36

Exercise 2.6

Give the person and number of the underlined verbs and then translate the following English sentences into Latin.

1. We <u>loved</u> and praised the queen. (1 + 6)
2. They were not <u>carrying</u> money. (1 + 4)
3. The sailors were not <u>killing</u> the woman. (1 + 5)
4. The queen does not <u>praise</u> the sailors. (1 + 5)
5. You (pl.) were not <u>praising</u> the women. (1 + 4)
6. The queen <u>praised</u> the sailor and the girls. (1 + 6)

Total: 36

Exercise 2.7

1. Study the passage below (do not write a translation) and answer the questions which follow. Complete sentences are not required.

Marcus and Flavia share an intimate dinner together.

1   Marcus erat agricola. Flavia erat puella. Marcus ad villam Flaviae festinabat. Marcus aquam portabat. agricola in villam ambulabat. Flavia in villa laborabat. cenam parabat. Flavia cenam parabat et Marcus cantabat.

     Flavia prope agricolam laborabat. agricola prope Flaviam stabat. Flavia cum agricola
5   cantabat. agricola cum puella laborabat. puella cenam parabat et agricola aquam portabat.

     Marcus cenam laudat. Marcus Flaviam laudat. agricola et puella cenam amant et cantant.

     e villa festinant agricola et puella et in via stant. per viam festinant. agricola puellam amat. agricola cenam amat. agricolam puella amat. cenam puella amat.

    a) Marcus ad villam Flaviae festinabat. (line 1)
        What was Marcus doing at the start of the story? (2)
    b) Marcus aquam portabat (lines 1–2)
        How was Marcus helping? (1)
    c) Flavia cenam parabat et Marcus cantabat. (lines 2–3)
        When Marcus went into the country house, who was doing what? (2)
    d) Flavia prope agricolam laborabat. agricola prope Flaviam stabat. (line 4)
        How do we find out in these lines that Marcus and Flavia enjoyed each other's company? (2)
    e) Marcus cenam laudat. Marcus Flaviam laudat. agricola et puella cenam amant et cantant. (line 6)
        How do we find out that the dinner was a success? (3)
    f) e villa festinant agricola et puella et in via stant. (line 7)
        What happens after dinner? (2)
    g) agricola puellam amat. agricola cenam amat. (lines 7–8)
        What are we told about the girl and the dinner in these lines? (2)
    h) cenam puella amat. (line 8)
        What are we told about the dinner in this sentence? (1)

Total: 15
➜

2   Translate the passage above into good English.

Total: 30

3   Study the passage above and answer the questions which follow. Complete sentences are not required.
    a) This question tests your knowledge of the origins of English words.
        Complete the table below. One example has been completed for you.   **(4)**

Latin word from passage	Meaning of the Latin word	An English word which comes from the Latin word
portabat (line 2)	he carried	portable
laborabat (line 4)		
viam (line 7)		

    b) **ad villam** (line 1) Which case is **villam** in, and why?
         A nominative, because it is the subject
         B accusative, because it is the subject
         C accusative, because it is the object
         D accusative, because it is after the preposition **ad** **(1)**
    c) **ambulabat** (line 2) In which tense is this verb?
         A present
         B imperfect
         C nominative
         D perfect **(1)**
    d) **puella cenam parabat et agricola aquam portabat.** (line 5) This sentence has two objects. Which two of the following are the objects in this sentence?
         A puella
         B cenam
         C agricola
         D aquam **(2)**
    e) **agricolam puella amat.** (line 7) Which word is the subject of this sentence?
         A agricolam
         B puella
         C amat **(1)**
    f) **amat** (line 7) This means *she loves*. How would you say in Latin *she was loving*?
         A amant
         B amabant
         C amabat
         D amabit **(1)**

Total: 10

4   Translate the following sentences into Latin.
    a) They were carrying money. **(3)**
    b) The woman was praising the queen. **(4)**
    c) They are watching the girls. **(3)**
    d) We were carrying spears. **(3)**
    e) The queen was shouting and calling the girls. **(7)**

Total: 20

Chapter 3: 2nd conjugation verbs, present and imperfect tense; present infinitive; 2nd declension nouns; adjectives in -us and -er

Exercise 3.1

Translate the following Latin sentences into English.

1	femina dominum timebat.	(4)
2	poeta equum non habet.	(5)
3	nauta te videbat.	(4)
4	libertus gladium domino dabat.	(5)
5	Marcus in templo stabat.	(5)
6	pueri et puellae in villa ridebant.	(7)

Total: 30

Exercise 3.2

Translate the following English sentences into Latin.

1	The master was not carrying a sword.	(5)
2	They were not warning the Romans.	(4)
3	The boy was entering the temple.	(4)
4	The sailors and women do not fear the schoolmaster.	(7)
5	We were not destroying the towns.	(4)
6	The friends were praising the wine and the books.	(6)

Total: 30

Exercise 3.3

Translate the following Latin sentences into English.

1	Romani ad agrum non festinabant.	(6)
2	pueri contra magistrum pugnabant.	(5)
3	multi liberti cum poeta bono ridebant.	(7)
4	puer fessus ad templum magnum ambulabat.	(7)
5	feminae pericula belli non timebant.	(6)
6	pecuniam vestram videbamus.	(4)

Total: 35

Exercise 3.4

Translate the following English sentences into Latin.

1	The boys and girls do not have books.	(7)
2	The schoolmaster was warning the boys.	(4)
3	The Romans were building a town.	(4)
4	Horses do not fear water.	(5)
5	They were not destroying the temples.	(4)
6	The slave-boys and slave-girls feared the master.	(6)

Total: 30

Exercise 3.5

Translate the following Latin sentences into English.

1 Graeci scuta Romanorum timebant. (5)
2 incolae prope templum sacrum cantabant. (6)
3 nautae mali a magna insula navigabant. (7)
4 multi incolae deam nostram timebant. (6)
5 dominus saevus trans agrum festinabat. (6)
6 regina pulchra nos spectabat. (5)

Total: 35

Exercise 3.6

Translate the following English sentences into Latin.

1 We have books and horses. (5)
2 They did not fear the Romans. (4)
3 The Romans were not killing the boys. (5)
4 The schoolmaster does not fear the boy. (5)
5 You (pl.) were not destroying the temple. (4)
6 We praised the queen but feared the master. (7)

Total: 30

Exercise 3.7

Study the passage below (do not write a translation) and answer the questions which follow. Complete sentences are not required.

Marcus and Flavia enjoy each other's company.

1   Marcus erat agricola. Flavia erat puella pulchra. Marcus et Flavia amici erant. Minerva erat dea saeva. deam Minervam amici timebant.

    olim cenam magnam Flavia parabat. Marcus cenam amat. multum vinum Flavia parabat. Marcus vinum amat. Marcus Flaviam videt et clamat.

5   'Flavia, Flavia!' inquit. 'cenam amo, vinum amo, Flaviam amo!'

    Flavia ridet et ad murum villae festinat. agricolam videt et ridet. Flavia agricolam amat. Marcus in villam intrabat et cenam bonam laudabat. Marcus Flaviam laudabat. Marcus Flaviam laudabat et ridebat.

1 Marcus erat agricola. (line 1)
   How is Marcus described? (2)
2 Flavia erat puella pulchra. (line 1)
   How is Flavia described? (2)
3 Minerva erat dea saeva. (lines 1–2)
   Who was Minerva? (1)
4 deam Minervam amici timebant. (line 2)
   What did the friends think of Minerva? (2)
5 multum vinum Flavia parabat. Marcus vinum amat. (lines 3–4)
   How did Flavia make sure that Marcus would enjoy the dinner? (1)
6 'cenam amo, vinum amo, Flaviam amo!' (line 5)
   How does Marcus express his appreciation? (3)
7 Marcus in villam intrabat et cenam bonam laudabat. Marcus Flaviam laudabat. Marcus Flaviam laudabat et ridebat. (lines 7–8)
   Describe in your own words what happens at the end of the story (4)

Total: 15

Exercise 3.8

Translate the passage below into good English.

Marcus shows Flavia what he thinks of her and Flavia responds.

1   Marcus prope Flaviam sedet. Flavia est puella
     pulchra. Marcus Flaviam spectat. Marcus Flaviam
     amat. Marcus est agricola. Marcus est agricola
     pulcher. Flavia prope Marcum sedet. Flavia Marcum
5   spectat. agricolam pulchrum amat.

     Flavia Marco multum vinum dat. cibum et multum
     vinum agricolae pulchro dat. Marcus vinum
     et cibum bonum amat. Flavia Marcum <u>basiat</u>.
     Marcus <u>rubet</u> et e villa festinat. trans agrum
10   magnum et per viam festinat sed ridet et cantat.
     Flaviam amat.

basio, -are = I kiss
rubeo, -ere = I blush

Total: 30

Exercise 3.9

Study the passage below and answer the questions which follow. Complete sentences are not required.

Marcus is given a lesson in bravery.

1   Marcus per viam festinabat. per viam festinabat et fessus erat. prope muros templi magni
     stabat. dominum videbat. dominum saevum videbat et timebat. dominus equum magnum
     habebat et ridebat.

     Marcus in templum intrabat. parvum puerum videbat. puer librum sacrum habebat et cum
5   amico ridebat. Marcus puerum vocabat et monebat. 'dominus in via est!' inquit. 'dominus
     saevus cum equo stabat. dominum timeo.'

     respondebat puer 'dominus non est saevus' inquit. 'dominum malum non timeo.'

     Marcus et puer e templo festinabant et in viam ambulabant. dominus prope viam stabat et
     flebat. dominus miser est. amicus pueri e templo festinabat et dominum vocabat.

10   'dominos Romanos' inquit 'non timeo. puer Romanus sum.'

1 This question tests your knowledge of the origins of English words. Complete the table below. One
   example has been completed for you.   (4)

Latin word from passage	Meaning of the Latin word	An English word which comes from the Latin word
muros (line 1)	walls	mural
videbat (line 2)		
miser (line 9)		

2 per viam (line 1) Which case is **viam** in and why?
   A nominative, because it is the subject
   B accusative, because it is the subject
   C accusative, because it is the object
   D accusative, because it is after the preposition **per**   (1)

3 **magnum** (line 2) Which part of speech is this word?
   A noun
   B verb
   C adjective
   D preposition   (1)

➡

4   puer librum sacrum habebat et cum amico ridebat. (lines 4–5)
   a) Which word is the object in this sentence:
        A   puer
        B   librum
        C   cum
        D   amico
   b) In which case is the word **sacrum**?
        A   nominative
        B   accusative
        C   genitive
        D   ablative   (2)

5   'dominum malum non timeo.' (line 7) This means *I do not fear the bad master.* How would you change
    the word **malum** if you wished to say in Latin *I do not fear the bad masters*?
        A   malus
        B   mali
        C   malos
        D   malis   (1)

6   'dominos Romanos' inquit 'non timeo.' (line 10) **non timeo** means *I do not fear.* How would you say in
    Latin *You (pl.) do not fear*?
        A   non timebam
        B   non timetis
        C   non times
        D   non timemus   (1)

                                                                            Total: 10

Exercise 3.10

Translate the following sentences into Latin.

1   The Romans fear the horse.   (4)
2   The master was looking at the book.   (4)
3   They were preparing the swords.   (3)
4   I was not carrying books.   (4)
5   You (pl.) have wine and horses.   (5)

                                                                            Total: 20

Chapter 4: 3rd and 4th conjugation verbs; questions; adverbs

Exercise 4.1

Give the 1st person singular of the present tense of the underlined verbs and then translate the following Latin sentences into English.

1	puer bonus librum <u>legebat</u>.	(1 + 5)
2	e templo <u>discedemus</u>.	(1 + 4)
3	Romani per agrum <u>currebant</u>.	(1 + 5)
4	libertus bonus epistulam domino <u>legebat</u>.	(1 + 6)
5	regina saeva incolas <u>regebat</u>.	(1 + 5)
6	amicos ad templum <u>ducebatis</u>.	(1 + 5)

Total: 36

Exercise 4.2

Give the 1st person singular of the present tense of the underlined verbs and then translate the following Latin sentences into English.

1	puellae fessae <u>dormiunt</u>.	(1 + 4)
2	ad templum magnum Romani <u>veniunt</u>.	(1 + 6)
3	poetam pulchrum <u>audimus</u>.	(1 + 4)
4	prope murum oppidi magni <u>dormit</u>.	(1 + 6)
5	trans aquam cum nauta <u>venis</u>.	(1 + 6)
6	verba magistri <u>auditis</u>.	(1 + 4)

Total: 36

Exercise 4.3

Give the 1st person singular of the present tense of the underlined verbs and then translate the following Latin sentences into English.

1	cur verba domini saevi <u>timetis</u>?	(1 + 5)
2	ubi <u>est</u> amicus bonus agricolae?	(1 + 6)
3	quis in oppido novo <u>regit</u>?	(1 + 6)
4	Marcusne in villa tua <u>laborabat</u>?	(1 + 7)
5	feminaene equum <u>timebant</u>?	(1 + 5)
6	cur pecuniam pueris <u>dabat</u>?	(1 + 5)

Total: 40

Exercise 4.4

Give an English word that is derived from the underlined Latin words and then translate the following Latin sentences into English.

1	<u>amici</u> vinum in villa bibebant.	(1 + 6)
2	Romani <u>dominum</u> magnopere timebant.	(1 + 5)
3	<u>agricolae</u> igitur ex agris discedunt.	(1 + 6)
4	cur <u>dormit</u> poeta in templo?	(1 + 6)
5	magistri saevi <u>pueros</u> numquam amant.	(1 + 6)
6	quid ad villam <u>ducis</u>?	(1 + 5)

Total: 40

Exercise 4.5

Give the part of speech of the underlined words and then translate the following Latin sentences into English.

1	librosne <u>sacros</u> amatis?	(1 + 5)
2	cur aquam altam <u>timebat</u> nauta?	(1 + 6)
3	reginam <u>novam</u> incolae timebant.	(1 + 5)
4	ubi <u>sunt</u> sagittae et scuta?	(1 + 6)
5	cibum et vinum Marcus <u>magnopere</u> laudabat.	(1 + 7)
6	dominus igitur <u>pecuniam</u> movebat.	(1 + 5)

Total: 40

Exercise 4.6

Translate the following English sentences into Latin.

1	They do not have horses.	(4)
2	You (pl.) do not fear the sailors.	(4)
3	The Romans were praising the girls and women.	(6)
4	The boys do not fear the schoolmaster.	(5)
5	You (sing.) do not like the dinner.	(4)
6	We have swords but fear the Romans.	(7)

Total: 30

Exercise 4.7

Study the passage below (do not write a translation) and answer the questions which follow. Complete sentences are not required.

Trouble in the classroom.

1   Sextus et Flavia amici sunt. in <u>ludo</u> laborant. scribunt. Sextus Flaviam non amat. Flaviam non amat quod <u>superba</u> est. puellas superbas non amat. Flavia Sextum non amat. Sextum non amat quod
5   puer <u>molestus</u> est. Flavia pueros <u>molestos</u> non amat. subito Sextus Flaviam <u>vexat</u>. Sextus puellas saepe <u>vexat</u>. Flavia igitur Sextum <u>castigat</u>.

Sextus Flaviam iterum <u>vexat</u>. pugnant. magister Sextum et Flaviam videt. 'quid facitis?' clamat.
10   'cur pugnatis?' Sextus et Flavia non iam pugnant. magistrum spectant. 'Sextus me semper <u>vexat</u>,' respondet Flavia. 'Flavia me semper <u>vexat</u>,' respondet Sextus. magister iratus est. Sextum punit. Sextus <u>flet</u>. magister Flaviam <u>quoque</u> punit.
15   Flavia quoque flet. Flavia et Sextus non laeti sunt. magistrum non amant.

ludus, -i, m. = school

superbus, -a, -um = proud, arrogant
molestus, -a, -um = annoying
vexo, -are = I annoy
prater + acc. = besides
castigo, -are = I chastise

punio, -ire = I punish
fleo, flere = I cry, weep
quoque = also

1   Sextus et Flavia amici sunt. (line 1)
    How are Sextus and Flavia described?   (2)
2   in ludo laborant. scribunt. (lines 1–2)
    What are they doing?   (2)
3   Flaviam non amat quod puella superba est. puellas superbas non amat. (lines 2–3)
    Why doesn't Sextus like Flavia?   (1)

→

4 subito Sextus Flaviam vexat. Sextus puellas saepe vexat. Flavia igitur Sextum castigat. (lines 5–7)
How does Flavia respond to Sextus's irritating behaviour? (2)

5 magister Sextum et Flaviam videt. 'quid facitis?' clamat. 'cur pugnatis?' (lines 8–10)
What happens when the schoolmaster sees what is going on? (2)

6 magister iratus est. Sextum punit. Sextus flet. (lines 13–14)
How does the schoolmaster react with Sextus, and what effect does this have on Sextus? (3)

7 Flavia et Sextus non laeti sunt. magistrum non amant. (lines 15–16)
How do Sextus and Flavia feel and what opinion of the schoolmaster do they have at the end of the story? (3)

Total: 15

Exercise 4.8

Translate the passage below into good English.

Marcus finds Flavia crying.

1	Flavia amicum habet. amicus Flaviae Marcus est. Marcus amicam habet. amica Marci Flavia est. Marcus per viam ambulat. Flavia <u>quoque</u> per viam ambulat. Flavia ad <u>ludum</u> festinat. <u>flet</u>. flet quod	quoque = also ludus, -i, m. = school
5	Sextus <u>eam</u> in ludo semper <u>vexat</u>. Sextum non amat quod puer malus est. Marcus Flaviam videt. 'Flavia,' statim rogat Marcus, 'cur fles?' Flavia Marco respondet: 'O Marce, fleo quod Sextus in ludo me <u>vexat</u>. deinde magister me <u>punit</u>. vir malus est.	fleo, -ere = I cry, weep eam = her vexo, -are = I annoy punio, -ire = I punish
10	Sextum numquam punit. Sextum non amo. puer malus est.' Marcus iratus est quod Flavia flet. Flaviam <u>basiat</u>. Flavia iam laeta est quod Marcus eam basiat. rident amici. Marcus et Flavia ad ludum ambulant. laeti sunt.	basio, -are = I kiss

Total: 30

Exercise 4.9

Study the passage below and answer the questions which follow. Complete sentences are not required.

Marcus teaches Sextus a lesson.

1 Flavia cum Marco ad ludum ambulat. Flavia Marcum amat. amicus bonus est. Flavia Sextum non amat. puer malus est. iam ad ludum appropinquant. multi discipuli prope ludum ludunt. Marcus Sextum non videt.

Marcus ludum intrat. ibi pueri laborant. libros legunt et scribunt. Marcus pueros spectat.
5 Sextum videt et ridet. ad Sextum currit. Sextum pulsat. Sextum iterum iterumque pulsat. 'hercle!' clamat Sextus. 'cur me pulsas?' Marcus desistit.

'te pulso quod tu Flaviam semper vexas,' respondet Marcus. 'Flavia amica mea est. tu puer malus es, Sexte!'

Marcus Sextum iterum pulsat, deinde discedit. Sextus non laetus est. flet. Marcus puer malus est.

➔

1   This question tests your knowledge of the origins of English words. Complete the table below. One
    example has been completed for you.   (4)

Latin word from passage	Meaning of the Latin word	An English word which comes from the Latin word
ambulat (line 1)	she walks	ambulatory
videt (line 3)		
libros (line 4)		

2   **ad ludum** (line 1) Which case is **ludum** in and why?
    A   nominative, because it is the subject
    B   accusative, because it is the subject
    C   accusative, because it is the object
    D   accusative, because it is after the preposition **ad**   (1)
3   **bonus** (line 1) In which case is this adjective?
    A   nominative
    B   accusative
    C   genitive
    D   ablative   (1)
4   **currit** (line 5) Which conjugation is this verb?

    A   1st
    B   2nd
    C   3rd
    D   4th   (1)
5   **laetus** (line 9) Which part of speech is this word:
    A   noun
    B   verb
    C   adjective
    D   adverb   (1)
6   **est** (line 9) From which verb does this come?
    A   edo
    B   moneo
    C   et
    D   sum   (1)
7   **respondet Marcus.** (line 7) This means *Marcus responds*. How would you say in Latin *Marcus was
    responding*?
    A   respondat
    B   respondebant
    C   respondebat
    D   respondit   (1)

Total: 10

Chapter 5: Mixed conjugation verbs; numerals 1–10; filius, deus and vir

Exercise 5.1

Translate the following Latin sentences into English.

1 Troiani Graecos semper timebant. (5)
2 diu Graeci Troiam capere cupiebant. (6)
3 consilium Graecorum Troiani non timent. (6)
4 'quid facitis, Graeci?' inquiunt. 'cur equum in aquam iacitis?' (10)
5 dea saeva patriam Troianorum numquam amabat. (7)
6 Troiani oppidum novum aedificare cupiebant. (6)

Total: 40

Exercise 5.2

Translate the following Latin sentences into English.

1 quattuor filios habebat dominus clarus. (6)
2 septem templa in oppido magno aedificabant. (7)
3 novem filias habebat regina pulchra. (6)
4 puer parvus octo libros in villam portabat. (8)
5 ad Graeciam igitur nautae navigabant. (6)
6 'Troiamne capere cupitis?' inquit dominus. (7)

Total: 40

Exercise 5.3

Identify the Latin subject in the following sentences. If the subject is 'in the verb', write down the Latin verb that contains the subject. Then translate the sentences into English.

1 'cur virum malum timebas?' (1 + 5)
2 tres Troiani ex insula parva navigabant. (1 + 7)
3 dominus tuus consilium novum numquam capit. (1 + 7)
4 amici vestri multa consilia capiebant. (1 + 6)
5 quinque templa in oppido aedificare cupiebat. (1 + 7)
6 nauta fessus hastas novas in viam iaciebat. (1 + 8)

Total: 46

Exercise 5.4

Identify the Latin object in the following sentences. If there is no object, write 'none'. Then translate the following Latin sentences into English.

1 deus saevus filios deae necare cupit. (1 + 7)
2 in villa magna dominus fessus dormiebat. (1 + 7)
3 in libro pueri miseri non scribebat. (1 + 7)
4 agricola Romanus sex agros habebat. (1 + 6)
5 pueri miseri in libro non scribebant. (1 + 7)
6 viri saevi nos magnopere timebant. (1 + 6)

Total: 46

Exercise 5.5

Identify the Latin preposition in the following sentences. If there is no preposition, write 'none'. Then translate the sentences into English.

1	in villa cum novem amicis nauta bibebat.	(1 + 8)
2	servus domini decem equos trans agrum ducebat.	(1 + 8)
3	Romani templum sacrum in oppido novo aedificabant.	(1 + 8)
4	tres filiae magistri in via cantabant.	(1 + 7)
5	novus magister pueris libros dabat.	(1 + 6)
6	ubi est filius clarus Troiani saevi?	(1 + 7)

Total: 50

Exercise 5.6

Translate the following English sentences into Latin.

1	The son fears the man.	(4)
2	They hear the Romans.	(3)
3	The Romans love the gods.	(4)
4	The Roman sees the horses.	(4)
5	You (pl.) do not like the men.	(4)
6	The god loves the son and the woman.	(6)

Total: 25

Exercise 5.7

Study the passage below (do not write a translation) and answer the questions which follow. Complete sentences are not required.

Marcus and Flavia encounter some drunken sailors.

1 Marcus et Flavia in oppido sunt. <u>tabernam</u> intrant.   taberna, -ae, f. = inn
    tabernam intrant et sedent. cibum consumere et vinum
    bibere cupiunt. in taberna manent. cibus bonus est. Flavia
    cibum amat. vinum bonum est. Marcus et Flavia laeti sunt.

5 quattuor nautae quoque in taberna sunt. prope Marcum
    et Flaviam stant. nautae vinum bonum amant et multum
    bibunt. mox nautae <u>ebrii</u> sunt. Flavia nautas ebrios spectat.   ebrius, -a, -um = drunk
    nautas timet. Marco itaque, 'Marce,' inquit, 'nautae ebrii
    sunt. <u>perterrita</u> sum. discedere cupio.' Marcus nautas   perterritus, -a, -um = terrified
10 spectat. nautas spectat et iratus est. Marcus Flaviam e
    taberna ducit. quattuor nautae quoque e taberna ambulant.

1 Marcus et Flavia in oppido sunt. tabernam intrant. (line 1)
   Where are Sextus and Flavia and what are they doing?   (2)
2 cibum consumere et vinum bibere cupiunt. (lines 2–3)
   Why do they go into the inn?   (2)
3 cibus bonus est Flavia cibum amat. vinum bonum est. Marcus et Flavia laeti sunt. (lines 3–4)
   Why are Marcus and Flavia happy?   (1)
4 quattuor nautae quoque in taberna sunt. prope Marcum et Flaviam stant. (lines 5–6)
   Who else is in the inn and what do they do?   (3)
5 mox nautae ebrii sunt. (line 7)
   What happens when the sailors drink the wine?   (2)
6 Flavia nautas ebrios spectat. nautas timet. (lines 7–8)
   What effect does this have on Flavia?   (2)
7 Marcus nautas spectat. nautas spectat et iratus est. Marcus Flaviam e taberna ducit. (lines 9–11)
   What does Marcus think of the sailors and what does he do to make Flavia feel better?   (3)

Total: 15

Exercise 5.8

Translate the passage below into good English.

The drunken sailors confront Marcus and Flavia; Marcus tells them to get lost.

1   Marcus et Flavia e <u>taberna</u> ambulant quod Flavia
     quattuor nautas <u>ebrios</u> timet. nautae quoque e
     taberna ambulant. 'Marce! nautas timeo,' clamat Flavia.
     festinare constituunt. nautae quoque per viam iam
5   festinant. 'nautas timeo, Marce!' clamat Flavia. currunt.
     nautae quoque currunt. sic nautae Marcum et Flaviam
     mox capiunt. nauta clamat: 'quid hic facitis?'

     Marcus respondet: '<u>domum</u> ambulamus.' nauta
     rogat: 'quis est puella?' Marcus iratus respondet:
10   'puella Flavia est. amica mea est.'

     nauta clamat: 'amica tua? Flavia pulchra est. amasne
     me, Flavia?'

     nautae rident. 'ubi est pecunia vestra?' clamat nauta.
     Marcus iam magnopere iratus est. 'pecuniam non
15   habemus,' respondet. subito nautae discedunt.

taberna, -ae, f. = inn
ebrius, -a, -um = drunk

domum = (to) home

Total: 30

Exercise 5.9

Study the passage below and answer the questions which follow. Complete sentences are not required.

Marcus's horsey friend to the rescue.

1   Flavia timet. Flavia nautas saevos timet et fugere cupit. Marcus puellam pulchram per viam
     ducit et domum festinat.
     Marcus Flaviam vocat et 'cur times?' inquit.
     'nautae ebrii et saevi sunt. quattuor nautas saevos timeo.'
5   Marcus Flaviam per viam ducit et ad villam amici festinat. amicus Marci equos habet. nautae
     aquam magnopere amant sed equos timent. amicus Marci novem equos habet et ridet.
     'nautae mali equos meos magnopere timent. tuti estis.'

1   This question tests your knowledge of the origins of English words. Complete the table below. One
    example has been completed for you.   (4)

Latin word from passage	Meaning of the Latin word	An English word which comes from the Latin word
fugere (line 1)	to flee	fugitive
nautae (line 4)		
amici (line 5)		

2   saevos (line 4) Which case is this noun in and why?
    A nominative, because it agrees with the subject
    B accusative, because it agrees with the subject
    C accusative, because it agrees with the object
    D genitive, because it means *of*   (1)
3   pulchram (line 1) Which part of speech is this word?
    A noun
    B verb
    C adjective
    D preposition   (1)

4   times (line 3)
   a) Which person is this word?
       A   1st
       B   2nd
       C   3rd   (1)
   b) Which number is this word?
       A   singular
       B   plural   (1)
5   saevos (line 1) This adjective means *savage*. What would it become (keeping it in the same case) if there were only one sailor?
       A   saevas
       B   saevus
       C   saevum
       D   saevi   (1)
6   nautae mali equos meos magnopere timent. (line 7) This means *the bad sailors fear my horses very much*. How would the word **timent** change if you wished to say in Latin *they were fearing my horses very much*?
       A   timet
       B   timebant
       C   timabant
       D   timant   (1)

                                                                    Total: 10

Exercise 5.10

Translate the following sentences into Latin.

1   The masters are looking at the wine.   (4)
2   You (pl.) were destroying the wall.   (3)
3   I was not warning the girl.   (4)
4   Romans love wine.   (4)
5   You (sing.) fear the god and the men.   (5)

                                                                    Total: 20

Chapter 6: Perfect tense; principal parts

Exercise 6.1

Give the 1st person singular of the present tense of the underlined verbs, and then translate the following Latin sentences into English.

1 Troiani Graecos non <u>timuerunt</u>.	(1 + 5)
2 Graeci Troiam <u>oppugnaverunt</u>.	(1 + 4)
3 consilium Graecorum Troiani <u>audiverunt</u>.	(1 + 5)
4 'quid <u>fecistis</u>?' inquiunt. 'cur equum prope aquam posuistis?'	(2 + 9)
5 deus patriam Troianorum <u>amavit</u>.	(1 + 5)
6 Troiani oppidum novum <u>aedificaverunt</u>.	(1 + 5)
	Total: 40

Exercise 6.2

Give the 1st person singular of the present tense of the underlined verbs, and then translate the following Latin sentences into English.

1 quattuor filios <u>spectavit</u> dominus.	(1 + 5)
2 septem templa in oppido novo <u>aedificavi</u>.	(1 + 7)
3 novem filias <u>amavit</u> regina nova.	(1 + 6)
4 puer parvus sex equos in agrum <u>duxit</u>.	(1 + 8)
5 Troiani in Graeciam non <u>navigaverunt</u>.	(1 + 6)
6 maritus dominae epistulam ad amicum <u>misit</u>.	(1 + 7)
	Total: 45

Exercise 6.3

Give the person and number of the underlined verbs and then translate the following Latin sentences into English.

1 libertus hortum dominae <u>paravit</u>.	(1 + 5)
2 magistri irati e villa magna <u>discesserunt</u>.	(1 + 7)
3 domina saeva libertum bonum non <u>terruit</u>.	(1 + 7)
4 cur, domine, captivos fessos in hortum <u>duxisti</u>?	(1 + 8)
5 filius domini libertos in turbam <u>duxit</u>.	(1 + 7)
6 captivi in silva non <u>manserunt</u>.	(1 + 6)
	Total: 46

Exercise 6.4

Give the tense of the underlined verbs and then translate the following Latin sentences into English.

1 Romani prope silvam manere <u>constituerunt</u>.	(1 + 6)
2 liberti cibum dominae non <u>consumpserunt</u> .	(1 + 6)
3 filii viri in horto <u>ludebant</u>.	(1 + 6)
4 epistulamne liberto <u>ostendisti</u>?	(1 + 5)
5 dominus tuus epistulam longam <u>tenebat</u>.	(1 + 6)
6 domina libertos manere <u>iussit</u>.	(1 + 5)
	Total: 40

Exercise 6.5

Give the 1st person singular of the present tense of the underlined verbs, and then translate the following Latin sentences into English.

1	cenamne <u>consumpsisti</u>?	(1 + 3)
2	cur turbam libertorum in hortum <u>duxistis</u>?	(1 + 7)
3	maritus meus librum in loco novo <u>posuit</u>.	(1 + 8)
4	pecuniam in templum <u>portavimus</u>.	(1 + 5)
5	domina epistulam libertis <u>dedit</u>.	(1 + 5)
6	iram mariti tui numquam <u>timuisti</u>.	(1 + 6)

Total: 40

Exercise 6.6

Translate the following English sentences into Latin.

1	We were always praising the dinner.	(4)
2	I do not fear the horses.	(4)
3	The Roman is not a sailor.	(5)
4	He was entering the country-house.	(3)
5	You (pl.) do not fear the master.	(4)
6	The women were often carrying wine.	(5)

Total: 25

Exercise 6.7

Study the passage below (do not write a translation) and answer the questions which follow. Complete sentences are not required.

Marcus gets his come-uppance.

1　Flavia e <u>taberna</u> cucurrit. flebat sed magnopere irata erat. Marcus et Valeria in taberna manserunt. Marcus Valeriam spectavit. Valeria Marcum spectavit. tandem Valeria Marcum rogavit: 'quis erat
5　puella pulchra, Marce?' Marcus respondit: 'puella pulchra Flavia erat,' inquit. 'amica mea est ... erat.'

'amica tua?!' clamavit Valeria. irata erat. 'duasne amicas habes, Marce? Flaviam et me amas? <u>eheu</u>! irata sum.'

10　Marcus tamen Valeriae respondere non cupivit. <u>rubuit</u>. 'te non amo, Marce,' inquit Valeria. 'puer malus es. tu amicus meus non es. <u>vale</u>!' puella misera Marcum <u>pulsavit</u> et irata e taberna festinavit. Marcus in taberna <u>attonitus</u> manebat.
15　<u>solus</u> erat.

taberna, -ae, f. = inn

eheu! = oh dear!

rubeo, -ere, rubui = I blush

vale = goodbye
pulso, -are, avi = I hit

attonitus, -a, -um = astonished
solus, -a, -um = alone

1	Flavia e taberna cucurrit. (line 1) What did Flavia do at the start of the story?	(2)
2	flebat sed magnopere irata erat. (lines 1–2) What sort of mood was she in?	(2)
3	Marcus et Valeria in taberna manserunt. (line 2) What did Marcus and Valeria do?	(2)
4	'quis erat puella pulchra, Marce?' (lines 4–5) What question does Valeria ask Marcus?	(2)
5	'puella pulchra Flavia erat,' inquit. 'amica mea est ... erat.' (lines 5–6) How does Marcus respond?	(2)

→

6 'amica tua?!' clamavit Valeria. irata erat. (line 7)
What effect does Marcus's answer have on Valeria? (2)
7 'te non amo, Marce,' inquit Valeria. 'puer malus es. tu amicus meus non es. vale!' (lines 11–12)
What does Valeria tell Marcus in these lines? (3)
8 Marcus tamen ... solus erat. (lines 10–15)
Translate these lines into good English. (30)

Total: 45

Exercise 6.8

Translate the passage below into good English.

Flavia helps Valeria take her mind of things.

1 Flavia et Valeria amicae erant. Flavia Valeriam amabat et
Valeria Flaviam amabat. puellae Marcum non amabat.

Flavia et Valeria per viam ambulabant. Flavia
fabulam longam narrabat. 'Graeci oppidum
5 magnum' inquit 'capere cupiebant. oppidum Troiam
oppugnabant et cum multis Troianis pugnabant.
multos Troianos necaverunt et multos ceperunt.'

'cur Troiam capere cupiebant Graeci?' inquit Valeria.

'Graeci Troianos non amabant. dominum Troiae non
10 amabant. filium domini non amabant.'

'cur dominum non amabant?' inquit Valeria. 'cur
filium non amabant? non <u>intellego</u>.'   intellego = I understand

'filius domini Troiani puellam amavit. puella erat
filia domini Graeci. puella erat Helena. multi Graeci
15 Helenam amabant. multi Graeci <u>servare</u>   servo, -are, -avi = I save, protect, look after
<u>promiserunt</u>.'   promitto, -ere, promisi (3) = I promise

Total: 30

Exercise 6.9

Study the passage below and answer the questions which follow. Complete sentences are not required.

Flavia continues her story.

1 Paris erat filius domini Troiani. Paris notus erat. Paris Helenam magnopere amabat et ad
insulam Cretam navigavit. tum e Graecia navigavit. cum Helena ad patriam Troianam
navigavit. Graeci irati erant et ad patriam Troianam navigaverunt.

Paris bene pugnabat et multos Graecos necavit. unus Graecorum erat Patroclus. Patroclus
5 notus erat et Helenam capere cupivit. sed Troiani Patroclum miserum necaverunt et multos
Graecos magnopere terruerunt.

1 This question tests your knowledge of the origins of English words. Complete the table below. One
example has been completed for you. (4)

Latin word from passage	Meaning of the Latin word	An English word which comes from the Latin word
filius (line 1)	son	filial
insulam (line 2)		
notus (line 5)		

→

2 **domini** (line 1) In which case is this word and why?
    A nominative, because it is the subject
    B dative, because it means *to*
    C accusative, because it is the object
    D genitive, because it means *of* (1)

3 **Helena** (line 2) In which case is this word and why?
    A nominative, because it is the subject
    B dative, because it means *to*
    C accusative, because it means *of*
    D ablative, because it is after a preposition (1)

4 **ad** (line 1) Which part of speech is this word?
    A noun
    B adjective
    C preposition
    D adverb (1)

5 **erat** (line 1) Which tense is this verb in?
    A present
    B imperfect
    C perfect (1)

6 **capere** (line 5) Which part of the verb is this?
    A present tense
    B present infinitive
    C perfect tense
    D imperative (1)

7 **terruerunt** (line 6) Which tense is this verb in?
    A present
    B imperfect
    C perfect (1)

Total: 10

Exercise 6.10

Translate the following sentences into Latin.

1 The Romans are building temples. (4)
2 The girl does not call the queen. (5)
3 They were entering the villa. (3)
4 The god was often warning the sailors. (5)
5 They were not building walls. (4)
6 You (sing.) always watch the women. (4)

Total: 25

Chapter 7: Temporal and causal clauses; **adsum** and **absum**; imperatives

Exercise 7.1

Translate into English:

1	absum	(1)
2	adest	(1)
3	aderat	(1)
4	aderant	(1)
5	aberam	(1)
6	aderam	(1)
7	adsunt	(1)
8	absunt	(1)
9	adsumus	(1)
10	aberatis	(1)

Total: 10

Exercise 7.2

Translate the following Latin sentences into English.

1	in horto adsum.	(4)
2	in villa adestis.	(4)
3	in templo adsumus.	(4)
4	in foro adsunt.	(4)
5	in insula aderant.	(4)
6	regina in villa adest.	(5)
7	ego in foro adsum.	(5)
8	ancillae in villa aderant.	(5)
9	Troiani in oppido aderant.	(5)
10	nos in villa adsumus.	(5)

Total: 45

Exercise 7.3

Translate the following Latin sentences into English.

1	olim liberti, ubi domina aberat, hortum delere constituerunt.	(10)
2	Graeci, quod bellum longum et saevum erat, prope oppidum diu aderant.	(13)
3	Troiam oppugnabant quod Troianos non amabant.	(7)
4	'cur hic manes?' rogavit libertus. 'cur domina abest?'	(11)
5	deus incolas laudavit quod patriam Troianorum amavit.	(9)
6	dominus saevus aberat. Troiani igitur oppidum novum aedificaverunt.	(10)

Total: 60

Exercise 7.4

Translate the following Latin sentences into English.

1	ubi agricolam vidit, Lucia in villam festinavit.	(8)
2	quod agricolam vidit, Flavia in villam festinavit.	(8)
3	ubi domina Iuliam cepit, maritum vocavit.	(7)
4	libertus, quod legere amabat, librum filio ostendit.	(8)
5	magister Graecus, quod fessus erat, in villa diu aderat.	(10)
6	Romani saevi in proelium hastas magnas semper portabant.	(9)

Total: 50

Exam Practice Questions

Exercise 7.5

Translate the following Latin sentences into English.

1. multi pueri laeti semper in horto aderant. (8)
2. pueri magnopere timebant quod magister saevus aderat. (8)
3. diu incolae non timebant quod regina nostra aberat. (9)
4. quis in horto adest? cur domina abest? (8)
5. Romani, quod fortiter pugnabant, Graecos saepe terruerunt. (8)
6. iterum et iterum libertus ancillam cibum parare iussit. (9)

Total: 50

Exercise 7.6

Translate the following Latin sentences into English.

1. 'festina in hortum, Marce! dominus ibi adest.' (9)
2. 'magistrum audi, puer, quod saevus est.' (8)
3. 'verba domini audite, liberti, et epistulas scribite.' (9)
4. 'maritum in villam duc, o femina misera.' (7)
5. 'pecuniam tene, Marce, et cibum domino para.' (9)
6. 'magistro respondete, puellae, quod iratus est.' (8)

Total: 50

Exercise 7.7

Write down the imperatives and then translate the following Latin sentences into English.

1. 'equos in agros magnos ducite, agricolae.' (1 + 7)
2. 'pugnate fortiter, Romani, prope muros oppidi magni!' (1 + 9)
3. 'quod regina irata in templum venit, bene cantate!' (1 + 10)
4. 'pecuniam domino da, o liberte miser, quod iratus est!' (1 + 9)
5. 'quod cum Graecis pugnatis, auxilium sociis date!' (1 + 9)
6. 'in silva manete, socii, et cibum consumite!' (2 + 9)

Total: 60

Exercise 7.8

Translate the following English sentences into Latin.

1. The schoolmaster was often praising the books. (5)
2. She was carrying money and letters. (5)
3. I do not watch the friends. (4)
4. The queen sees the dinner and the wine. (6)
5. You (pl.) do not fear the gods. (4)
6. They were often carrying swords and spears. (6)

Total: 30

Exercise 7.9

Study the passage below (do not write a translation) and answer the questions which follow. Complete sentences are not required.

Marcus shows who is boss.

1   Marcus et Flavia et quattuor nautae in via stant.
      Marcus magnopere iratus est. nautas discedere
      iubet. nautae, quod Marcum non timent, rident.
      Marco et Flaviae clamant: 'date nobis pecuniam
5   vestram. vinum <u>emere</u> cupimus.' Marcus nautas   emo, emere, emi = I buy
      terrere constituit. gladium novum habet. gladius
      bonus et validus est. Marcus gladium suum capit et
      ad nautas statim currit. clamat. Flavia <u>perterrita</u> est.   perterritus, -a, -um = terrified
      Marcus cum nautis pugnat. fortiter pugnat. bene
10   pugnat. nautae tamen gladios non habent. itaque
      Marcus nautas mox superat. nautae fugiunt. Marcus
      Flaviam spectat. 'pecunia nostra tuta est. nos tuti
      sumus,' inquit. 'te amo, Marce,' respondet Flavia.

1   Marcus et Flavia et quattuor nautae in via stant. (line 1)
    Who is standing in the road?   (2)
2   Marcus magnopere iratus est. nautas discedere iubet. (lines 2–3)
    What does Marcus say to the sailors?   (2)
3   nautae, quod Marcum non timent, rident. (line 3)
    Why do the sailors laugh?   (1)
4   Marco et Flaviae clamant: 'date nobis pecuniam vestram. vinum emere cupimus.' (lines 4–5)
    Explain in your own words what is happening here.   (2)
5   Marcus gladium suum capit et ad nautas statim currit. (lines 7–8)
    What action does Marcus take against the sailors?   (2)
6   nautae tamen gladios non habent. (line 10)
    What advantage does Marcus have over the sailors?   (2)
7   'pecunia nostra tuta est. nos tuti sumus.' (lines 12–13)
    What is Marcus able to say to Flavia at the end of the story to reassure her?   (4)

Total: 15

Exercise 7.10

Translate the passage below into good English.

Marcus: Flavia's hero.

1   Marcus et Flavia tuti erant. Flavia non iam <u>perterrita</u>   perterritus, -a, -um = terrified
      erat. Flavia Marcum laudabat. 'Marce, tu vir fortis et
      validus es. ego laeta sum quod tuti sumus. nautae
      te timebant. etiam ego te timebam. quod nautae te
5   timebant, pugnare non cupiebant.'

      Marcus Flaviae dixit: 'Flavia, ego quoque laetus sum
      quod nos tuti sumus.'

      'Marce, veni ad villam meam. cibum habeo. cenam
      bonam paravi. tu <u>heros</u> meus es.'   heros, herois, m. = hero
10   Marcus laetus erat. cibum amabat. cenas Flaviae
      quoque amabat. Marcus et Flavia igitur ad villam
      Flaviae festinaverunt.

Total: 30

Exercise 7.11

Study the passage below and answer the questions which follow. Complete sentences are not required.

Caught in the act.

1	olim Flavia cenam in villa parare cupiebat. Marcus	
	cenas Flaviae amabat. in villa tamen Flavia multum	
	cibum non habebat. in oppidum igitur ambulare et	
	cibum ibi <u>emere</u> constituit. itaque e villa festinavit	emo, emere, emi = I buy
5	et per viam ad oppidum ambulavit. in via <u>taberna</u>	taberna, -ae, f. = inn
	aderat. Flavia, ubi ad tabernam venit, intrare et	
	vinum emere constituit. ubi tamen tabernam	
	intravit, Marcum vidit. Marcus puellam <u>basiabat</u>!	basio, -aare, avi = I kiss
	Marcus, ubi Flaviam vidit, statim <u>rubuit</u>. 'Marce!'	rubeo, -ere, rubui = I blush
10	clamavit Flavia. 'quid facis?'	
	'nihil facio,' respondit Marcus. 'Valeria amica mea	
	est. Valeria amica mea nova est.' 'puer malus	
	es, Marce,' inquit Flavia. 'te <u>odi</u>.' e taberna Flavia	odi = I hate
	cucurrit et ad villam festinavit. irata erat. magnopere	
15	irata erat.	

1 This question tests your knowledge of the origins of English words. Complete the table below. One example has been completed for you. **(4)**

Latin word from passage	Meaning of the Latin word	An English word which comes from the Latin word
parare (line 1)	to prepare	preparation
constituit (line 4)		
vidit (line 9)		

2 **cenas** (line 2) Which case is this noun in and why?
   A nominative, because it is the subject
   B dative, because it means *to*
   C accusative, because it is the object
   D genitive, because it means *of*   **(1)**

3 **habebat** (line 3) Which tense is this verb in?
   A present
   B imperfect
   C perfect   **(1)**

4 **per** (line 5) Which part of speech is this word?
   A noun
   B adjective
   C preposition
   D adverb   **(1)**

5 **intrare** (line 6) Which part of the verb is this?
   A present tense
   B present infinitive
   C perfect tense
   D imperative   **(1)**

→

6 est (line 12)
   a) In which tense is this verb?
      A present tense
      B present infinitive
      C perfect tense   (1)
   b) Give its 1st person singular, present tense
      A edo
      B eram
      C sum
      D ego   (1)

Total: 10

Exercise 7.12

Translate the following sentences into Latin.

1 We were shouting and destroying the temple.   (6)
2 The schoolmaster is carrying books and a letter.   (6)
3 He sees the sword.   (3)
4 The girls do not like the master.   (5)
5 I was watching the queen and calling.   (6)
6 You (pl.) often praise the queen.   (4)

Total: 30

Chapter 8: Revision of Level 1

Exercise 8.1

Translate the following into English:

1 amaverunt. (2)
2 currunt. (2)
3 videmus. (2)
4 scribebas. (2)
5 pugno. (2)
6 respondet. (2)
7 respondit. (2)
8 manebamus. (2)
9 fuisti. (2)
10 clamant. (2)

Total: 20

Exercise 8.2

Translate the following into English:

1 ducis. (2)
2 dicis. (2)
3 luserunt. (2)
4 mittimus. (2)
5 movimus. (2)
6 discessistis. (2)
7 oppugnabas. (2)
8 ostenditis. (2)
9 paravit. (2)
10 posui. (2)

Total: 20

Exercise 8.3

Translate the following into English:

1 videmus. (2)
2 superaverunt. (2)
3 eratis. (2)
4 portabatis. (2)
5 audiunt. (2)
6 necavit. (2)
7 necant. (2)
8 movit. (2)
9 iussit. (2)
10 dat. (2)

Total: 20

Exercise 8.4

Translate the following into English:

1 constituerunt. (2)
2 cepit. (2)
3 cupiebam. (2)
4 ducebat. (2)
5 iecimus. (2)
6 laudatis. (2)
7 steterunt. (2)
8 portavisti. (2)
9 mittis. (2)
10 festinabamus. (2)

Total: 20

Exercise 8.5

Translate the following into English:

1 celeriter currebamus. (3)
2 fortiter pugnabat. (3)
3 diu navigaverunt. (3)
4 numquam ludo. (3)
5 bene scribis. (3)
6 saepe flebant. (3)
7 diu dormivi. (3)
8 tandem discesserunt. (3)
9 subito intravit. (3)
10 semper bibit. (3)

Total: 30

Exercise 8.6

Translate the following into English:

1 Romani magnum oppidum aedificaverunt. (5)
2 nauta pericula non timebat. (5)
3 turba feminarum in via stabat. (6)
4 multa verba dixisti. (4)
5 Romani multa templa deleverunt. (5)

Total: 25

Exercise 8.7

Translate the following into English:

1 oppidum novum muros altos habet. (6)
2 multi nautae celeriter appropinquant. (5)
3 hodie laboro. heri tamen nihil feci. (7)
4 Romani multa scuta portabant. (5)
5 multi viri boni in proelio pugnaverunt. (7)

Total: 30

Exercise 8.8

Translate the following into English:

1 liberti in templum sacrum festinaverunt. (6)
2 olim multi Romani clari erant. (6)
3 dominus malus servum miserum
   non laudat. (6)
4 feminae pulchrae cibum bonum parabant. (6)
5 pueri mali magistros numquam audiunt. (6)

Total: 30

Exercise 8.9

Translate the following into English:

1 magister puerum verbis iratis terruit. (6)
2 gladiis et scutis semper pugnamus. (6)
3 dominus multam pecuniam Marco dedit. (6)
4 virum malum hasta mea necavi. (6)
5 poeta clarus librum bonum legebat. (6)

Total: 30

Exercise 8.10

Translate the following into English:

1 verba nautarum mala erant. (5)
2 turbae Romanorum veniunt. (4)
3 muri templi alti et validi sunt. (7)
4 amicus pueri cantabat. (4)
5 verba magistri numquam audimus. (5)

Total: 25

Exercise 8.11

Translate the following into English:

1 ludere amant. (3)
2 Flavia pugnare cupiebat. (4)
3 dominus Brutum laborare iussit. (5)
4 laborare numquam cupio. (4)
5 libertus currere constituit. (4)

Total: 20

Exercise 8.12

Translate the following into English:

1 lente ambulate, pueri! (4)
2 librum scribe, poeta! (4)
3 equos movete, agricolae! (4)
4 vinum bibe, amice! (4)
5 arma relinquite, nautae! (4)

Total: 20

Exercise 8.13

Translate the following into English:

1 puer in via stabat. (5)
2 incolae contra barbaros[1] pugnaverunt. (5)
3 in magno periculo sumus. (5)
4 libertus per portam[2] cucurrit. (5)
5 puella cum amicis ludit. (5)

Total: 25

   1 barbarus, -i, m. = barbarian
   2 porta, -ae, f. = gate

Exercise 8.14

Translate the following into English:

1 agricolane caelum diu spectabat? (6)
2 magisterne verba mala dixit? (6)
3 incolaene murum delent? (5)
4 puerine scuta habent? (5)
5 Britannine[1] multos agros et prata[2] habebant? (8)

Total: 30

1 Britanni, -orum , m. pl. = the Britons

2 pratum, -i, n. = meadow

Exercise 8.15

Give the person, number, tense and 1st person singular of the present tense of the following verbs and then translate:

1 rident. (5)
2 oppugnabat. (5)
3 ponebamus. (5)
4 dedistis. (5)
5 steterunt. (5)
6 laboraverunt. (5)
7 constituunt. (5)
8 cucurristis. (5)
9 scripserunt. (5)
10 parabamus. (5)

Total: 50

Exercise 8.16

Give the person, number, tense and 1st person singular of the present tense of the following verbs, and then translate:

1 veniunt. (5)
2 erat. (5)
3 portabas. (5)
4 necas. (5)
5 biberunt. (5)
6 dormiebas. (5)
7 iussit. (5)
8 monet. (5)
9 cepisti. (5)
10 dicebant. (5)

Total: 50

Exercise 8.17

Give and translate the following verb parts:

1 The 1st person singular, imperfect tense of amo. (2)
2 The 2nd person plural, present tense of sum. (2)
3 The 2nd person singular, perfect tense of video. (2)
4 The 3rd person plural, perfect tense of porto. (2)
5 The 1st person plural, imperfect tense of timeo. (2)

Total: 10

Exercise 8.18

Give and translate the following verb parts:

1 The 3rd person singular, present tense of video. (2)
2 The 2nd person plural, imperfect tense of deleo. (2)
3 The 1st person plural, perfect tense of laudo. (2)
4 The 3rd person plural, present tense of festino. (2)
5 The 2nd person singular, perfect tense of moneo. (2)

Total: 10

Exercise 8.19

Give and translate the following verb parts:

1 The 3rd person singular, perfect tense of **sum**. (2)
2 The 1st person singular, imperfect tense of **teneo**. (2)
3 The 2nd person singular, present tense of **rego**. (2)
4 The 3rd person singular, present tense of **capio**. (2)
5 The 2nd person singular, imperfect tense of **audio**. (2)

Total: 10

Exercise 8.20

Give the case of the underlined words and translate the sentences:

1 nautae <u>feminas</u> non timebant. (1 + 5)
2 <u>agricolae</u> agros amant. (1 + 4)
3 oppida <u>muros</u> habebant. (1 + 4)
4 magistri <u>pueros</u> puniebant. (1 + 4)
5 <u>puellae</u> deos laudabant. (1 + 4)

Total: 26

Exercise 8.21

Translate the following into English:

1 pueri semper currunt et clamant. (6)
2 Iulia et Valeria sunt puellae. (6)
3 agricolae <u>argentum</u>[1] et aurum amant. (6)
4 saepe currimus et ludimus. (6)
5 amici rident et ludunt. (6)
6 <u>legatus</u>[2] est fessus sed laetus . (6)
7 puer cibum et aquam habet. (6)
8 contra Romanos et Graecos pugnamus. (6)
9 agricolae hastas et sagittas habent. (6)
10 pueri intrant et laborant. (6)

Total: 60

1 argentum, -i, n. = silver
2 legatus, -i, m. = ambassador

Exercise 8.22

Translate the following into English:

1 Marcus et Sextus sunt pueri. (6)
2 rideo et ludo. (5)
3 puer et puella currunt. (5)
4 <u>pirata</u>[1] ex <u>provincia</u>[2] discedit. (5)
5 currunt et ludunt. (5)
6 nauta ventum et <u>undas</u>[3] timet. (6)
7 magister pueros et puellas monet. (6)
8 dominus intrat et <u>avunculum</u>[4] vocat. (7)
9 puella intrat et amicum videt. (7)
10 pueri et puellae rident et ludunt. (8)

Total: 60

1 pirata, -ae, c. = pirate
2 provincia, -ae, f. = province
3 unda, -ae, f. = wave
4 avunculus, -i, m. = uncle

Exercise 8.23

Translate the following into English:

1   Romulus et Remus Romani erant. (6)
2   semper ridemus et ludimus. (6)
3   Valeria et Aurelia Romanae sunt. (6)
4   magister Sextum et Marcum vocat. (6)
5   Sextus et Marcus magistrum audiunt. (6)
6   magister puerum et puellam spectabat. (6)
7   puer agricolas et nautas timebat. (6)
8   Latini[1] cibum et aquam habebant. (6)
9   discipuli[2] fessi et miseri erant. (6)
10 templum sacrum et pulchrum erat. (6)

Total: 60

1 Latinus, -a, -um = Latin

2 discipulus, -i, m. = pupil

Exercise 8.24

Translate the following into English:

1   terruisti. (2)
2   rogaverunt. (2)
3   deleverunt. (2)
4   misimus. (2)
5   vidit. (2)
6   audivisti. (2)
7   constituerunt. (2)
8   clamavistis. (2)
9   reximus. (2)
10 venit. (2)

Total: 20

Exercise 8.25

Translate the following into English:

1   dixit. (2)
2   iussit. (2)
3   cucurrimus. (2)
4   capit. (2)
5   fecisti. (2)
6   mansimus. (2)
7   cepistis. (2)
8   appropinquaverunt. (2)
9   bibi. (2)
10 fuit. (2)

Total: 20

Exercise 8.26

Give the tense of the underlined verbs and transate the sentences into English:

1   appropinquabam. (1 + 2)
2   servus laborat. (1 + 3)
3   amicus pugnabat. (1 + 3)
4   puer bonus est. (1 + 4)
5   nauta navigavit. (1 + 3)

Total: 20

Exercise 8.27

Give the case of the underlined words and translate the sentences into English:

1   libri boni sunt. (1 + 4)
2   gladios portabatis. (1 + 3)
3   bella timemus. (1 + 3)
4   nautae magnas hastas iecerunt. (1 + 5)
5   servi muros altos aedificabant. (1 + 5)

Total: 25

Exercise 8.28

Give and translate the following verb parts:

1   The 1st person singular, imperfect tense of **maneo**. (2 + 2)
2   The 2nd person plural, perfect tense of **navigo**. (2 + 2)
3   The 3rd person singular, present tense of **aedifico**. (2 + 2)
4   The 1st person singular, perfect tense of **sto**. (2 + 2)
5   The 3rd person plural, perfect tense of **sum**. (2 + 2)

Total: 20

Exercise 8.29

Give the case of the underlined words and translate the sentences into English:

1 <u>puellae</u> non cantant.   (1 + 4)
2 dona <u>pulchra</u> sunt.   (1 + 4)
3 incolae <u>muros</u> aedificabant.   (1 + 4)
4 pueri <u>scuta</u> portaverunt.   (1 + 4)
5 <u>puellae</u> magistros timent.   (1 + 4)

Total: 25

Exercise 8.30

Give the person, number, tense and 1st person singular of the present tense of the following verbs, and then translate:

1 vocavit.   (4 + 2)
2 appropinquabant.   (4 + 2)
3 iecisti.   (4 + 2)
4 oppugnamus.   (4 + 2)
5 iussit.   (4 + 2)

Total: 30

Exercise 8.31

Keeping the same person and number, put the following verbs into the imperfect tense and translate your answer:

1 appropinquaverunt.   (1 + 2)
2 vocavit.   (1 + 2)
3 navigavi.   (1 + 2)
4 oppugnavisti.   (1 + 2)
5 iussit.   (1 + 2)
6 iusserunt.   (1 + 2)
7 superavimus.   (1 + 2)
8 stetit.   (1 + 2)
9 deleverunt.   (1 + 2)
10 dedimus.   (1 + 2)

Total: 30

Exercise 8.32

Translate the passage below into good English.

Discord gatecrashes the wedding party of Peleus and the goddess Thetis.

1   olim <u>in monte Olympo</u> di et deae <u>festum celebrabant</u>. cibum consumebant et vinum bibebant. festum celebrabant quod Peleus <u>Thetim in matrimonium ducebat</u>. Thetis dea erat. Peleus
5   vir <u>mortalis</u> erat. di et deae laeti erant. ridebant. subito tamen Discordia, dea mala, intravit. <u>ceteri</u> di, ubi Discordiam viderunt, non laeti erant. non iam ridebant. non ridebant quod Discordiam non amabant. clamaverunt: 'quid cupis, Discordia? cur
10   hic ades? te non amamus. statim discede!'
     Discordia respondit: 'audite, di! audite, deae! <u>donum</u> habeo. donum pulchrum habeo. hic est.' deinde Discordia <u>pomum</u> prope cibum <u>deposuit</u>. risit et discessit. di et deae ad pomum
15   appropinquaverunt. pomum spectaverunt.

in monte Olympo = on Mount Olympus
festum celebro, -are, -avi (1) = I hold a celebration
Thetim = accusative case of Thetis (a sea nymph)
in matrimonium duco (3) = I marry
mortalis = mortal
ceteri = the other

donum, -i, n. = gift
pomum, -i, n. = apple
depono, deponere, deposui = I put down

Total: 30

Exercise 8.33

Study the passage below (do not write a translation) and answer the questions which follow. Complete sentences are not required.

The wasp.

1 Orbilius magister erat. olim in <u>ludo</u> laborabat. multi <u>discipuli</u> aderant. Marcus quoque aderat. discipuli bene laborabant. Orbilius igitur laetus erat.	ludus, -i, m. = school discipulus, -i, m. = pupil
subito <u>vespa</u> ludum intravit. Marcus et amici vespam 5 audiverunt, deinde viderunt. non iam laborabant. vespam spectabant. Orbilius, quod discipuli non laborabant, magnopere iratus erat. vespam statim necare igitur constituit.	vespa, -ae, f. = wasp
vespa iam in magno periculo erat. in muro erat. 10 Orbilius vespam vidit. ad vespam festinavit. vespam necavit. vespam cepit et discipulis ostendit. '<u>ecce!</u>' Marco et amicis clamavit, 'vespam necavi! nunc laborate, pueri.'	ecce! = look!

1   olim in ludo laborabat. (line 1)
    What was Orbilius doing?   **(2)**
2   multi discipuli aderant. Marcus quoque aderat. (lines 1–2)
    Who else was there?   **(2)**
3   subito vespa ludum intravit. (line 4)
    What happened to disturb the peace and quiet in the room?   **(1)**
4   Orbilius, quod discipuli non laborabant, magnopere iratus erat. (lines 6–7)
    Explain in your own words why Orbilius became angry.   **(2)**
5   vespam statim necare igitur constituit. (lines 7–8)
    What did the master plan to do?   **(2)**
6   vespam cepit et discipulis ostendit. (line 11)
    After carrying out his plan, what did the master do to show that it had succeeded?   **(3)**
7   'vespam necavi! nunc laborate, pueri.' (lines 12–13)
    How did the master try to put the disturbance behind him?   **(3)**

Total: 15

Exercise 8.34

Translate the passage below into good English.

Marcus takes a stand.

1 Marcus erat puer bonus. discipuli Marcum amabant
quod bonus erat sed magistrum magnopere
timebant. magister discipulos non amabat quod
saevus erat. Marcum non amabat quod piger erat.
5 Marcus laborare non amabat.

olim magister in ludo de vespis clamabat. magister
vespas timebat et semper eas necabat.

Marcus vespas magnopere amabat et magistrum
impedire constituit. librum magnum igitur cepit et
10 ad magistrum iratum ruit.

'discede, vir male!' clamavit. 'vespa perterritus est.
cur eam terres?'

discipuli, Marci amici, ridebant et ad magistrum
ruerunt. magister attonitus e ludo festinavit et in
15 viam cucurrit.

discipulus, -i, m. = pupil

piger = lazy

ludus, -i, m. = school

vespa, -ae, f. = wasp

eas = them

impedio (4) = I obstruct

ruo, ruere, rui (3) = I rush

perterritus, -a, -um = terrified

eam = it (feminine)

attonitus, -a, -um = astonished

Total: 30

Exercise 8.35

Study the passage below and answer the questions which follow. Complete sentences are not required.

Orbilius gets the last laugh.

1 Orbilius, magister saevus, in via stabat. iratus erat.
iratus semper erat. Marcus et amici in ludo

aderant et ridebant. magistrum non amabant et,
quod Marcus eum superavit, laeti erant. magister
5 tamen consilium cepit. multas vespas vidit et eas
pellere in ludum constituit. septem vespas per
ianuam ludi pepulit et ipse in via mansit.

subito perterriti discipuli clamaverunt et in viam
ruerunt. vespae in viam discipulos miseros
10 fugaverunt. ridebat magister saevus.

ludus, -i, m. = school

eum = him

vespa, -ae, f. = wasp

eas = them

pello, pellere, pepuli (3) = I drive

ianua, -ae, f. = door

ipse = he himself

perterritus, -a, -um = terrified

discipulus, -i, m. = pupil

ruo, ruere, rui (3) = I rush

fugo, -are, -avi = I chase away

1 This question tests your knowledge of the origins of English words. Complete the table below. One
example has been completed for you. (4)

Latin word from passage	Meaning of the Latin word	An English word which comes from the Latin word
magister (line 1)	master	magistrate
iratus (line 1)		
constituit (line 6)		

2 **via** (line 1) Which case is this noun in, and why?
   A nominative, because it is the subject
   B dative, because it means *to*
   C ablative, because it is after a preposition
   D ablative, because it means *by* (1)

3 **erat** (line 1) Which tense is this verb in?
   A present
   B imperfect
   C perfect (1)

4 **subito** (line 8) Which part of speech is this word?
   A noun
   B adjective
   C verb
   D adverb (1)

5 **constituit** (line 6) In which person is this verb?
   A 1st
   B 2nd
   C 3rd (1)

6 **septem** (line 6) Which part of speech is this word?
   A conjunction
   B adverb
   C numeral
   D preposition (1)

7 **ridebat** (line 10) This means *he was laughing*. How would you say in Latin *he has laughed*?
   A ridet
   B riduit
   C risit
   D ridavit (1)

Total: 10

Exercise 8.36

Translate the following sentences into Latin.

1 The friends prepare wine and dinner. (6)
2 The god was watching the girls and boys. (6)
3 We were not afraid of the Romans. (3)
4 You (sing.) carry a spear and a sword. (5)

Total: 20

Level 2

Chapter 9: 3rd declension nouns; agreement of adjectives with 3rd declension nouns

Exercise 9.1

Translate the following into English:

1 comitem vidi. (3)
2 dux currit. (3)
3 uxorem meam amo. (4)
4 rex regit. (3)
5 mulierem amamus. (3)
6 fratrem et sororem habeo. (5)
7 rex uxorem pulchram habet. (5)
8 multos milites vidimus. (4)
9 ad montem altum appropinquabamus. (5)
10 parentes mei iam veniunt. (5)

Total: 40

Exercise 9.2

Translate the following into English:

1 Marcus frater Aureliae est. (5)
2 Aurelia soror Marci est. (5)
3 puella cibum patri parabat. (5)
4 puella sororem non amat. (5)
5 servi ad montem festinant. (5)
6 in montibus sunt multae viae. (6)
7 rex matrem patremque amabat. (5)
8 rex uxorem pulchram habebat. (5)
9 patrem bonum habeo. (4)
10 soror mea mala est. (5)

Total: 50

Exercise 9.3

Translate the following into English:

1 captivus cum milite semper pugnat. (6)
2 homo cum comite saepe cantat. (6)
3 frater dominae iratus est. (5)
4 rex terram bene regit. (5)
5 rex pecuniam militi dat. (5)
6 libertus pecuniam regis capit. (5)
7 uxor mea fratrem clarum habet. (6)
8 frater matris meae clarus erat. (6)
9 Romanus multa dona mulieri dedit. (6)
10 uxor regis pulchra est. (5)

Total: 55

Exercise 9.4

Give the correct form of the following nouns:

1 The nominative plural of **rex, regis**, m. (1)
2 The genitive singular of **comes, comitis**, c. (1)
3 The dative plural of **dux, ducis**, m. (1)
4 The ablative singular of **homo, hominis**, c. (1)
5 The genitive plural of **miles, militis**, m. (1)
6 The dative singular of **lux, lucis**, f. (1)
7 The ablative plural of **mulier, mulieris**, f. (1)
8 The accusative singular of **parens, parentis**, c. (1)
9 The accusative plural of **clamor, clamoris**, m. (1)
10 The vocative singular of **uxor, uxoris**, f. (1)

Total: 10

Exercise 9.5

Give the correct form of the following nouns:

1	The genitive singular of **corpus, corporis**, n.	(1)
2	The nominative plural of **flumen, fluminis**, n.	(1)
3	The dative singular of **iter, itineris**, n.	(1)
4	The vocative singular of **rex, regis**, m.	(1)
5	The dative plural of **nomen, nominis**, n.	(1)
6	The accusative singular of **flumen, fluminis**, n.	(1)
7	The ablative singular of **corpus, corporis**, n.	(1)
8	The accusative plural of **iter, itineris**, n.	(1)
9	The ablative plural of **parens, parentis**, c.	(1)
10	The genitive plural of **comes, comitis**, c.	(1)

Total: 10

Exercise 9.6

Give the case and number of the following. If more than one answer is possible, give all possibilities.

1	regem	(1)
2	hominum	(1)
3	parentis	(1)
4	clamoribus	(2)
5	duces	(3)
6	mulieris	(1)
7	uxor	(2)
8	militem	(1)
9	ducibus	(2)
10	lucis	(1)

Total: 15

Exercise 9.7

Translate the following into English:

1	dux validus corpus magnum habet.	(6)
2	homo flumen altum diu spectabat.	(6)
3	milites itinera longa faciebant.	(5)
4	nomen regis Tarquinius erat.	(5)
5	clamores Troianorum equos terrebant.	(5)
6	milites hominem miserum in flumen iecerunt.	(7)
7	liberti dominae regem timebant.	(5)
8	milites Romani comites laudaverunt.	(5)
9	multa itinera trans montes faciebamus.	(6)
10	corpora hominum multorum spectabas.	(5)

Total: 55

Exercise 9.8

Translate the following into Latin:

1	I prepare a good dinner.	(4)
2	We see the small boy.	(4)
3	I have a savage master.	(4)
4	They were watching the famous Roman.	(4)
5	He was carrying many books.	(4)
6	The villa was beautiful.	(4)
7	I love the good women.	(4)
8	The queen is beautiful.	(4)
9	The girls are unhappy.	(4)
10	The Romans were carrying swords.	(4)

Total: 40

Exercise 9.9

Translate the following into Latin:

1 They were walking out of the country-house. (4)
2 The sailors were fighting with the Romans. (5)
3 They were building a villa near the temple. (5)
4 They were carrying many books into the country-house. (6)
5 They have big swords and spears. (6)
6 The Romans were fighting with swords. (4)
7 You (sing.) were walking towards the unhappy slave-girl. (5)
8 Sailors do not fear the gods. (5)
9 We were walking with the unhappy man. (5)
10 The boys were always friends. (5)

Total: 50

Exercise 9.10

Translate the following into Latin:

1 We were watching the bad schoolmaster. (4)
2 The girl walks with the woman. (5)
3 I was afraid of the savage schoolmaster. (4)
4 The Romans were destroying the great temple. (5)
5 We were walking towards the temple with the money. (6)
6 They were walking out of the great temple. (5)
7 The unhappy girl walks into the villa. (6)
8 They are fighting with swords and spears. (4)
9 The girls were always unhappy. (5)
10 The friends do not like big dinners. (6)

Total: 50

Exercise 9.11

Translate the following into English:

1 Marcus et Sextus milites Romani erant. (5)
2 Valeria et Aurelia mulieres Romanae sunt. (5)
3 matrem pulchram et patrem iratum habeo. (7)
4 soror mea parentes nostros non amabat. (7)
5 nautae lucem claram diu spectabant. (6)
6 milites trans flumen navigare non cupiebant. (6)
7 cur rex equum terrebat? (5)
8 milites Romani urbem hastis et sagittis oppugnaverunt. (7)
9 mater et pater regis irati erant. (6)
10 frater meus captivos Troianos capiebat. (6)

Total: 60

Exercise 9.12

Give the case and number of the underlined nouns and then translate the sentences:

1	ad flumen <u>milites</u> festinabant.	(1 + 5)
2	libertus <u>parentes</u> non iam habebat.	(1 + 5)
3	puellae ad <u>mulierem</u> subito appropinquabant.	(1 + 5)
4	<u>dona</u> pulchra semper amavistis.	(1 + 5)
5	<u>viri</u> feminas claras laudaverunt.	(1 + 5)
6	<u>mons</u> altus pulcher est.	(1 + 5)
7	puer <u>parentes</u> claros amat.	(1 + 5)
8	rex cum <u>uxore</u> habitabat.	(1 + 5)
9	<u>ducis</u> uxor bellum timet.	(1 + 5)
10	mater ducis <u>militibus</u> cantabat.	(1 + 5)

Total: 60

Exercise 9.13

Give the correct form of the following nouns:

1	The nominative plural of **nomen, nominis**, n.	(1)
2	The accusative singular of **iter, itineris**, n.	(1)
3	The genitive singular of **corpus, corporis**, n.	(1)
4	The ablative plural of **flumen, fluminis**, n.	(1)
5	The dative plural of **homo, hominis**, c.	(1)
6	The dative singular of **iter, itineris**, n.	(1)
7	The ablative singular of **nomen, nominis**, n.	(1)
8	The accusative plural of **corpus, corporis**, n.	(1)
9	The nominative singular of **parens, parentis**, c.	(1)
10	The vocative singular of **flumen, fluminis**, n.	(1)

Total: 10

Exercise 9.14

Give the case and number of the underlined nouns and then translate the sentences:

1	nauta <u>mare</u> non timet.	(1 + 5)
2	<u>iter</u> militum longum erat.	(1 + 5)
3	milites <u>corpus</u> regis portabant.	(1 + 5)
4	multa <u>itinera</u> longa fecimus.	(1 + 5)
5	aqua <u>fluminis</u> alta erat.	(1 + 5)
6	sunt in <u>urbe</u> multa templa.	(1 + 6)
7	oppida et <u>urbes</u> amo.	(1 + 5)
8	nomen <u>regis</u> Sextus erat.	(1 + 5)
9	pater meus trans <u>mare</u> solus saepe navigat.	(1 + 8)
10	amici <u>itinere</u> longo fessi erant.	(1 + 6)

Total: 65

Exercise 9.15

Give the tense of the underlined verbs and then translate the sentences:

1 multa corpora e templo <u>portabamus</u>.   (1 + 6)
2 iter iuvenum et longum et miserum <u>erat</u>.   (1 + 7)
3 rex lucem claram et montes altos <u>vidit</u>.   (1 + 7)
4 nomen urbis Roma <u>erat</u>.   (1 + 5)
5 puellae iuvenes pulchros saepe <u>amant</u>.   (1 + 6)
6 pater multam pecuniam iuveni <u>dedit</u>.   (1 + 6)
7 matrem patremque in urbe heri <u>spectabam</u>.   (1 + 7)
8 corpus magnum nauta <u>habebat</u>.   (1 + 5)
9 ad flumen altum mox <u>venimus</u>.   (1 + 6)
10 itinere fessi, diu <u>dormivimus</u>.   (1 + 5)

Total: 70

Exercise 9.16

Translate the following into Latin:

1 You (pl.) are fighting with the bad man.   (5)
2 We are afraid of the savage schoolmaster.   (4)
3 The temple is big.   (4)
4 The Romans were fighting in the temple.   (5)
5 She was calling the unhappy boy.   (4)
6 I do not have a friend.   (4)
7 I saw many women and girls.   (6)
8 We often prepare dinner.   (4)
9 You (sing.) have a small horse.   (4)
10 The unhappy queen fears the gods.   (5)

Total: 45

Exercise 9.17

Translate the following into Latin:

1 The miserable boy was afraid of the master.   (5)
2 The unhappy sailors never have money.   (6)
3 Famous men often fight with swords.   (6)
4 We were often watching the beautiful women.   (5)
5 The woman is preparing the dinner with a friend.   (6)
6 The boys always fear the savage schoolmaster.   (6)
7 She was walking to the large country-house.   (5)
8 At last they had wine and money.   (6)
9 The god was warning the unhappy sailors.   (5)
10 The friends were shouting in the temple.   (5)

Total: 55

Exercise 9.18

Give the case and number of the following nouns and translate:

1 O reges! (1 + 1)
2 cum uxore (1 + 1)
3 ad flumen (1 + 1)
4 in itinere (1 + 1)
5 cum comite (1 + 1)
6 in lucem (1 + 1)
7 uxori (1 + 1)
8 militum (1 + 1)
9 duci (1 + 1)
10 in flumine (1 + 1)

Total: 20

Exercise 9.19

Give the correct form of the following nouns:

1 The genitive singular of **rex, regis**, m. (1)
2 The nominative plural of **uxor, uxoris**, f. (1)
3 The dative singular of **mater, matris**, f. (1)
4 The vocative singular of **pater, patris**, m. (1)
5 The dative plural of **frater, fratris**, m. (1)
6 The accusative singular of **mons, montis**, m. (1)
7 The ablative singular of **soror, sororis**, f. (1)
8 The accusative plural of **mater, matris**, f. (1)
9 The ablative plural of **frater, fratris**, m. (1)
10 The genitive plural of **pater, patris**, m. (1)

Total: 10

Exercise 9.20

Translate the following into English:

1 montem altum vidi. (4)
2 pater iratus currit. (4)
3 uxorem meam amo. (4)
4 rex clarus bene regebat. (5)
5 matrem nostram amamus. (4)
6 et fratrem et sororem habeo. (5)
7 rex sororem pulchram habet. (5)
8 multos montes vidimus. (4)
9 ad montem altum appropinquabamus. (5)
10 uxor mea iam dormit. (5)

Total: 45

Exercise 9.21

Give the case and number of the underlined nouns and then translate the sentences:

1 Marcus <u>frater</u> Aureliae est. (1 + 5)
2 Aurelia soror <u>Marci</u> est. (1 + 5)
3 puella cibum <u>patri</u> parabat. (1 + 5)
4 puella <u>sororem</u> non amat. (1 + 5)
5 servi ad <u>montem</u> festinant. (1 + 5)
6 in <u>montibus</u> sunt multae viae. (1 + 6)
7 <u>rex</u> matrem patremque amabat. (1 + 5)
8 rex <u>uxorem</u> pulchram habebat. (1 + 5)
9 <u>patrem</u> bonum habeo. (1 + 4)
10 <u>soror</u> mea mala est. (1 + 5)

Total: 60

Exercise 9.22

Give the part of speech of the underlined words and then translate the sentences:

1 puer cum sorore semper <u>pugnabat</u>. (1 + 6)
2 puella <u>cum</u> fratre saepe pugnat. (1 + 6)
3 pater pueri mali <u>iratus</u> est. (1 + 6)
4 rex bonus terram <u>bene</u> regit. (1 + 6)
5 rex multam <u>pecuniam</u> sorori dat. (1 + 6)
6 libertus pecuniam regis clari <u>capit</u>. (1 + 6)
7 mater <u>mea</u> fratrem clarum habet. (1 + 6)
8 frater <u>matris</u> meae clarus erat. (1 + 6)
9 puer multa dona matri <u>dedit</u>. (1 + 6)
10 uxor <u>nova</u> regis pulchra est. (1 + 6)

Total: 70

Exercise 9.23

In the following sentences, give the English subject of the sentence and translate this noun into Latin:

1 The son of the king loves wine. (1 + 1)
2 The women saw the queen. (1 + 1)
3 The men were destroying the walls. (1 + 1)
4 Was the man fighting with the farmers? (1 + 1)
5 The horses are tired. (1 + 1)
6 The Romans' swords terrify the Greeks. (1 + 1)
7 The walls of the town are large. (1 + 1)
8 Sailors always fear the water. (1 + 1)
9 The Romans always praise the gods. (1 + 1)
10 Why is the queen calling the friends? (1 + 1)

Total: 20

Exercise 9.24

In the following sentences, give the person, number and tense of the verb and translate it into Latin:

1	I have a good brother.	(2 + 2)
2	My sister is beautiful.	(2 + 2)
3	The wife of the master was preparing the dinner.	(2 + 2)
4	We see the high mountains.	(2 + 2)
5	Our parents like many gifts.	(2 + 2)
6	Mountains are not tall.	(2 + 2)
7	The king prepared a present for his parents.	(2 + 2)
8	Both the brother and the sister were shouting.	(2 + 2)
9	I am entering my father's country-house.	(2 + 2)
10	We were always warning the unhappy boys.	(2 + 2)

Total: 40

Exercise 9.25

In the following sentences, give the preposition and translate it and the noun it goes with into Latin:

1	We were walking towards the walls of the town.	(1 + 2)
2	The girl is singing with the schoolmaster.	(1 + 2)
3	The mother and father are hurrying to the country-house.	(1 + 2)
4	They were fighting in the street.	(1 + 2)
5	We are running from the town.	(1 + 2)
6	You (sing.) were preparing the dinner near the temple.	(1 + 2)
7	The sailors hurry out of the villa.	(1 + 2)
8	The wretched men were working in the town.	(1 + 2)
9	The bad masters were carrying money out of the temple.	(1 + 2)
10	At last the boys carry the books into the country-house.	(1 + 2)

Total: 30

Exercise 9.26

Give the case and number of the underlined nouns and then translate the sentences:

1	Marcus et Sextus <u>pueri</u> Romani sunt.	(1 + 7)
2	Brutus et Aurelia parentes <u>pueri</u> sunt.	(1 + 7)
3	O <u>dux</u>, matrem bonam et patrem clarum habes.	(1 + 9)
4	soror mea <u>dominam</u> saevam saepe timebat.	(1 + 7)
5	dux et <u>comites</u> et milites saepe monebat.	(1 + 8)
6	vir magnam turbam <u>militum</u> vidit.	(1 + 6)
7	milites <u>lucem</u> diu spectabant.	(1 + 5)
8	<u>milites</u> Romani oppidum hastis et sagittis oppugnaverunt.	(1 + 8)
9	mater et pater <u>regis</u> irati erant.	(1 + 7)
10	frater meus <u>corpus</u> magnum habet.	(1 + 6)

Total: 80

Exercise 9.27

Put into the singular and translate your answer:

1	reges festinabant.	(2 + 3)
2	puellae fratres habebant.	(3 + 4)
3	puellae non appropinquabant.	(2 + 4)
4	dona amavistis.	(2 + 3)
5	viri feminas puniverunt.	(3 + 4)

Total: 30

Exercise 9.28

Put into the plural and translate your answer:

1	mons altus est pulcher.	(4 + 5)
2	puer patrem amat.	(3 + 4)
3	rex sororem habebat.	(3 + 4)
4	uxor bellum timet.	(3 + 4)
5	mater discessit.	(2 + 3)

Total: 35

Exercise 9.29

Study the passage below (do not write a translation) and answer the questions that follow. Complete sentences are not required.

On Mount Olympus the three goddesses Juno, Athena and Venus argue over the golden apple.

1   dei deaeque in monte Olympo erant. <u>pomum</u>
     spectabant. pomum pulchrum erat. pomum <u>aureum</u>
     erat. verba in pomo erant: 'pomum aureum feminae
     <u>pulcherrimae</u> est.'

5   Iuno regina deorum erat. et soror et uxor <u>Iovis</u> erat.
     dea Iuno pomum spectavit. verba legit. 'ego dea
     pulcherrima sum,' clamavit. 'pomum igitur meum est.'

     dea Athena pomum spectavit. verba legit. 'erras,
     Iuno,' inquit. 'pomum meum est. pomum meum

10   est quod ego pulcherrima sum.' dea Venus pomum
     spectavit. verba legit. '

     'deae,' inquit. 'ego pulcherrima sum. pomum igitur
     meum est. pomum <u>mihi</u> tradite!'

     sic tres deae de pomo aureo <u>disputabant</u>. <u>omnes</u>

15   pomum aureum habere cupiebant. ad Iovem
     appropinquare igitur constituerunt. Iuppiter et pater
     et rex deorum erat.

pomum, -i, n. = apple
aureus, -a, -um = golden
pulcherrimus, -a, -um = the most beautiful

Iuppiter, Iovis, m. = Jupiter

mihi = to me
disputo, -are, -avi (1) = I argue
omnes = (they) all

1 dei deaeque in monte Olympo erant. (line 1)
   Where were the gods and goddesses? **(2)**
2 pomum spectabant. (lines 1–2)
   What were they doing? **(3)**
3 'pomum aureum feminae pulcherrimae est.' (lines 3–4)
   What was written on the apple? **(4)**
4 et soror et uxor Iovis erat. (line 5)
   How was Juno's relationship with Jupiter unusual? **(4)**
5 'ego dea pulcherrima sum,' clamavit. (lines 6–7)
   What did Juno claim on reading the writing on the apple? **(2)**
6 dea Athena ... mihi tradite! (lines 8–13)
   Translate these lines into good English. **(30)**
7 Give the meaning of the following words, and for each one, give an English word which comes from the Latin word.
   a) constituerunt (line 16) **(2)**
   b) pater (line 16) **(2)**
8 cupiebant (line 15) In which tense is this verb? **(1)**
9 habere (line 15) Give the 1st person singular, present tense of this verb. **(1)**
10 erat (line 17)
   a) Give the 1st person singular, present tense of this verb. **(1)**
   b) In which tense is this verb? **(1)**
   c) Give the person of this verb. **(1)**
   d) Give the number of this verb. **(1)**

Total: 55

Exercise 9.30

Translate the following English sentences into Latin.

1 The friends love money. **(4)**
2 The man was carrying wine and a book. **(6)**
3 The friends do not warn the master. **(5)**
4 We were shouting and praising the wine. **(5)**

Total: 20

Chapter 10: Non-increasing 3rd declension nouns; the future tense

Exercise 10.1

Translate the following into English:

1 rex cives Romanos diu regebat. (6)
2 dux cum hostibus pugnabat. (5)
3 nautae Romani naves in mare portaverunt. (7)
4 senem Romanum in templo exspectabamus. (6)
5 Romani iuvenes validos saepe laudabant. (6)
6 ubi sunt comites hostium? (5)
7 iuvenis cives ceteros magnopere timebat. (6)
8 dominus mulierem caram diu amabat. (6)
9 senex miser iuvenem in medium mare iecit. (8)
10 regina captivos ceteros liberavit. (5)

Total: 60

Exercise 10.2

Translate the following into English:

1 iuvenes ad mare appropinquabant. (5)
2 urbes magnas diu spectabamus. (5)
3 naves hostium iuvenis diu exspectabat. (6)
4 cur corpora hostium in mediam urbem portatis? (8)
5 in medios hostes festinavimus. (5)
6 iter longum ad mare nostrum* faciebamus. (7)
7 domina maritum carum prope montes necavit. (7)
8 fabulas longas iuvenibus narrabam. (5)
9 per montes altos milites Romani diu errabant. (8)
10 cives ceteros liberaverunt. (4)

* The Romans referred to the Mediterranean Sea as 'mare nostrum'. Why do you think this was?

Total: 60

Exercise 10.3

Give the correct form of the following nouns:

1 The nominative plural of iuvenis, iuvenis, c. (1)
2 The genitive singular of civis, civis, c. (1)
3 The dative plural of hostes, hostium, m.pl. (1)
4 The ablative singular of mare, maris, n. (1)
5 The genitive plural of miles, militis, m. (1)
6 The genitive plural of senex, senis, m. (1)
7 The ablative plural of urbs, urbis, f. (1)
8 The genitive plural of iuvenis, iuvenis, c. (1)
9 The accusative plural of hostes, hostium, m.pl. (1)
10 The genitive plural of civis, civis, c. (1)

Total: 10

Exercise 10.4

Give the correct form of the following nouns:

1 The genitive singular of **iuvenis, iuvenis**, c. (1)
2 The nominative plural of **mare, maris**, n. (1)
3 The dative singular of **miles, militis**, m. (1)
4 The vocative singular of **civis, civis**, c. (1)
5 The dative plural of **navis, navis**, f. (1)
6 The accusative singular of **mons, montis**, m. (1)
7 The ablative singular of **urbs, urbis**, f. (1)
8 The accusative plural of **civis, civis**, c. (1)
9 The genitive plural of **urbs, urbis**, f. (1)
10 The genitive singular of **senex, senis**, m. (1)

Total: 10

Exercise 10.5

Give the case and number of the underlined nouns and then translate the sentences:

1 iuvenes Romani in templum <u>hostium</u> festinaverunt. (1 + 7)
2 Romani urbem in septem <u>montibus</u> aedificaverunt. (1 + 7)
3 Romani cum hostibus prope <u>mare</u> pugnabant. (1 + 7)
4 regina <u>nomina</u> civium non amabat. (1 + 6)
5 senex in urbe cum <u>muliere</u> habitabat. (1 + 7)
6 naves magnas <u>hostium</u> spectabamus. (1 + 5)
7 nautae Romani per <u>mare</u> diu errabant. (1 + 7)
8 libertus cum <u>iuvene</u> valido approbinquabat. (1 + 6)
9 cum <u>comitibus</u> in montibus habitabatis. (1 + 6)
10 domina servum carum <u>parentum</u> liberare constituit. (1 + 7)

Total: 75

Exercise 10.6

Put into the singular and translate your answer*:

1 flumina longa sunt. (3 + 3)
2 urbes diu oppugnabatis. (2 + 3)
3 dona spectavimus. (2 + 2)
4 pueri montes viderunt. (3 + 3)
5 poetae cantabant. (2 + 2)

Total: 25

You will not be required to do this in the exam.

Exercise 10.7

Put into the plural and translate your answer*:

1 iuvenis currit. (2 + 2)
2 iter longum est. (3 + 3)
3 iam advenio. (1 + 2)
4 rex urbem cepit. (3 + 3)
5 urbs pulchra erat. (3 + 3)

Total: 25

You will not be required to do this in the exam.

Exercise 10.8

Translate the following into Latin:

1 She loves letters. (3)
2 The queen has many sons. (5)
3 He has a beautiful villa. (4)
4 The slaves attacked the town with spears. (5)
5 The savage god was destroying the town. (5)
6 The queen's sons feared the gods. (5)
7 The men saw the girl in the town. (6)
8 We were entering the temple with swords. (5)
9 The sailors are not afraid of the horses. (5)
10 The bad girl watches the horses near the walls. (7)

Total: 50

Exercise 10.9

Study the passage below (do not write a translation) and answer the questions that follow. Complete sentences are not required.

Jupiter passes the buck to Paris, prince of Troy.

1   tres deae, ubi ad <u>Iovem</u> venerunt, <u>haec</u> verba
       dixerunt:'Iuppiter, <u>pomum aureum</u> nos tres deae
       cupimus. quis est <u>pulcherrima</u>? lege! nunc lege!' Iuppiter
       <u>perterritus</u> erat. iram dearum timebat. 'deae,' inquit,'vos
5   <u>omnes</u> pulchrae estis. vos omnes corpora pulchra
       habetis. legere non cupio. iuvenem tamen <u>scio</u>, <u>Paridem</u>
       nomine. prope urbem Troiam habitat. feminas pulchras
       amat. Paris pulcherrimam leget. Paridem rogate!' tres
       deae iratae erant. Paridem tamen rogare constituerunt.
10   itaque ad urbem iter fecerunt. iter longum non erat.
       mox igitur Paridem invenerunt. Paris, ubi lucem claram
       vidit, timebat. deae iuveni fabulam de pomo aureo
       narraverunt. 'Iuppiter nos ad te misit, Paris. te deam
       pulcherrimam legere iubet. nunc lege!

Iuppiter, Iovis, m. = Jupiter
pomum, -i, n. = apple
aureus, -a, -um = golden
pulcherrimus, -a, -um = the most beautiful
perterritus, -a, -um = terrified
omnes = all
scio, -ire, -ivi (4) = I know
Paris, Paridis, m. = Paris (a son of the King of Troy)

1 **tres deae, ubi ad Iovem venerunt.** (line 1)
  What do the goddesses do at the start of the story?   **(2)**

2 **'Iuppiter, pomum aureum nos tres deae cupimus. quis est pulcherrima?'** (lines 2–3)
  What do the goddesses ask Jupiter, and what is it they want?   **(2 + 2)**

3 **iram dearum timebat.** (line 4)
  Why does Jupiter not wish to answer their question?   **(2)**

4 **vos omnes pulchrae estis. vos omnes corpora pulchra habetis.** (lines 5–6)
  What reason does Jupiter give for not being able to give the goddesses a straight answer?   **(4)**

5 **iuvenem tamen scio, Paridem nomine. prope Troiam habitat.** (lines 6–7)
  What type of person does Jupiter suggest might take over the task, and where was he to be found?   **(1 + 2)**

6 **feminas pulchras ... nunc lege!** (lines 7–14)
  Translate these lines into good English.   **(30)**

7 Give the meaning of the following words, and for each one, give an English word which comes from the Latin word.
     a) **iratae** (line 9)   **(2)**
     b) **iuvenem** (line 6)   **(2)**

8 **rogate** (line 8) What part of the verb is this?   **(1)**

9 **urbem** (line 7) In which case is this noun?   **(1)**

10 **claram** (line 11) Give the gender of this adjective.   **(1)**

11 **timebat** (line 12) This means *he was afraid*. How would you say in Latin *they were afraid*?   **(1)**

12 **misit** (line 13) Give the Latin subject of this verb?   **(1)**

13 **nunc** (line 14) What part of speech is this word?   **(1)**

14 Translate the following English sentences into Latin.
     a) We never fear the gods.   **(4)**
     b) The good boy was calling the bad slave.   **(6)**
     c) Many women watch the queen.   **(5)**
     d) The Romans were building large walls.   **(5)**

Total: 75

Exam Practice Questions

Exercise 10.11

Translate the following into English:

1 portabimus.	(2)
2 delebit.	(2)
3 sedebitis.	(2)
4 necabunt.	(2)
5 appropinquabo.	(2)
6 superabis.	(2)
7 errabit.	(2)
8 tenebunt.	(2)
9 intrabis.	(2)
10 clamabimus.	(2)
11 liberabunt.	(2)
12 dabimus.	(2)
13 narrabitis.	(2)
14 exspectabis.	(2)
15 narrabunt.	(2)
16 ridebitis.	(2)
17 videbit.	(2)
18 laborabimus.	(2)
19 cantabitis.	(2)
20 monebimus.	(2)

Total: 40

Exercise 10.12

Translate the following into English:

1 aedificabunt.	(2)
2 iubebo.	(2)
3 respondebitis.	(2)
4 stabunt.	(2)
5 pugnabimus.	(2)
6 oppugnabunt.	(2)
7 clamabit.	(2)
8 terrebitis.	(2)
9 delebunt.	(2)
10 dabitis.	(2)
11 appropinquabimus.	(2)
12 delebit.	(2)
13 manebo.	(2)
14 rogabo.	(2)
15 ridebimus.	(2)
16 videbo.	(2)
17 sedebimus	(2)
18 stabit.	(2)
19 monebitis.	(2)
20 habitabunt.	(2)

Total: 40

Exercise 10.13

Translate the following into Latin:

1 We are building.	(1)
2 They walk.	(1)
3 I was loving.	(1)
4 He shouts.	(1)
5 We destroy.	(1)
6 You (sing.) have.	(1)
7 I enter.	(1)
8 They were praising.	(1)
9 We advise.	(1)
10 She kills.	(1)
11 I was preparing.	(1)
12 You (sing.) carry.	(1)
13 They were fighting.	(1)
14 She watches.	(1)
15 You (pl.) are.	(1)
16 We fear.	(1)
17 You (sing.) see.	(1)
18. We were calling.	(1)
19. She is.	(1)
20 He is destroying.	(1)

Total: 20

Exercise 10.14

Give the person and number of the following verbs, and then translate them into English:

1 manebit.	(1 + 2)
2 oppugnabitis.	(1 + 2)
3 manebimus.	(1 + 2)
4 necabis.	(1 + 2)
5 tenebo.	(1 + 2)
6 videbimus.	(1 + 2)
7 spectabunt.	(1 + 2)
8 vocabunt.	(1 + 2)
9 terrebit.	(1 + 2)
10 festinabitis.	(1 + 2)
11 monebo.	(1 + 2)
12 appropinquabitis.	(1 + 2)
13 tenebitis.	(1 + 2)
14 intrabis.	(1 + 2)
15 rogabunt.	(1 + 2)
16 delebo.	(1 + 2)
17 vocabis.	(1 + 2)
18 habebunt.	(1 + 2)
19 aedificabunt.	(1 + 2)
20 parabimus.	(1 + 2)

Total: 60

Exercise 10.15

Give the person and number of the following verbs, and then translate them into English:

1	regemus.	(1 + 2)
2	consumet.	(1 + 2)
3	legam.	(1 + 2)
4	erunt.	(1 + 2)
5	advenietis.	(1 + 2)
6	bibemus.	(1 + 2)
7	curram.	(1 + 2)
8	curremus.	(1 + 2)
9	trades.	(1 + 2)
10	mittet.	(1 + 2)
11	constituemus.	(1 + 2)
12	ludemus.	(1 + 2)
13	eris.	(1 + 2)
14	leges.	(1 + 2)
15	fugiam.	(1 + 2)
16	constituetis.	(1 + 2)
17	mittent.	(1 + 2)
18	ludent.	(1 + 2)
19	cupietis.	(1 + 2)
20	discedam.	(1 + 2)

Total: 60

Exercise 10.16

Translate the following into English:

1	fugiet.	(1)
2	ostendemus.	(1)
3	eritis.	(1)
4	dormies.	(1)
5	scribemus.	(1)
6	current.	(1)
7	accipient.	(1)
8	capiemus.	(1)
9	dormiet.	(1)
10	erit.	(1)
11	discedemus.	(1)
12	dormiam.	(1)
13	punient.	(1)
14	veniam.	(1)
15	ero.	(1)
16	capietis.	(1)
17	iaciam.	(1)
18	accipies.	(1)
19	pones.	(1)
20	dicet.	(1)

Total: 20

Exercise 10.17

Translate the following into English:

1	currit.	(1)
2	curret.	(1)
3	regimus.	(1)
4	regemus.	(1)
5	festinabit.	(1)
6	festinamus.	(1)
7	est.	(1)
8	erit.	(1)
9	clamabit.	(1)
10	bibet.	(1)
11	bibit.	(1)
12	ostendent.	(1)
13	ostendunt.	(1)
14	puniet.	(1)
15	punit.	(1)
16	videmus.	(1)
17	videbimus.	(1)
18	manebunt.	(1)
19	manent.	(1)
20	erunt.	(1)

Total: 20

Exercise 10.18

Translate the following into English:

1	portabitis.	(1)
2	parant.	(1)
3	dabo.	(1)
4	delemus.	(1)
5	vocabimus.	(1)
6	delebis.	(1)
7	dormiemus.	(1)
8	narrabit.	(1)
9	habent.	(1)
10	legis.	(1)
11	dormimus.	(1)
12	intramus.	(1)
13	ridebitis.	(1)
14	leges.	(1)
15	habebo.	(1)
16	advenient.	(1)
17	fugiet.	(1)
18	fugit.	(1)
19	capiunt.	(1)
20	habebis.	(1)

Total: 20

Exercise 10.19

Give the tense of the verb and then translate the sentences.

1	heri <u>discipula</u>[1] laborabat.	(1 + 4)
2	hodie <u>socii</u>[2] pugnant.	(1 + 4)
3	cras <u>sacerdos</u>[3] fugiet.	(1 + 4)
4	heri oppidum oppugnabamus.	(1 + 4)
5	hodie oppidum oppugnamus.	(1 + 4)
6	cras oppidum capiemus.	(1 + 4)
7	saepe pueri currebant.	(1 + 4)
8	pueri numquam currunt.	(1 + 4)
9	cras pueri current.	(1 + 4)
10	olim puellas pulchras spectabam.	(1 + 5)
11	hodie multas puellas pulchras specto.	(1 + 6)
12	cras multas puellas pulchras spectabo.	(1 + 6)
13	heri Romani scuta portabant.	(1 + 5)
14	hodie Romani scuta portant.	(1 + 5)
15	cras Romani scuta portabunt.	(1 + 5)
16	olim regina patriam regebat.	(1 + 5)
17	magister <u>pietatem</u>[4] Romanorum laudat.	(1 + 5)
18	quis vinum novum consumet?	(1 + 5)
19	cur iuvenes in templo pugnabant?	(1 + 6)
20	novem senes ad montem appropinquabant.	(1 + 6)

Total: 115

1 discipulua, -ae, f. = pupil

2 socius, -i, m. = ally

3 sacerdos, sacerdotis, c. = priest

4 pietas, pietatis, f. = piety

Exercise 10.20

Give the tense of the verb in the following sentences and then translate the verb into Latin.

1	Many young men were walking into the mountains.	(1 + 2)
2	The old man was shouting in the garden.	(1 + 2)
3	My father was praising the unhappy citizens.	(1 + 2)
4	The angry soldiers were attacking the walls.	(1 + 2)
5	The boys often hurry to school.	(1 + 2)

Total: 15

Exercise 10.21

Give the object in the following sentences and then translate the object into Latin:

1	I shall drink wine tomorrow.	(1 + 1)
2	Pupils will never praise teachers.	(1 + 1)
3	The young man will carry the books to the town.	(1 + 1)
4	Marcus will never prepare dinner again.	(1 + 1)
5	The farmer will always lead the horses into the fields.	(1 + 1)

Total: 10

Exercise 10.22

Translate the following into English:

1	ad urbem appropinquabo.	(4)
2	rex uxorem pulchram habet.	(5)
3	femina maritum validum habet.	(5)
4	senex vinum et libros ad mare portabat.	(8)
5	iter in montes mox faciemus.	(6)
6	ceteri milites iuvenem fessum diu exspectabant.	(7)
7	dux civium urbem claram defendebat.	(6)
8	senex ancillam miseram mox liberabit.	(6)
9	o cives, montes et mare diu spectabitis.	(7)
10	novem iuvenes in mare ducemus.	(6)

Total: 60

Exercise 10.23

Give the person and number of the verb in the following sentences and then translate the verb into Latin.

1	The water of the river is deep.	(1+2)
2	The wife of the king will not have money.	(1+2)
3	We walked down from the mountain.	(1+2)
4	You (pl.) carried the king on the journey.	(1+2)
5	They will fight in the city tomorrow.	(1+2)

Total: 15

Exercise 10.24

Study the passage below (do not write a translation) and answer the questions that follow. Complete sentences are not required.

Paris faces a dilemma.

1　Paris perterritus erat. respondit tamen: 'certe, pulchrae estis, deae. nunc legere non cupio. ad me cras venite! cras constituam.'

　　deae Paridi 'nos cras veniemus,' inquiunt. iratae
5　discesserunt. secreto tamen Iuno ad Paridem appropinquavit. Paridi 'si pomum mihi trades,' inquit, 'ego te virum potentissimum faciam.' tum dea discessit.

　　Athena quoque ad Paridem secreto
10　appropinquavit. Paridi 'si tu me leges,' inquit, 'ego te virum sapientissimum faciam.' tum dea discessit. postea, Venus ad Paridem secreto appropinquavit. Paridi 'si tu me leges,' inquit, 'ego tibi feminam pulcherrimam dabo. femina
15　uxor tua erit.' tum discessit. Paris solus nunc erat.

Paris, Paridis, m. = Paris
perterritus, -a, -um = terrified
certe = indeed
nos = we
secreto = in secret
si = if
pomum, -i, n. = apple
mihi = to me
te = you (accusative)
potentissimus, -a, -um = very powerful
me = me
sapientissimus, -a, -um = very wise
tibi = to you
pulcherrimus, -a, um = very beautiful

➤

1   respondit tamen: 'certe pulchrae estis, deae.' (line 1)
    What does Paris say to the goddesses?   (2)
2   nunc legere non cupio (line 2)
    How does this affect his ability to make a decision?   (2)
3   ad me cras venite! (lines 2–3)
    What does Paris ask the goddesses to do?   (3)
4   cras constituam. (line 3)
    What will he do when they do this?   (2)
5   iratae discesserunt. (lines 4–5)
    What effect does this conversation have on the goddesses?   (2)
6   secreto tamen Iuno ad Paridem appropinquavit. Paridi 'si pomum mihi trades,' inquit,
    'ego te virum potentissimum faciam.' (lines 5–7)
    How does the goddess Juno hope to get an advantage in the contest?   (4)
7   Athena quoque ... nunc erat. (lines 9–16)
    Translate these lines into good English.   (30)
8   Give the meaning of the following words, and for each one, give an English word which comes from
    the Latin word.
        a) feminam (line 14)   (2)
        b) solus (line 15)   (2)
9   leges (line 13) In which tense is this verb?   (1)
10 feminam (line 14) In which case is this noun?   (1)
11 dabo (line 14) This means *I shall give*. How would you say in Latin *they were giving*?   (1)
12 discessit (line 15) What is the 1st singular of the present tense of this verb?   (1)
13 nunc (line 15) What part of speech is this word?   (1)
14 erat (line 16) In which tense is this verb?   (1)
15 Translate the following English sentences into Latin.
        a) Boys are always happy.   (5)
        b) Masters never praise the slaves.   (5)
        c) We carry many books to the schoolmaster.   (6)
        d) The Romans were building temples.   (4)

Total: 75

Chapter 11: Questions with nonne and num; nemo and nihil; numerals 11–20; personal pronouns; the pluperfect tense

Exercise 11.1

Translate the following into English:

1 ludit. (2)
2 num timet? (2)
3 nonne ridet? (2)
4 pugnabant. (2)
5 ambulabantne? (2)
6 num laborabatis? (2)
7 effugerunt. (2)
8 navigabimusne? (2)
9 nonne fugistis? (2)
10 num advenerunt? (2)

Total: 20

Exercise 11.2

Translate the following into English:

1 Achilles bene pugnabat. (4)
2 nonne Achilles bene pugnabat? (5)
3 num Graeci bene pugnabant? (5)
4 miles validus est. (4)
5 nonne miles validus est? (5)
6 num miles validus est? (5)
7 Hector miles clarus erat. (5)
8 nonne Hector clarus erat? (5)
9 num Hector miles clarus erat? (6)
10 nonne Hector dux Troianorum erat? (6)

Total: 50

Exercise 11.3

Translate the following into English:

1 nonne cives urbem bene defendebant? (6)
2 num puer Troianum conspexit? (5)
3 num Graeci Romanos vicerunt? (5)
4 num cives validi mortem timent? (6)
5 nonne mulierem in urbe heri conspexisti? (7)
6 nonne matrem tuam amas? (5)
7 nonne Graeci multa arma collegerunt? (6)
8 num femina maritum necare cupiebat? (5)
9 nonne milites Romani in proelio bene pugnaverunt? (8)
10 num Troiani ex urbe magna effugiebant? (7)

Total: 60

Exercise 11.4

Translate the following into Latin:

1 We were shouting with the sailors. (4)
2 You (pl.) fear the queen. (3)
3 She prepares the dinner with the boy. (5)
4 A famous woman was preparing the money in the villa. (7)
5 The master, however, is not afraid of the Romans. (6)

Total: 25

Exercise 11.5

Translate the following into Latin:

1 Boys often fight with good girls. (7)
2 The Romans never fight in the town. (6)
3 You (sing.) were praising the gods in the temple. (5)
4 I was not building the walls near the villa. (6)
5 The small boy was fighting with a big spear. (6)

Total: 30

Exam Practice Questions

Exercise 11.6

Translate the following into English:

1. tu ludis; ego laboro. (4)
2. nos Romani sumus; vos Graeci estis. (6)
3. nos vos non amamus. (4)
4. vos nos non amatis. (4)
5. ego te non amo. (4)
6. tu me non amas. (4)
7. nemo me vidit. (3)
8. ego puellam amo. (3)
9. puella me non amat. (4)
10. te in urbe vidi. (4)

Total: 40

Exercise 11.7

Translate the following into English:

1. hostes nos spectant. (4)
2. Romani nos non amant. (5)
3. pater meus te amat. (5)
4. te puniam, serve! (4)
5. quis me vocat? (4)
6. magister te vocat. (4)
7. femina vos spectabat. (4)
8. quis pecuniam mihi dabit? (5)
9. ego multam pecuniam tibi dabo. (6)
10. puellae nobiscum ludent. (4)

Total: 45

Exercise 11.8

Translate the following into English:

1. cur Paris[1] prope me stabat? (6)
2. hostes contra nos saepe pugnabant. (6)
3. pater meus pecuniam tibi dabit. (6)
4. legati[2], dominus argentum[3] vobis dabit. (6)
5. num Poeni[4] ad me festinabunt? (6)
6. nonne amici mecum ludent? (5)
7. pauci comites nobiscum cantabant. (5)
8. magister dona nobis numquam dat. (6)
9. senex donum mihi, tibi pecuniam dedit. (7)
10. cur magister te, non me, amat? (7)

Total: 60

1 Paris, Paridis, m. = Paris (the son of King Priam of Troy)

2 legatus, -i, m. = ambassador

3 argentum, -i, n. = silver

4 Poenus, -a, -um = Carthaginian

Exercise 11.9

Give the person, number and tense of the verbs in these sentences, and then translate the verbs into Latin:

1. The Romans were fighting with me. (3 + 2)
2. They were watching the soldiers with you. (3 + 2)
3. I am carrying money to you. (3 + 2)
4. He often prepares dinner for us. (3 + 2)
5. Why were they destroying the walls? (3 + 2)
6. We do not often walk with you. (3 + 2)
7. The wife of the king was calling us. (3 + 2)
8. The teacher often enters the temple. (3 + 2)
9. Surely he was not praising the leader of the enemy? (3 + 2)
10. Why was my mother warning the master? (3 + 2)

Total: 50

Exercise 11.10

Translate the following into English:

1 barbam[1] cruentam[2] Hectoris[3] miseri vidi. (6)
2 hasta magna Hectorem miserum vulneravit. (6)
3 sacerdos[4] Troianos stultos[5] iterum monebat. (6)
4 auriga[6] equum magnum celeremque comprehendit[7]. (6)
5 rex clarus equites[8] statim collegit. (6)

Total: 30

1 barba, -ae, f. = beard

2 cruentus, -a, -um = bloodstained

3 Hector, Hectoris, m. = Hector (son of King Priam of Troy)

4 sacerdos, sacerdotis, m. = priest

5 stultus, -a, -um = stupid

6 auriga, -ae, m. = charioteer

7 comprehendo, -ere, comprehendi, comprehensum = I seize

8 eques, equitis, m. = horseman; in plural, cavalry

Exercise 11.11

Translate the following into English:

1 dividimus[1] muros et moenia[2] pandimus[3] urbis. (8)
2 primus ante omnes Laocoon[4] decurrit[5] ab arce[6]. (8)
3 inde magnam hastam in latus[7] equi contorsit[8]. (8)
4 pastores[9] iuvenem magno clamore ad regem trahebant[10]. (8)
5 Laocoon sacerdos[11] taurum[12] magnum ad[13] aram[14] mactabat[15]. (8)

Total: 40

1 divido, -ere, divisi, divisum = I break through

2 moenia, moenium, n. pl. = fortifications

3 pando, -ere, pandi, pansum = I throw open

4 Laocoon = a Trojan priest

5 decurro, decurrere, decucurri, decursum = I run down

6 arx, arcis, f. = citadel

7 latus, lateris, n. = side

8 contorqueo, -ere, contorsi, contortum = I hurl

9 pastor, pastoris, m. = shepherd

10 traho, -ere, traxi, tractum = I drag

11 sacerdos, sacerdotis, m. = priest

12 taurus, -i, m. = bull

13 ad (+ acc.) = at

14 ara, arae, f. = altar

15 macto, -are, -avi, -atum = I sacrifice

Exercise 11.12

Give the case and number of the underlined words and then translate the sentences into English:

1 milites in proelio fortiter pugnaverunt. (1 + 6)
2 civem in urbe heri conspexi. (1 + 6)
3 multae naves insulam contra hostes defendebant. (1 + 7)
4 milites in proelio bene pugnabant. (1 + 6)
5 Romani bella contra Graecos saepe gerebant. (1 + 7)
6 arma militum Romanorum nova erant. (1 + 6)
7 comites ab insula in navibus sine mora discesserunt. (1 + 9)
8 hostes multos cives armis vulneraverunt. (1 + 6)
9 magister, quod ego numquam laborabam, me non amabat. (1 + 9)
10 copiae hostium multa vulnera a nobis acceperunt. (1 + 8)

Total: 80

Exam Practice Questions

Exercise 11.13

Give the tense of the underlined words and then translate the sentences into English:

1	cives Romani hostes numquam <u>timebunt</u>.	(1 + 6)
2	contra miltes Troianos dux bene <u>pugnabat</u>.	(1 + 7)
3	urbem muris magnis <u>defendebunt</u>.	(1 + 5)
4	milites hastis sagittisque urbem <u>oppugnabant</u>.	(1 + 6)
5	senes et parentes puellarum ducem hostium magnopere <u>timent</u>.	(1 + 9)
6	tandem in urbem iter <u>faciemus</u>.	(1 + 6)
7	comites ducis filios mulieris <u>salutaverunt</u>.	(1 + 6)
8	nonne mortem <u>timetis</u>?	(1 + 4)
9	Troiani septem milites <u>occiderunt</u>.	(1 + 5)
10	num vulnera militum mala <u>erant</u>?	(1 + 6)

Total: 70

Exercise 11.14

Study the passage below and answer the questions that follow.

The Greeks realise that capturing Troy will not be a five-minute job.

1　Protesilaus mortuus erat. Graeci contra muros
　　Troiae ruerant. fortiter et diu sub muris
　　pugnaverant, sed frustra. multos Troianos
　　vulneraverant, multos Troianos occiderant, sed
5　urbem non ceperant.

　　<u>Agamemnon</u>, frater Menelai, dux Graecorum erat.　　Agamemnon, Agamemnonis,
　　non laetus erat. militibus, 'comites,' inquit, 'Troiam　　m. = Agamemnon
　　hodie non capiemus. muri Troiae alti et validi
　　sunt. cives Troiani quoque validi sunt. muros bene
10　defendunt. ego vos <u>castra</u>
　　<u>ponere</u> iubeo. bene dormite! cras contra hostes　　castra, -orum, n.pl. = camp
　　iterum pugnabimus.'　　castra pono = I pitch camp

　　postquam milites Graeci verba Agamemnonis audiverunt,
　　castra posuerunt. fessi erant et mox dormiebant.

1	Translate the passage into good English.	(30)
2	**muros** (line 1) Explain the connection between **muros** and the English word *mural*.	(2)
3	**laetus** (line 7)	
	a) In which case is this adjective?	(1)
	b) Why is this case used?	(1)
4	**capiemus** (line 8) Give the 1st person singular of the present tense of this verb.	(1)
5	**defendunt** (line 10)	
	a) Give the person and number of this verb.	(1)
	b) In which tense is this verb?	(1)
6	**verba** (line 13)	
	a) In which case is this noun?	(1)
	b) Why is this case used?	(1)
7	**fessi** (line 14) What part of speech is this word?	(1)

Total: 40

Exercise 11.15

Translate the underlined words into Latin*:

1 They had built a <u>temple</u>. (1)
2 He had seen the <u>queen</u>. (1)
3 You (sing.) had destroyed the <u>walls</u>. (1)
4 We had walked <u>to</u> the town. (1)
5 I <u>often</u> fight with my friends. (1)
6 You (pl.) had punished the <u>bad</u> boy. (1)
7 He had made a journey into the <u>town</u>. (1)
8 She had sent a <u>letter</u> to my friend. (1)
9 We <u>always</u> listen to the master. (1)
10 They had carried the <u>wine</u> into the villa. (1)

Total: 10

* *Your teacher may ask you to translate the whole sentence.*

Exercise 11.16

Translate the following into English:

1 amaveramus. (2)
2 ceperant. (2)
3 audiveras. (2)
4 rexerat. (2)
5 dederam. (2)
6 duxerat. (2)
7 monueramus. (2)
8 terruerat. (2)
9 responderant. (2)
10 miseram. (2)

Total: 20

Exercise 11.17

Translate the following into English:

1 posuerat. (2)
2 cucurrerant. (2)
3 discesseras. (2)
4 legeram. (2)
5 dormiveramus. (2)
6 ambulaveramus. (2)
7 fugerat. (2)
8 feceratis. (2)
9 riseramus. (2)
10 deleveras. (2)

Total: 20

Exercise 11.18

Translate the following into English:

1 manseramus. (2)
2 viderant. (2)
3 pugnaverat. (2)
4 intraverant. (2)
5 ceperat. (2)
6 monueras. (2)
7 biberat. (2)
8 dixerat. (2)
9 luseramus. (2)
10 occideratis. (2)

Total: 20

Exercise 11.19

Translate the following into English:

1 magister iratus erat quod riseramus. (7)
2 puer librum non legerat. (5)
3 pueri mali fuerant. (4)
4 puella puerum vulneraverat. (4)
5 verba non audiveramus. (4)
6 dominus laetus erat quod bene dormiverat. (8)
7 iuvenes bene laboraverant. (4)
8 uxor tandem discesserat. (4)
9 domina cibum paraverat. (4)
10 amicus multam pecuniam tibi dederat. (6)

Total: 50

Exercise 11.20

Translate the following into English:

1	hostes laeti erant quod discesseramus.	(7)
2	di Romanos vicerant.	(4)
3	numquam urbem deleverant.	(4)
4	celeriter adveneramus.	(3)
5	multa oppida ceperant.	(4)
6	puer celeriter currebat quod magistrum viderat.	(8)
7	magister iratus libertum conspexerat.	(5)
8	milites validi cives terruerant.	(5)
9	tandem homo ducem occiderat.	(5)
10	miles malus sororem vulneraverat.	(5)

Total: 50

Exercise 11.21

Translate the following into English:

1	puer diu laboraverat.	(4)
2	dux iratus fuerat.	(4)
3	milites bene pugnaverant.	(4)
4	bene dormiveram.	(3)
5	puer miser non riserat.	(5)
6	proelium longum fuerat.	(4)
7	hostes multas terras superaverant.	(5)
8	dominus multos servos liberaverat.	(5)
9	rex hostium ad flumen festinaverat.	(6)
10	milites oppidum fortiter oppugnaverant.	(5)

Total: 45

Exercise 11.22

Translate the following into English:

1	duodecim iuvenes ex oppido cucurrerant.	(6)
2	nemo sedecim libros legerat.	(5)
3	nuntius fessus nihil dixerat.	(5)
4	senex multam aquam biberat.	(5)
5	femina undecim vulnera acceperat.	(5)
6	quattuordecim dona ad patrem miserat.	(6)
7	viginti milites in flumen festinaverant.	(6)
8	septendecim puellas non conspexeramus.	(5)
9	duodeviginti milites non bene pugnaverant.	(6)
10	undecim cives oppidum fortiter defenderant.	(6)

Total: 55

Exercise 11.23

Translate the underlined words into Latin*:

1	We had <u>never</u> conquered the enemy.	(1)
2	They had <u>often</u> seized the city.	(1)
3	He had wounded the <u>unhappy</u> king.	(1)
4	We had defended the <u>big</u> town.	(1)
5	I had seen the <u>beautiful</u> girl.	(1)

Total: 5

* Your teacher may ask you to translate the whole sentence.

Exercise 11.24

Translate the underlined words into Latin*:

1	The leader had destroyed <u>many</u> temples.	(1)
2	The soldier had wounded the friend with a <u>spear</u>.	(1)
3	The enemy had charged against the <u>town</u>.	(1)
4	The <u>sailors</u> had waited for the ship for a long time.	(1)
5	The Greeks had killed <u>many</u> Romans.	(1)

Total: 5

* Your teacher may ask you to translate the whole sentence.

Exercise 11.25

Give and translate the following:

1 The 3rd person plural, present tense
   of **voco**. (2)
2 The 1st person plural, imperfect tense
   of **habeo**. (2)
3 The 2nd person plural, present tense
   of **deleo**. (2)
4 The 2nd person singular, imperfect tense
   of **video**. (2)
5 The 3rd person singular, present tense
   of **paro**. (2)

Total: 10

Exercise 11.26

Give the person, number, tense and 1st person
singular of the present tense of the following, and
then translate:

1 defendemus. (4 + 2)
2 tradebat. (4 + 2)
3 vicerat. (4 + 2)
4 eritis. (4 + 2)
5 accepit. (4 + 2)

Total: 30

Exercise 11.27

Translate the underlined words into Latin*:

1 I do not <u>have</u> courage. (2)
2 The enemy <u>were</u> savage. (2)
3 We will <u>never</u> beat the <u>Romans</u>. (2)
4 They will seize the <u>big town</u> tomorrow. (2)
5 The <u>Romans</u> have <u>not</u> conquered
   the Greeks. (2)

Total: 10

** Your teacher may ask you to translate the
whole sentence.*

Exercise 11.28

Translate the underlined words into Latin*:

1 The man <u>has</u> great courage. (2)
2 The courage of the soldiers <u>was</u> famous. (2)
3 The citizens were <u>destroying</u> the town walls. (2)
4 The soldiers were attacking the city with
   <u>spears</u> and arrows. (2)
5 I <u>often</u> see my <u>friends</u> in the city. (2)

Total: 10

** Your teacher may ask you to translate the
whole sentence.*

Exercise 11.29

Keeping the same person and number, put the following verbs into the imperfect tense and translate your answer:

1 paraverunt. (1 + 2)
2 vocavit. (1 + 2)
3 monuimus. (1 + 2)
4 timuimus. (1 + 2)
5 aedificavistis. (1 + 2)
6 delevit. (1 + 2)
7 viderunt. (1 + 2)
8 clamabit. (1 + 2)
9 amabit. (1 + 2)
10 portaveram. (1 + 2)

Total: 30

Exercise 11.30

Study the passage below (do not write a translation) and answer the questions that follow. Complete sentences are not required.

Achilles and Hector.

1	Graeci Troiam oppugnaverant. urbem Troiam tamen non statim occupaverant. Troianos non vicerant. prope urbem Troiam igitur <u>castra</u> posuerant. diu copiae Graecorum urbem Troiam oppugnabant.
5	muros tamen delere non <u>poterant</u>. milites Graeci igitur irati, Troiani laeti erant.
	Priamus rex Troiae erat. multos liberos validos rex habebat. unus filiorum, nomine Hector, vir magnae virtutis erat. pro Troianis fortiter semper pugnabat
10	Hector. inter Graecos quoque erant multi milites validi. Achilles autem <u>validissimus</u> erat. Achilles amicum, Patroclum nomine, habebat. quod Hector Patroclum in proelio occiderat, Achilles Troianos magnopere <u>oderat</u>.

castra, -orum, n.pl. = camp

poterant = they were able

validissimus, -a, -um = strongest

oderat = (he) hated

1 urbem Troiam tamen non statim occupaverant. (lines 1–2)
   What was the state of the war between the Greeks and Trojans at this stage? (2)
2 prope urbem Troiam igitur castra posuerant. (line 3)
   How had the Greeks set about defending their position? (2)
3 diu copiae Graecorum urbem Troiam oppugnabant. (lines 3–4)
   Give and translate the word that tells us how long the Greeks were on the attack. (2)
4 muros tamen delere non poterant. (line 5)
   What was the difficulty that the Greeks faced? (2)
5 milites Graeci igitur irati. (lines 5–6)
   What effect did this have on the Greeks? (2)
6 Priamus ... oderat. (lines 7–13)
   Translate these lines into good English. (30)
7 inter (line 10) What part of speech is this word? (1)
8 erant (line 10) Give the tense of this verb. (1)
9 validos (line 7) In which case is this word? (1)
10 virtutis (line 9) In which case is this word? (1)
11 pugnabat (line 9) This verb means *he was fighting*. How would it change if you wished to say *they were fighting*? (2)
12 milites (line 10)
   a) In which declension is this word? (1)
   b) In which case is it? (1)
13 From the passage, give an example of the following:
   a) a preposition followed by the accusative case (1)
   b) a 3rd declension noun in the genitive case (1)
   c) a preposition followed by the ablative case (1)
14 prope urbem Troiam (line 3) Explain the connection between **urbem** and the English word *urban*. (2)
15 nomine Hector (line 8) Explain the connection between **nomine** and the English word *nominate*. (2)

Total: 55

Exercise 11.31

Translate the following into Latin.

1 The queen feared the famous gods. (5)
2 The wretched boys were warning the horse with a sword. (6)
3 The women walk towards the temple. (5)
4 Augustus was a good master. (4)

Total: 20

Chapter 12: 3rd declension adjectives; is, ea, id

Exercise 12.1

Translate the following into English:

1 Menelaus miles Graecus erat. is vir bonus erat. (10)
2 Helena uxor Menelai erat. ea femina pulchra erat. (10)
3 in urbe est forum. id est forum magnum. (10)
4 Marcus filium habet. eum amat. (7)
5 Marcus filiam habet. eam amat. (7)
6 Marcus filium et filiam habet. eos amat. (9)
7 Marcus filium habet. pecuniam ei dat. (8)
8 insula magna est. multi incolae in ea habitant. (10)
9 Marcus multos libros accepit. eos semper legit. (9)
10 Marcus uxorem pulchram habet. nomen eius est Aurelia. (10)

Total: 90

Exercise 12.2

Translate the following into English:

1 Aurelia quindecim amicos habet. amici eius clari sunt. (10)
2 Marcus et Aurelia septendecim servos habent. servi eorum boni sunt. (12)
3 Marcus pecuniam eis saepe dat. (6)
4 Marcus librum longum legit. sunt in eo multa verba. (10)
5 Marcus vinum bonum ad Aureliam misit. ea id nunc bibit. (12)
6 Marcus multa arma habet. arma eius nova sunt. (10)
7 dominus duodecim templa aedificaverat. ea amat. (8)
8 rex liberos amat. multam pecuniam eis saepe dat. (10)
9 puer aquam rogaverat. dominus eam ei dedit. (9)
10 forum novum est. id nunc spectamus. (8)

Total: 95

Exercise 12.3

Translate the following into English:

1 magister puerum malum non amabat. eum igitur puniebat. (10)
2 Protesilaus fortiter pugnabat. Troiani tamen eum mox occiderunt. (10)
3 Graeci contra Troianos ruerunt. sedecim ex eis necaverunt. (10)
4 miles fortis septem vulnera acceperat. vulnera eius mala erant. (11)
5 dominus servum bonum, Sextum nomine, habebat. eum heri liberavit. (11)
6 navis magna erat. erant in ea undeviginti nautae. (10)
7 magister multa verba dixit. nemo tamen ea audiebat. (10)
8 multae puellae appropinquabant. eas mox conspeximus. (8)
9 Romani milites boni erant. Graeci eos non superaverant. (10)
10 agricolae viginti agros habebant. agri eorum magni erant. (10)

Total: 100

Exercise 12.4

Translate the following into English:

1	ubi amicus venit, vir eum salutavit.	(8)
2	magister meus uxorem pulchram habet. eam saepe video.	(10)
3	femina pulchra erat. multi viri eam amabant.	(9)
4	urbs magna erat. Romani eam occupare constituerunt.	(9)
5	vinum domini bonum est. id saepe bibo.	(9)
6	Graeci multa arma collegerant. ea in navibus posuerunt.	(10)
7	Menelaus et Helena Graeci erant. is clarus, ea pulchra erat.	(12)
8	quod cives boni erant, dominus multam pecuniam eis dedit.	(11)
9	puer, quod puellam amabat, multa dona ei dabat.	(10)
10	nonne auxilio eorum urbem ingentem mox capiemus?	(7)

Total: 95

Exercise 12.5

Translate the underlined words into Latin*:

1	I <u>have</u> a brother. I like him.	(2)
2	He <u>has</u> a sister. I like her.	(2)
3	You (sing.) <u>have</u> a new name. I do not like it.	(2)
4	You (pl.) have many <u>horses</u>. I love them.	(1)
5	We have <u>many</u> daughters. I love them.	(2)
6	The <u>master</u> gave twenty presents to him.	(1)
7	I do not <u>like</u> his brother.	(2)
8	I was <u>watching</u> the girls; I did not like their mother.	(2)
9	Their weapons were new. They placed them <u>near</u> the walls.	(1)
10	I have nineteen friends. I gave <u>money</u> to them.	(1)

Total: 16

* *Your teacher may ask you to translate the whole sentence.*

Exercise 12.6

Put into the plural and translate your answer:

1	ambulabam.	(1 + 2)
2	nauta clamabat.	(2 + 3)
3	deum laudo.	(2 + 3)
4	puerum monebas.	(2 + 3)
5	puer amicum habet.	(3 + 4)

Total: 25

Exercise 12.7

Put into the plural and translate your answer:

1	regina spectat.	(2 + 3)
2	puellam vides.	(2 + 3)
3	amicum vocabas.	(2 + 3)
4	cum amico ambulas.	(3 + 4)
5	Romanus gladio non pugnat.	(3 + 5)

Total: 30

Exercise 12.8

Put into the singular and translate your answer:

1	amicos laudabant.	(2 + 2)
2	reginas monebant.	(2 + 2)
3	amicos laudatis.	(2 + 2)
4	puellae libros non portabant.	(3 + 4)
5	epistulas spectabant.	(3 + 3)

Total: 25

Exercise 12.9

Put into the singular and translate your answer:

1	Romani erant.	(2 + 3)
2	templa magna sunt.	(3 + 4)
3	nautae pugnabant.	(2 + 3)
4	agricolae ambulant.	(2 + 3)
5	monetis.	(1 + 2)

Total: 25

Exercise 12.10

Give and translate the following:

1 The 3rd person plural, imperfect tense of
   exspecto, -are, -avi, -atum.   (1 + 2)
2 The 3rd person singular, perfect tense of
   conspicio, -ere, conspexi, conspectum. (1 + 2)
3 The 1st person singular, future tense of
   ruo, -ere, rui, rutum.   (1 + 2)
4 The 2nd person plural, imperfect tense
   of occido, -ere, occidi, occisum.   (1 + 2)
5 The 2nd person singular, present tense
   of sum.   (1 + 2)

                                         Total: 15

Exercise 12.11

Give the person, number, tense and 1st person
singular of the present tense of the following, and
then translate:

1 conspexerant.   (4 + 2)
2 fugisti.   (4 + 2)
3 ruet.   (4 + 2)
4 occideratis.   (4 + 2)
5 accepimus.   (4 + 2)

                                         Total: 30

Exercise 12.12

Study the passage below (do not write a translation) and answer the questions that follow. Complete
sentences are not required.

Protesilaus: hero or half-wit?

1   quod venti <u>secundi</u> erant, Graeci naves paraverunt. deinde   secundus, -a, -um = favourable
      in eis trans mare celeriter navigaverunt. ubi autem naves
      ad terram appropinquaverunt, nemo e Graecis e navibus
      <u>descendere</u> cupiebat, nam dei Graecis sic dixerant: 'is <u>qui</u>   descendo, -ere, descendi (3) =
5   <u>primus</u> in terram Troianam descendet,' inquiunt, 'primus   I climb down, disembark
      <u>peribit</u>.'
                                                                    qui = who
      diu Graeci nihil fecerunt. inter eos autem erat miles,
      Protesilaus nomine. is, quod mortem non timebat,   primus = first
      clamavit: 'spectate me, comites! ego fortis sum.   peribit = he will die
10   ego audax sum. ego primus in terram Troianam
      descendam. sic ego clarus ero.'

      Protesilaus in terram statim descendit. ubi is
      descendit, ceteri Graeci descenderunt. postquam
      Protesilaus Troianos vidit, contra eos ruit. multos ex
15   eis occidit. tandem tamen, postquam multa vulnera
      accepit, miles clarus <u>periit</u>.   periit = he died

1 quod venti secundi erant, Graeci naves paraverunt. (line 1)
   How did the weather affect the Greeks' preparations?   (3)
2 deinde in eis trans mare celeriter navigaverunt. (lines 1–2)
   What did the Greeks do once their preparations were complete?   (3)
3 ubi autem naves ad terram appropinquaverunt, nemo e Graecis e navibus descendere cupiebat.
   (lines 2–4)
   What happened when the Greek ships approached land?   (3)
4 nam dei Graecis sic dixerant: 'is qui primus in terram Troianam descendet,' inquiunt, 'primus
   peribit.' (lines 4–6)
   a) Who had given a warning to the Greeks?   (1)
   b) In your own words, say what that warning was.   (5)
5 diu Graeci ... clarus ero'. (lines 7–11)
   Translate these lines into good English.   (30)

→

6   Protesilaus in terram ... clarus periit. (lines 12–16). Study these lines and answer the questions that follow. Complete sentences are not required.
   a) Give, in Latin, one example of each of the following:
       i)   a demonstrative pronoun;   (1)
       ii) a 3rd declension noun;   (1)
       iii) an adverb.   (1)
   b) vulnera (line 15) Explain the connection between this word and the English word *vulnerable*.   (2)
   c) eos (line 14)
       i)   In which case is this pronoun?   (1)
       ii) Why is this case used?   (1)
   d) accepit (line 16)
       i)   In which tense is this verb?   (1)
       ii) Give this verb's 1st person singular of the present tense.   (1)
   e) clarus (line 16) is in the nominative masculine singular. What would be the nominative masculine plural?   (1)

                                                                                                    Total: 55

Exercise 12.13

Translate the following into Latin:

1   I do not fear the gods.   (4)
2   The boy was building a big wall.   (5)
3   The slaves always kill the Romans.   (5)
4   The good men were walking with the master.   (6)

                                                                                                    Total: 20

Exercise 12.14

Translate the underlined words* into Latin:

1   We will rush against the <u>Romans</u> tomorrow.   (1)
2   We will attack the <u>town</u> with weapons.   (1)
3   Death will come to the old man <u>soon</u>.   (1)
4   The wounds of the king <u>are</u> bad.   (2)
5   The <u>sailors</u> were not present today because of the delay.   (1)

                                                                                                     Total: 6

* *Your teacher may ask you to translate the whole sentence.*

Exercise 12.15

Translate the following into English:

1 rex nobilis	(2)	11 filius felix	(2)
2 reges nobiles	(2)	12 iter difficile	(2)
3 mors difficilis	(2)	13 mariti crudeles	(2)
4 feminae difficiles	(2)	14 domina tristis	(2)
5 miles fortis	(2)	15 templi ingentis	(2)
6 milites fortes	(2)	16 cum captivis nobilibus	(3)
7 omnes puellae	(2)	17 in foro ingenti	(3)
8 viri tristes	(2)	18 ex horto pulchro	(3)
9 libertus fortis	(2)	19 cum captivis felicibus	(3)
10 vulnera crudelia	(2)	20 sine comitibus sapientibus	(3)

                                                                                                    Total: 45

Exercise 12.16

Translate the following into English:

1 omnia flumina	(2)	11 verba crudelia (2)
2 omnes hastae	(2)	12 verbum crudele (2)
3 dux fortis	(2)	13 liberti tristes (2)
4 duces fortes	(2)	14 nomen nobile (2)
5 feminae crudeles	(2)	15 domina tristis (2)
6 hostes fortes	(2)	16 ad reginam nobilem (3)
7 verbum facile	(2)	17 in horto ingenti (3)
8 liber difficilis	(2)	18 cum marito sapienti (3)
9 viri nobiles	(2)	19 prope forum ingens (3)
10 via difficilis	(2)	20 sine copiis audacibus (3)

Total: 45

Exercise 12.17

Give the case and gender of the underlined words, and translate the sentences into English:

1 dominum crudelem habebatis. (2 + 4)
2 verbum facile amas. (2 + 4)
3 omnia vina laudant. (2 + 4)
4 omnes libros lego. (2 + 4)
5 omnes partes spectabam. (2 + 4)
6 omnia non porto. (2 + 4)
7 silvam ingentem intrabamus. (2 + 4)
8 ducem fortem laudaverant. (2 + 4)
9 libertos tristes videt. (2 + 4)
10 omnes silvas laudo. (2 + 4)

Total: 60

Exercise 12.18

Give the tense of the underlined verbs, and translate the sentences into English:

1 dominus felix servum fortem liberaverat. (1 + 6)
2 omnes puellas amas. (1 + 4)
3 omnes non amo. (1 + 4)
4 libros difficiles magister laudavit. (1 + 6)
5 dominum crudelem gladio ingenti occiderunt. (1 + 6)
6 milites crudeles semper timebimus. (1 + 6)
7 milites fortes civem audacem laudaverant. (1 + 7)
8 puer fortis erat. (1 + 4)
9 omnia arma tibi dabit. (1 + 5)
10 nonne verba crudelia dominae sapientis audivisti? (1 + 7)

Total: 65

Exercise 12.19

Give the part of speech of the underlined words, and translate the sentences into English:

1 dominus vester est fortis et validus. (1 + 7)
2 ei milites sunt fortes validique. (1 + 7)
3 ea puella nobilis est. (1 + 5)
4 is liber difficilis est. (1 + 5)
5 dominus meus crudelis sed audax est. (1 + 7)
6 omnes tamen pueri laborant. (1 + 5)
7 cur tristis es, puer? (1 + 5)
8 tristis sum quod magister crudelis est. (1 + 8)
9 omnia verba difficilia sunt. (1 + 5)
10 num rex urbis nobilis est? (1 + 6)

Total: 70

Exercise 12.20

Give the case of the underlined words and translate the sentences into English:

1 magister <u>crudelis</u> omnes pueros punit.   (1 + 6)
2 librum facilem cum <u>magistro</u> legimus.   (1 + 6)
3 eam feminam <u>nobilem</u> non amabam.   (1 + 6)
4 omnes in <u>silvis</u> ludebant.   (1 + 5)
5 non omnes <u>magistri</u> crudeles sunt.   (1 + 6)
6 servi tristes dominum <u>crudelem</u> timent.   (1 + 6)
7 dominus <u>nobilis</u> cives laudat.   (1 + 5)
8 frater meus <u>omnia</u> parat.   (1 + 5)
9 itinera <u>difficilia</u> saepe facimus.   (1 + 5)
10 servi tristes sunt quod dominus saepe <u>crudelis</u> est.   (1 + 10)

Total: 70

Exercise 12.21

Translate the underlined words* into Latin:

1 A <u>large</u> wood (nominative)   (1)
2 Difficult <u>books</u> (nominative)   (1)
3 In the <u>savage</u> war   (1)
4 With the <u>happy</u> girl   (1)
5 Cruel <u>masters</u> (accusative)   (1)
6 On account of the <u>famous</u> soldiers   (1)
7 In the <u>large</u> wood   (1)
8 The <u>unhappy</u> soldiers (nominative)   (1)
9 <u>Bad</u> citizens (accusative)   (1)
10 With <u>savage</u> companions   (1)

Total: 10

* Your teacher may ask you to translate the whole phrase.

Exercise 12.22

Translate the underlined words* into Latin:

1 By an easy <u>road</u>   (1)
2 With the cruel <u>boy</u>   (1)
3 <u>With</u> the brave soldiers   (1)
4 All the <u>girls</u> (nominative)   (1)
5 By a cruel <u>spear</u>   (1)
6 Towards the noble <u>master</u>   (1)
7 With all the <u>spears</u>   (1)
8 Of a brave boy, <u>however</u>   (1)
9 <u>With</u> the noble girl   (1)
10 By a sad <u>book</u>   (1)

Total: 10

* Your teacher may ask you to translate the whole phrase.

Exercise 12.23

Translate the underlined words* into Latin:

1 The noble queen <u>was</u> sad.   (2)
2 All wise boys <u>like</u> wine.   (2)
3 The cruel king punished the <u>wretched</u> soldier.   (1)
4 All wars <u>are</u> cruel.   (2)
5 The wall was <u>famous</u> and huge.   (1)
6 The bold <u>men</u> had fought well.   (1)
7 We shall overcome all the <u>savage</u> enemy.   (1)
8 All the citizens <u>feared</u> the noble king.   (2)
9 We do not like the cruel <u>master</u>.   (1)
10 That king <u>is</u> noble.   (2)
11 The villas of all the citizens are <u>big</u>.   (1)
12 All the farmers worked well <u>in</u> the huge wood.   (1)
13 It is not easy to work with the cruel <u>slave girl</u>.   (1)
14 The brave citizen fought <u>near</u> the huge forum.   (1)
15 We came <u>to</u> the city by an easy journey.   (1)

Total: 20

* Your teacher may ask you to translate the whole sentence.

Exercise 12.24

Study the passage below (do not write a translation) and answer the questions that follow. Complete sentences are not required.

Achilles, angry because of Patroclus' death, tells Hector that he will kill him. Hector is not impressed.

1   Achilles iratus erat quod Hector Patroclum occiderat.
    Hectorem igitur occidere cupiebat. olim Troiani
    contra Graecos prope urbem Troiam pugnabant.
    omnes fortiter pugnabant. tum subito Achilles
5   Hectorem forte conspexit. ubi eum vidit, ei clamavit:
    'audi me, Hector!' inquit. 'ego sum Achilles, <u>fortissimus</u>   fortissimus, -a, -um = the bravest
    Graecorum. tu vir crudelis es. quod tu Patroclum,
    amicum meum, occidisti, ego te occidam!'

    Hector, ubi verba Achillis audivit, ei respondit: 'audi
10 verba mea, Achilles!' inquit. 'laetus sum quod ego
    Patroclum, amicum tuum, occidi. ego te non timeo. tu
    me non terres. tu fortis non es. tu audax non es. veni!
    pugna! <u>victoria</u> mihi facilis erit. ego te mox vincam!'   victoria, -ae, f. = victory

1   Achilles iratus erat quod Hector Patroclum occiderat. (line 1)
    Why was Achilles unhappy?   (2)
2   Hectorem igitur occidere cupiebat. (line 2)
    What did he intend to do about it?   (2)
3   olim Troiani contra Graecos prope urbem Troiam pugnabant. (lines 2–3)
    Where did the fighting take place?   (1)
4   omnes fortiter pugnabant. (line 4)
    Give and translate the word that tells us how they were fighting.   (1 + 1)
5   tum subito Achilles Hectorem forte conspexit. (lines 4–5)
    Give and translate the word that tells us that what happened next was unexpected.   (1 + 1)
6   ubi eum vidit, ei clamavit: 'audi me, Hector!' (lines 5–6)
    What did Achilles do when he saw Hector?   (2)
7   'ego sum Achilles, fortissimus Graecorum. tu vir crudelis es.' (lines 6–7)
    What contrast did Achilles make between himself and Hector?   (2)
8   'quod tu Patroclum, amicum meum, occidisti, ego te occidam!' (lines 7–8)
    What did Achilles threaten to do to Hector?   (2)
9   Hector ... mox vincam. (lines 9–13)
    Translate these lines into good English.   (30)
10 From the passage give, in Latin, one example of each of the following:
    a) a verb in the pluperfect tense.   (1)
    b) an imperative.   (1)
    c) a personal pronoun.   (1)
    d) a verb in the future tense.   (1)
11 urbem (line 3) In which case is this noun? Why is this case used?   (2)
12 conspexit (line 5) Give the tense and the 1st person singular of the present tense of this verb.   (2)
13 clamavit (line 5) Explain the connection between this word and the English word *exclamation*.   (1)
14 verba (line 10) Give the gender of this noun.   (1)

Total: 55

Chapter 13: Comparison of adjectives

Exercise 13.1

Translate the following into English:

1	magister clarior	(2)
2	femina sapientior	(2)
3	deus saevior	(2)
4	Romanus audacior	(2)
5	dux fortior	(2)
6	cives miseriores	(2)
7	agricolae iratiores	(2)
8	liberti sapientiores	(2)
9	montes altiores	(2)
10	proelia ferociora	(2)

Total: 20

Exercise 13.2

Translate the following into English:

1	in flumen altius	(3)
2	prope templa maiora	(3)
3	cum uxoribus pulchrioribus	(3)
4	sine copiis melioribus	(3)
5	super muros maiores	(3)
6	inter pueros minores	(3)
7	post proelia longiora	(3)
8	in mari altiore	(3)
9	cum magistris peioribus	(3)
10	propter parentes miseriores	(3)

Total: 30

Exercise 13.3

Translate the following into English:

1	hostes audacissimi	(2)
2	flumen altissimum	(2)
3	mulier crudelissima	(2)
4	miles fortissimus	(2)
5	milites fortissimi	(2)
6	uxor pulcherrima	(2)
7	liber longissimus	(2)
8	flumina longissima	(2)
9	maxima turba	(2)
10	iter difficillimum	(2)

Total: 20

Exercise 13.4

Translate the following into English:

1	omnes milites Romani audaciores erant.	(6)
2	soror puellae felicior est.	(5)
3	omnes magistri sapientiores sunt.	(5)
4	ea puella fratrem clariorem habet.	(6)
5	milites ducem feliciorem semper amabant.	(6)
6	poetae feminam crudelissimam timent.	(5)
7	omnes agricolae bene laborabant.	(5)
8	patrem sapientem puellae pulchrioris amamus.	(6)
9	ad urbem itinere faciliore venimus.	(6)
10	captivos plures mox capiemus.	(5)

Total: 55

Exercise 13.5

Translate the following into English:

1	amicus meus fortis est; amicus tuus fortior est.	(10)
2	is miles fortior est quam dux.	(7)
3	id flumen longum est; altissimum flumen longius est.	(10)
4	tuum corpus est longius quam meum.	(7)
5	ea puella sapientior est quam frater meus.	(8)
6	magistri sapientiores sunt quam pueri.	(7)
7	magistri Graeci sapientissimi saepe sunt.	(6)
8	templum Romanum altius est quam villa mea.	(8)
9	liber meus non facilis sed difficillimus est.	(8)
10	milites Romani fortiores erant quam milites Graeci.	(9)

Total: 80

Exercise 13.6

Translate the following into English:

1   milites audaciores sunt quam cives Troiani. (7)
2   ea puella pulcherrima est; puellam pulchriorem numquam vidi. (10)
3   is magister Romanus iratissimus erat; magistrum iratiorem numquam vidi. (11)
4   miles Romanus audacissimus erat; militem audaciorem numquam vidi. (10)
5   ea mulier tristissima erat; mulierem tristiorem numquam vidi. (10)
6   Achilles miles fortissimus sed crudelissimus erat. (7)
7   Romani saepe audaciores erant quam Graeci. (8)
8   urbes Graecae pulchriores erant quam urbes Romanae. (8)
9   omnes mulieres sapientiores erant quam viri. (8)
10 Romani clari erant, sed Graeci clariores quam Romani erant. (11)

Total: 90

Exercise 13.7

Translate the underlined words* into Latin:

1   Brutus was a very wise <u>man</u>. (1)
2   You (sing.) <u>were building</u> a very high wall. (2)
3   The enemy <u>had</u> very daring soldiers. (2)
4   We <u>warn</u> the very fortunate king. (2)
5   She <u>fears</u> her very cruel master. (2)
6   The tired <u>horses</u> made very long journeys. (1)
7   The queen <u>praises</u> the very brave citizens. (2)
8   He <u>loves</u> his very dear wife. (2)
9   You (pl.) <u>were building</u> a very sacred temple. (2)
10 She <u>prepares</u> very good dinners. (2)

Total: 18

* Your teacher might ask you to translate the whole sentence.

Exercise 13.8

Translate the underlined words* into Latin:

1   She <u>shouts</u> with very happy words. (2)
2   We <u>were looking</u> at the higher wall. (2)
3   You (sing.) <u>were calling</u> the very angry teacher. (2)
4   I was not <u>fighting</u> with the very lucky boys. (2)
5   He <u>has</u> the name of a wiser man. (2)
6   They often walk with a more beautiful <u>girl</u>. (1)
7   It <u>is</u> a present for the very famous king. (2)
8   He <u>fears</u> the anger of very cruel masters. (2)
9   He gave them <u>money</u> after the very long war. (1)
10 He carried <u>books</u> to the city on an easier journey. (1)

Total: 17

* Your teacher might ask you to translate the whole sentence.

Exercise 13.9

Translate the underlined words* into Latin:

1   My <u>son</u> is very tall and very famous. (1)
2   Marcus <u>is</u> wiser than Flavia. (2)
3   Aren't the boys wiser than the <u>girls</u>? (1)
4   The temple is <u>not</u> taller than the walls of the city. (1)
5   They were looking at the very beautiful <u>girls</u>. (1)

Total: 6

* Your teacher might ask you to translate the whole sentence.

Exercise 13.10

1 Translate the passage below into good English. (30)

Achilles fights Hector.

1 Achilles Hectorem spectabat. Hector Achillem
spectabat. Hector vir fortissimus et audacissimus
erat. Achilles tamen fortior et audacior quam
Hector erat. subito Hector hastam suam iecit.
5 hasta ad Achillem <u>volavit</u>. in scuto tamen
Achillis <u>haesit</u>. Achilles, ubi hastam Troiani vidit,
risit. deinde Hectori ita verba crudelia dixit:
'tu me non occidisti, Hector,' inquit. 'ego sum
fortior quam tu. ego sum fortissimus omnium
10 Graecorum. nunc ego te occidam.' ita dixit et
hastam ad Hectorem iecit. hasta in corpore
Hectoris haesit. Hector ad terram <u>cecidit</u>
mortuus. Achilles laetissimus erat. risit.

volo, -are, volavi (1) = I fly

haereo, -ere, haesi (2) = I stick

cado, -ere, cecidi (3) = I fall

2 From the passage give, in Latin, and translate one example of each of the following:
  a) a personal pronoun in the accusative. (1 + 1)
  b) a comparative adjective. (1 + 1)
  c) a superlative adjective (1 + 1)
3 iecit (line 4)
  a) Give the Latin subject and the Latin object of this verb; (2)
  b) Give the person, number and tense of this verb. (3)
  c) Give the 1st person singular of the present tense of this verb. (1)
4 Hectorem (line 11) In which case is this noun? Why is this case used? (2)
5 audacior (line 3) Explain the connection between this word and the English word *audacious*. (2)
6 corpore (line 11) In which case is this noun and why is this case used? (2)
7 terram (line 12) In which case is this noun and why is this case used? (2)

Total: 50

Exercise 13.11

Translate the underlined words* into Latin:

1 The <u>famous</u> leader was very bold. (1)
2 I have a very lucky <u>friend</u>. (1)
3 The leader threw many spears <u>into</u> the temple. (1)
4 Very wise men often <u>fear</u> death. (2)
5 Many <u>spears</u> wounded the very brave leader. (1)
6 The swords of the enemy <u>were</u> longer than the arrows. (2)
7 The <u>walls</u> of the town were huge. (1)
8 We attack the city with <u>many</u> spears. (1)
9 The courage of the good citizen <u>always</u> frightened the very wise king. (1)
10 The soldiers' <u>swords</u> were very long. (1)

Total: 12

* *Your teacher might ask you to translate the whole sentence.*

Exercise 13.12

Translate the following into English:

1 ego sum libertus bonus, sed tu es melior. (10)
2 nonne Sextus puer pessimus est? (6)
3 Iulius Caesar erat dux optimus. (6)
4 nostrum templum est maius quam muri oppidi. (8)
5 Alexander miles melior erat quam Iulius Caesar. (8)
6 cibus matris tuae optimus erat. (6)
7 naves maximae ad insulam minimam appropinquabant. (7)
8 ego plus pecuniae habeo quam tu. (7)
9 Italia maior est quam Britannia. (6)
10 Britannia minor est quam Italia. (6)

Total: 70

Exercise 13.13

Translate the following into English:

1 ea silva minima est. (5)
2 puer maior quam puella est. (6)
3 plurimi milites audaces oppidum occupaverunt. (6)
4 magister pessimus omnium magistrorum erat. (6)
5 Romani meliores sunt quam Graeci. (6)
6 Troiani peiores sunt quam Graeci. (6)
7 milites Romani optimi erant. (5)
8 Romani milites meliores quam Graeci habebant. (7)
9 Graeci milites peiores quam Romani habebant. (7)
10 cives plurimi maximum oppidum defendebant. (6)

Total: 60

Exercise 13.14

Translate the following into English:

1 vulnus meum pessimum est. (5)
2 vulnus peius numquam accepi. (5)
3 montes Italiae maiores sunt quam montes Britanniae. (9)
4 muri Troiae olim maximi erant. (6)
5 milites in maximo periculo erant. (6)
6 agricola plurimos et maximos agros habet. (7)
7 sunt in silvis plurimi equi. (6)
8 in maiore nave quam ea numquam navigavi. (8)
9 Graeci templa maiora et meliora quam Romani aedificaverant. (9)
10 templa Romanorum minora et peiora erant quam Graecorum. (9)

Total: 70

* *Your teacher might ask you to translate the whole sentence.*

Exercise 13.15

Translate the underlined words* into Latin:

1 He was a very bad <u>boy</u>. (1)
2 They were very good <u>girls</u>. (1)
3 The leader <u>had</u> very many soldiers. (2)
4 The <u>Romans</u> had very many ships. (1)
5 We <u>always</u> want very good leaders. (1)
6 You (pl.) were building a bigger <u>temple</u>. (1)
7 They live in a very small <u>villa</u>. (1)
8 We all <u>fear</u> the very fierce war. (2)
9 Smaller girls <u>do not fear</u> the cruel woman. (3)
10 My mother <u>praises</u> the very good teacher. (2)

Total: 15

* *Your teacher might ask you to translate the whole sentence.*

Exercise 13.16

Give the case of the underlined words and translate the sentences into English:

1 libertus <u>uxorem</u> pulcherrimam amat. (1 + 5)
2 verba <u>sapientissima</u> numquam audiebamus. (1 + 5)
3 <u>naves</u> maximas celeriter parabant. (1 + 5)
4 Graeci saevissimi <u>cives</u> terruerant. (1 + 5)
5 mulieres pulcherrimae <u>viros</u> non laudant. (1 + 6)
6 corpora maxima <u>milites</u> Romani habent. (1 + 6)
7 templa maxima prope muros <u>urbis</u> aedificaverunt. (1 + 7)
8 dux audax milites in <u>forum</u> maximum duxit. (1 + 8)
9 num <u>scutum</u> maximum habes? (1 + 5)
10 cur novem maximi pueri in <u>silvis</u> legebant? (1 + 8)

Total: 70

Exercise 13.17

Give the case of the underlined words and translate the sentences into English:

1 plurimae feminae maritos <u>nobiles</u> amabant. (1 + 6)
2 nauta ex <u>aqua</u> altissima festinavit. (1 + 6)
3 puer multa dona <u>parentibus</u> dedit. (1 + 6)
4 domina <u>saevissima</u> servos puniebat. (1 + 5)
5 Romani copias maximas in <u>proelium</u> duxerant. (1 + 7)
6 iter Romam <u>via</u> longissima fecimus. (1 + 6)
7 lucem clarissimam <u>omnes</u> spectabant. (1 + 5)
8 agricola caelum <u>pulcherrimum</u> laudabat. (1 + 6)
9 equi agros <u>maximos</u> semper amant. (1 + 6)
10 magister <u>iratissimus</u> pueros puellasque terrebat. (1 + 7)

Total: 70

Exercise 13.18

Give the part of speech of the underlined words and translate the sentences into English:

1 plurimi cives hostes timebant et <u>ex</u> urbe effugiebant. (1 + 10)
2 Romani bella <u>saeviora</u> quam Graeci gerebant. (1 + 7)
3 quamquam <u>dux</u> multos hostes vicerat, nemo eum laudavit. (1 + 10)
4 omnes milites mortem <u>in</u> bello timent. (1 + 7)
5 cives Graeci sapientiores <u>erant</u> quam cives Romani. (1 + 9)
6 milites Romani multa oppida occupaverant <u>et</u> multos hostes vicerant. (1 + 11)
7 plurimas puellas pulcherrimas in <u>urbe</u> heri conspexi. (1 + 8)
8 milites Romani pro civibus Romanis <u>semper</u> fortiter pugnabant. (1 + 9)
9 ei servi dominum crudelissimum habebant. <u>eum</u> non amabant. (1 + 10)
10 cives muros oppidi <u>contra</u> hostes maxima virtute defendebant. (1 + 9)

Total: 100

Exercise 13.19

Give the part of speech of the underlined words* and translate them into Latin:

1 I am running <u>towards</u> the bigger wall. (1 + 1)
2 I found <u>money</u> in the smaller street. (1 + 1)
3 The luckiest slaves escaped from the <u>country-house</u>. (1 + 1)
4 The king <u>had</u> more money than me. (1 + 2)
5 The <u>savage</u> leader had seized the biggest town. (1 + 1)
6 The biggest wall saved the <u>temple</u>. (1 + 1)
7 The Romans conquered the Greeks with very long <u>spears</u>. (1 + 1)
8 The farmer led the smallest horse <u>into</u> the street. (1 + 1)
9 The <u>sons</u> of the very brave leader feared the enemy. (1 + 1)
10 The brave soldier <u>kills</u> his best friend with a sword. (1 + 2)

Total: 22

* *Your teacher might ask you to translate the whole sentence.*

Exercise 13.20

Study the passage below (do not write a translation) and answer the questions that follow. Complete sentences are not required.

Achilles mistreats Hector's body.

1 Achilles vir crudelissimus erat. corpus Hectoris <u>currui</u> suo <u>pedibus</u> <u>vinxit</u>. deinde corpus Hectoris circum muros Troiae <u>traxit</u>. omnes cives Troiani, ubi corpus viderunt, tristissimi erant.

5 Paris filius <u>Priami</u> erat. frater igitur Hectoris erat. quod Achilles Hectorem occiderat, iratissimus erat. arma cepit, ex urbe cucurrit, in proelium ruit. Achillem mox invenit. crudelia verba sic ei dixit: 'Achilles, vir pessimus es,' inquit. 'nemo peior est

10 quam tu. Hectorem, fratrem meum, occidisti. ego tamen miles melior sum quam tu. numquam effugies. nemo te servabit. te nunc occidam.'

tum Paris hastam in Achillem misit. hasta in <u>calce</u> Achillis <u>haesit</u>. Achilles ad terram mortuus <u>cecidit</u>.

currui (dative) = to (his) chariot
pes, pedis, m. = foot
vincio, -ire, vinxi (4) = I tie
traho, -ere, traxi (3) = I drag
Priamus, -i, m. = Priam (the King of Troy)
calx, calcis, f. = heel
haereo, -ere, haesi (2) = I stick
cado, -ere, cecidi (3) = I fall

1 Achilles vir crudelissimus erat. (line 1)
  How is Achilles described? (2)
2 corpus Hectoris currui suo pedibus vinxit. (lines 1–2)
  How did Achilles first mistreat Hector's body? (3)
3 deinde corpus Hectoris circum muros Troiae traxit. (lines 2–3)
  What did he do then to mistreat it even more? (4)
4 omnes cives Troiani, ubi corpus viderunt, tristissimi erant. (lines 3–4)
  Explain in your own words the effect this had on the Trojans. (6)
5 Paris filius ... nunc occidam. (lines 5–12)
  Translate these lines. (30)
6 From the passage give, in Latin, one example of each of the following:
  a) a superlative adjective; (1)
  b) a comparative adjective; (1)
  c) a preposition; (1)
  d) a verb in the pluperfect tense. (1)
7 misit (line 13) Give the Latin subject and the Latin object of this verb. (2)
8 terram (line 14) In which case is this noun? Why is this case used? (2)
9 mortuus (line 14) Give the gender of this word. With which noun does it agree? (2)

Total: 55

Chapter 14: possum; reflexive pronouns

Exercise 14.1

Translate the following into English:

1	potest.	(1)	11	possum.	(1)
2	potestis.	(1)	12	poteramus.	(1)
3	poterat.	(1)	13	potuit.	(1)
4	potuerat.	(1)	14	potuerunt.	(1)
5	poterit.	(1)	15	potueramus.	(1)
6	potuimus.	(1)	16	possunt.	(1)
7	posse.	(1)	17	poterunt.	(1)
8	potueras.	(1)	18	possumus.	(1)
9	poteras.	(1)	19	potuistis.	(1)
10	potes.	(1)	20	potero.	(1)

Total: 20

Exercise 14.2

Translate the following into English:

1 laborare non possum. (3)
2 effugere potest. (2)
3 vincere possumus. (2)
4 cantare non poteram. (3)
5 fugere poterant. (2)
6 errare possum. (2)
7 currere non poteramus. (3)
8 oppugnare potuerunt. (2)
9 dormire non possum. (3)
10 pugnare non poteras. (3)

Total: 25

Exercise 14.3

Translate the following into English:

1 comites ad insulam navigare poterant. (6)
2 hostes vincere numquam poterimus. (5)
3 milites urbem occupare non poterant. (6)
4 liberti ex oppido effugere non poterant. (7)
5 milites oppidum clarum capere poterunt. (6)
6 Romani hastas iacere non poterant. (6)
7 is rex bene regere non potest. (7)
8 cives urbem bene defendere non poterant. (7)
9 Romanus felix vinum malum bibere non potest. (8)
10 in forum hodie venire non potuimus. (7)

Total: 65

Exercise 14.4

Give the case of the underlined words, and then translate the sentences into English:

1 quis ad <u>forum</u> cras venire poterit? (1 + 7)
2 num <u>iter</u> longum facere hodie poterimus? (1 + 7)
3 milites flumen <u>altum</u> defendere non possunt. (1 + 7)
4 dominus eum <u>servum</u> liberare non poterat. (1 + 7)
5 <u>comites</u> celeriter currere non poterant. (1 + 6)
6 magistri <u>omnia</u> facere non possunt. (1 + 6)
7 Graeci Romanos in proelio <u>crudeli</u> superare non poterant. (1 + 9)
8 vir <u>fessus</u> librum longum scribere non poterit. (1 + 8)
9 multam pecuniam filio <u>meo</u> dare non poteram. (1 + 8)
10 milites fessi contra hostes <u>audaces</u> bene pugnare non poterant. (1 + 10)

Total: 85

Exercise 14.5

Translate the underlined words* into Latin:

1 I can read the <u>book</u>. (1)
2 We could not escape <u>from</u> the town. (1)
3 I will <u>soon</u> not be able to walk. (1)
4 You (sing.) <u>cannot</u> walk. (1)
5 They could not destroy the <u>walls</u> of the town. (1)
6 I can sail with the happy <u>sailors</u>. (1)
7 He could sing with his <u>friends</u>. (1)
8 They will be able to come <u>immediately</u>. (1)
9 They could not see the <u>money</u>. (1)
10 You (pl.) can depart from the <u>country-house</u>. (1)

Total: 10

* Your teacher might ask you to translate the whole sentence. Note, these sentences require the use of the present infinitive, which will not be tested at Level 2, but it is good practice.

Exercise 14.6

Translate the underlined words* into Latin:

1 The boy cannot drink <u>wine</u>. (1)
2 The citizens will not be able to defend the <u>town</u>. (1)
3 The citizens have <u>not</u> been able to overcome the king. (1)
4 The enemy could not find the citizens' <u>money</u>. (1)
5 The leader could not prepare <u>many</u> forces. (1)
6 Aren't you (pl.) able to see the <u>villa</u>? (1)
7 Why can you (sing.) not read that <u>book</u>? (1)
8 My friends can destroy the <u>wall</u>. (1)
9 The sad <u>slave</u> was able to see his mother. (1)
10 We are not able to prepare the <u>dinner</u> for the mistress. (1)

Total: 10

* Your teacher might ask you to translate the whole sentence. Note, these sentences require the use of the present infinitive, which will not be tested at Level 2, but it is good practice.

Exercise 14.7

Give the case of the underlined words and translate the sentence.

1 mox ex <u>urbe</u> effugiam. (1 + 5)
2 rex nobilis in <u>foro</u> adest. (1 + 6)
3 comites <u>Romani</u> urbem defendere poterant. (1 + 6)
4 quis <u>captivum</u> videre potest? (1 + 5)
5 Marcus, quod <u>amicum</u> exspectabat, discedere non poterat. (1 + 9)
6 cives, quod dominum videre poterant, e <u>villa</u> cucurrerunt. (1 + 10)
7 <u>cives</u> in foro aderant quod discedere non poterant. (1 + 10)
8 <u>hostes</u> superare non possumus. (1 + 5)
9 milites, quod <u>hostes</u> in proelio superaverant, salutabamus. (1 + 9)
10 num dux <u>hostium</u> milites fessos ad montes reducere potest? (1 + 10)

Total: 85

Exercise 14.8

Give the person, number, tense and 1st person singular of the present tense of the following, and then translate into English:

1 poterat.   (4 + 2)
2 fuit.   (4 + 2)
3 reduxerunt.   (4 + 2)
4 eramus.   (4 + 2)
5 advenisti.   (4 + 2)

Total: 30

Exercise 14.9

Study the passage below (do not write a translation) and answer the questions that follow. Complete sentences are not required.

The Greeks despair of taking Troy, but Ulysses comes up with a plan.

1 diu Graeci urbem Troiam oppugnabant. post multos <u>annos</u> fessi erant. quamquam fortiter pugnabant, urbem capere non poterant. 'quid faciemus?' inquiunt. 'num urbem capiemus?

annus, -i, m. = year

5 muri Troiae altissimi et maximi sunt. eos delere numquam poterimus. <u>domum</u> redire debemus.'

domum = home

Ulixes, miles audacissimus Graecorum, ubi verba comitum audivit, iratus erat. magna voce

clamavit: 'audite me, Graeci! nolite <u>stulti</u> esse! nos
10 Graeci sapientiores quam Troiani sumus. domum redire non debetis! Troiam mox capiemus. consilium habeo. consilium optimum habeo. consilio meo urbem delebimus. equum <u>ligneum</u> maximum aedificate!' Graeci igitur equum ligneum maximum aedificaverunt.

stultus, -a, -um = stupid

ligneus, -a, -um = wooden

1 diu Graeci urbem Troiam oppugnabant. (line 1)
   What are we told about the Greeks and Troy in this opening sentence?   (2)
2 quamquam fortiter pugnabant, urbem capere non poterant. (lines 2–3)
   What level of success were the Greeks enjoying?   (3)
3 muri Troiae altissimi et maximi sunt. (line 5)
   Why did the Greeks think they would be unable to capture Troy?   (3)
4 Ulixes, miles audacissimus Graecorum, ubi verba comitum audivit, iratus erat. (lines 7–8)
   Who was Ulysses and what did he think of the Greeks' attitude?   (4)
5 'nolite stulti esse!' (line 9)
   What does this mean?   (1)
6 'nos Graeci sapientiores quam Troiani sumus.' (lines 9–10)
   What advantage did Ulysses think the Greeks had over the Trojans?   (2)
7 Ulixes ... aedificaverunt. (lines 7–14) From these lines give, in Latin, one example of each of the following:
   a) a superlative adjective;   (1)
   b) a comparative adjective;   (1)
   c) an imperative.   (1)
8 consilium (line 12) In which case is this noun? Why is this case used?   (2)
9 delebimus (line 13) Give the tense of this verb.   (1)
10 equum (line 14) Give the gender of this noun.   (1)
11 equum ligneum maximum. (line 13) Explain the connection between the Latin word **maximum** and the English word *maximum*.   (2)
12 aedificaverunt (line 14) Give the person of this verb.   (1)

Total: 25

Exercise 14.10

Translate the following into Latin:

1 The temple was large. (4)
2 We fear the savage spears. (4)
3 They were attacking the town with swords. (4)
4 The Romans were unhappy. (4)
5 She is walking with a friend. (4)

Total: 20

Exercise 14.11

Translate the following into Latin:

1 The queen was walking to the villa. (5)
2 The master was not entering the temple. (5)
3 They always have many horses. (5)
4 The sailors feared the savage man. (5)

Total: 20

Exercise 14.12

Translate the following into English:

1 is puer se amat. (5)
2 Romani se liberare constituerunt. (5)
3 Troiani se defendere paraverunt. (5)
4 puella pulcherrima se semper spectat. (6)
5 dux milites iter secum facere iussit. (7)
6 liberti sapientes se numquam laudant. (6)
7 cives Troiani se fortiter defendebant. (6)
8 is miles se gladio suo vulneravit. (7)
9 cives tristes hostibus se tradiderunt. (6)
10 post proelium multi captivi se liberabant. (7)

Total: 60

Exercise 14.13

Translate the following into English:

1 num senex mortuus est? (5)
2 muulti manserunt, pauci effugerunt. (6)
3 nolite me hic relinquere, comites! (5)
4 clamores multorum senum audivimus. (5)
5 milites fortes se servare cupiunt. (6)
6 bene pugnate pro patria, cives! (5)
7 Graeci non fortiores sunt quam nos. (7)
8 nonne milites Graeci felicissimi erant? (6)
9 vos tuti estis, nos in magno periculo sumus. (10)
10 quis nos vincere poterit? (5)

Total: 60

Exercise 14.14

Give the case of the underlined words and then translate the sentences into English:

1 senex et <u>fortis</u> et audax erat. (1 + 7)
2 num puer miser in media <u>via</u> stat? (1 + 8)
3 non omnes cives <u>fortes</u> erant. (1 + 6)
4 nonne dux id <u>oppidum</u> occupare mox poterit? (1 + 8)
5 <u>nostri</u> Graecos vincere non poterant. (1 + 6)
6 milites ducem <u>felicem</u> semper amant. (1 + 6)
7 pater meus <u>gladio</u> se vulneravit. (1 + 6)
8 Graeci, ubi Troiam occupaverunt, Helenam ad <u>Graeciam</u> reduxerunt. (1 + 10)
9 nonne Troiani urbem <u>suam</u> bene defendebant? (1 + 7)
10 clamores <u>earum</u> feminarum magni erant. (1 + 6)

Total: 80

Exercise 14.15

Give the tense of the underlined verbs and then translate the sentences into English:

1 di deaeque, ubi deam Discordiam <u>viderunt</u>, iratissimi erant. (1 + 10)
2 Menelaus, ubi Paris Helenam cepit, nuntios ad omnes comites <u>misit</u>. (1 + 12)
3 Graeci, ubi de Helena <u>audiverunt</u>, copias ad Menelaum miserunt. (1 + 11)
4 copiae Graecorum, ubi trans mare <u>navigaverunt</u>, Troiam oppugnaverunt. (1 + 10)
5 Achilles, ubi Hectorem occidit, laetus <u>erat</u>. (1 + 8)
6 Graeci, ubi equum magnum aedificaverunt, eum prope urbem <u>reliquerunt</u>. (1 + 11)
7 Graeci, ubi equum prope urbem reliquerunt, <u>discesserunt</u>. (1 + 9)
8 Troiani, ubi equum maximum viderunt, <u>timebant</u>. (1 + 8)
9 multi Troiani, ubi Graecos in media urbe viderunt, <u>fugerunt</u>. (1 + 11)
10 Graeci, ubi urbem Troiam <u>deleverunt</u>, ad Graeciam navigaverunt. (1 + 10)

Total: 110

Exercise 14.16

Write down the adjectives and then translate the following sentences into English:

1 nauta, quamquam nobilissimus est, aquam timet. (1 + 8)
2 Achilles, quamquam miles audax erat, pugnare non cupiebat. (1 + 10)
3 Graeci, quamquam urbem clarissimam oppugnaverunt, eam armis capere non poterant. (1 + 12)
4 hostes, quamquam milites meliores habebant, non bene pugnaverunt. (1 + 10)
5 ego, quamquam sapientior sum quam multi homines, multam pecuniam non habeo. (3 + 13)
6 Troiani, quamquam urbem suam defenderunt, eam servare non poterant. (1 + 11)
7 miles, quamquam fessus erat, diu pugnabat. (1 + 8)
8 liberti, quamquam dominus sapientissimus erat, eum non amabant. (1 + 10)
9 quamquam vox senis magna erat, eam audire non poteramus. (1 + 11)
10 cives validi, quamquam hostes timebant, contra eos pugnaverunt. (1 + 10)

Total: 115

Exercise 14.17

Give and translate the following verb parts:

1 The 1st person plural, present tense of **aedifico**. (1 + 2)
2 The 3rd person plural, imperfect tense of **habeo**. (1 + 2)
3 The 3rd person singular, imperfect tense of **paro**. (1 + 2)
4 The 3rd person singular, present tense of **specto**. (1 + 2)
5 The 2nd person plural, present tense of **sum**. (1 + 2)

Total: 15

Exercise 14.18

Give the person, number, tense and 1st person singular of the present tense of the following and then translate:

1 posuit. (4 + 2)
2 potuit. (4 + 2)
3 reduxerunt. (4 + 2)
4 effugisti. (4 + 2)
5 relinquemus. (4 + 2)

Total: 30

Exercise 14.19

Translate the following into Latin:

1 Good men do not fear the gods. (6)
2 The boys were praising the dinner. (4)
3 The Romans love famous women. (5)
4 I was walking with a good friend. (5)

Total: 20

Exercise 14.20

Translate the following into Latin:

1 Bad men and women destroy temples. (7)
2 Many women do not have money. (6)
3 The man loved the happy son. (5)
4 The horses were walking near the walls. (5)
5 Savage masters often kill unhappy men. (7)

Total: 30

Exercise 14.21

Keeping the same person and number, put the following verbs into the imperfect tense and translate your answer:

1 servavit. (1 + 2)
2 viderunt. (1 + 2)
3 superavi. (1 + 2)
4 aedificavimus. (1 + 2)
5 steterunt. (1 + 2)
6 timuerunt. (1 + 2)
7 delevistis. (1 + 2)
8 spectavit. (1 + 2)
9 responderunt. (1 + 2)
10 amavit. (1 + 2)

Total: 30

Exercise 14.22

Study the passage below (do not write a translation) and answer the questions that follow. Complete sentences are not required.

The Trojans see the horse.

1   Graeci equum ligneum maximum aedificaverant. antequam
     in navibus discesserunt, plurimos milites in equum
     posuerunt et equum in litore prope urbem reliquerunt.

     Troiani, ubi equum viderunt, e portis festinaverunt. attoniti
5   erant. diu equum spectabant. unus e Troianis sic dixit: 'Graeci
     discesserunt,' inquit. 'nonne eos vicimus? equus donum
     nobis est. eum in mediam urbem trahere debetis, cives!'

     Troianus secundus autem magna voce clamavit: 'num
     equus donum est? Graeci dona numquam dant. Graeci
10   homines fallaces sunt. nolite equum in urbem trahere,
     cives! eum delere debemus!' tandem tamen Troiani
     equum in urbem trahere constituerunt.

ligneus, -a, -um = wooden

litus, litoris, n. = shore

relinquo, -ere, reliqui (3)
= I leave behind, I abandon

porta, -ae, f. = gate

attonitus, -a, -um = amazed

traho, -ere, traxi = I drag
fallax, fallacis = deceitful

1 Graeci equum ligneum maximum aedificaverant. (line 1)
   What had the Greeks done? (2)
2 antequam in navibus discesserunt, plurimos milites in equum posuerunt et equum in litore
   prope urbem reliquerunt. (lines 1–3)
   What did the Greeks do before they left in their ships? (2 + 2)
3 Troiani, ubi equum viderunt, e portis festinaverunt. (line 4)
   What did the Trojans do when they saw the horse? (1)
4 attoniti erant. diu equum spectabant. (lines 4–5)
   What effect did it have on them? (2)
5 'Graeci discesserunt,' inquit. 'nonne eos vicimus?' (lines 5–6)
   What did one of the Trojans think had happened? (1 + 2)
6 'equus donum nobis est. eum in mediam urbem trahere debetis, cives!' (lines 6–7)
   What was his suggestion about the horse? (1 + 2)

➡

7 Troianus secundus ... trahere constituerunt. (lines 8–12)
  Translate these lines into good English. (30)
8 From the passage give, in Latin, an example of:
  a) a conjunction; (1)
  b) an adverb; (1)
  c) a preposition followed by the ablative case. (1)
9 discesserunt (line 6)
  a) Give the tense of this verb; (1)
  b) Give its 1st person singular, present tense; (1)
  c) What would it be in the imperfect tense? (1)
10 nobis (line 7) What is the case of this word? (1)
11 equum (line 12)
  a) Explain the connection between this Latin word and the English word *equestrian*. (2)
  b) What would this word be if it were in the plural, keeping the case the same? (1)

Total: 55

Exercise 14.23

Study the passage below (do not write a translation) and answer the questions that follow. Complete sentences are not required.

The fall of Troy.

1   Troiani equum in urbem <u>traxerunt</u>. laetissimi erant quod   traho, -ere, traxi = I drag
     Graeci discesserant. laetissimi erant quod Graecos vicerant.
     ea nocte igitur omnes cives <u>festum</u> <u>celebrabant</u>. multum   festum celebrare = to hold a
     cibi consumebant et multum vini bibebant. mox omnes   celebration
5   Troiani dormiebant. media nocte milites Graeci, <u>qui</u> in equo   qui = who
     erant, de equo <u>silentio</u> descenderunt. per vias urbis magnis   silentio = in silence
     clamoribus ruerunt. Troiani se defendere non poterant.
     Graeci saevi multos Troianos gladiis occiderunt. inter
     mortuos erat Priamus senex, rex Troiae. Graeci paucos
10   Troianos vivos reliquerunt. sic Graeci post decem <u>annos</u>   annus, -i, m. = year
     urbem Troiam <u>dolo</u> ceperunt. maximam partem urbis   dolus, -i, m. = trickery
     deleverunt. Helenam ad Graeciam reducere nunc poterant.

1 Troiani equum in urbem traxerunt. (line 1)
  What did the Trojans do with the horse? (1)
2 laetissimi erant quod Graeci discesserant. laetissimi erant quod Graecos vicerant. (lines 1–2)
  Give two reasons why the Trojans were so happy. (2 + 2)
3 multum cibi consumebant et multum vini bibebant. (lines 3–4)
  Say how the Trojans celebrated. (2)
4 mox omnes Troiani dormiebant. (lines 4–5)
  What happened after the celebration? (2)
5 media nocte milites Graeci, qui in equo erant, de equo silentio descenderunt. (lines 5–6)
  Describe what happened in the middle of the night. (4)
6 per vias urbis magnis clamoribus ruerunt. (lines 6–7)
  What did the Greeks then do? (2)
7 Troiani se defendere ... nunc poterant. (lines 7–12)
  Translate these lines into good English. (30)
8 From the passage give, in Latin, one example of each of the following:
  a) a verb in the pluperfect tense; (1)
  b) a preposition followed by the accusative case; (1)
  c) a superlative adjective. (1)
9 mortuos (line 9) Explain the connection between this word and the English word *mortuary*. (2)
10 urbis (line 11) In which case is this noun? Why is this case used? (2)
11 poterant (line 12) Give the 1st person singular of the present tense of this verb. (1)
12 ceperunt (line 11) Give the Latin subject and the Latin object of this verb. (2)

Total: 55

Chapter 15: Revision of Level 2

Exercise 15.1

Give the part of speech and meaning of the following Latin words:

1	clamor	(2)
2	comes	(2)
3	corpus	(2)
4	dux	(2)
5	flumen	(2)
6	homo	(2)
7	iter	(2)
8	lux	(2)
9	miles	(2)
10	mulier	(2)
11	nomen	(2)
12	parens	(2)
13	rex	(2)
14	uxor	(2)

Total: 28

Exercise 15.2

Give the part of speech and meaning of the following Latin words:

1	carus	(2)
2	ceteri	(2)
3	longus	(2)
4	medius	(2)
5	civis	(2)
6	hostes	(2)
7	iuvenis	(2)
8	mare	(2)
9	mons	(2)
10	navis	(2)
11	senex	(2)
12	urbs	(2)
13	appropinquo	(2)
14	erro	(2)

Total: 28

Exercise 15.3

Give the part of speech and meaning of the following Latin words:

1	exspecto	(2)
2	libero	(2)
3	narro	(2)
4	mortuus	(2)
5	pauci	(2)
6	solus	(2)
7	vivus	(2)
8	nonne?	(2)
9	num?	(2)
10	nemo	(2)
11	nihil	(2)
12	virtus	(2)
13	vox	(2)
14	vulnus	(2)

Total: 28

Exercise 15.4

Give the part of speech and meaning of the following Latin words:

1	duodecim	(2)
2	duodeviginti	(2)
3	quattuordecim	(2)
4	quindecim	(2)
5	sedecim	(2)
6	septendecim	(2)
7	tredecim	(2)
8	undecim	(2)
9	undeviginti	(2)
10	viginti	(2)
11	accipio	(2)
12	conspicio	(2)
13	effugio	(2)
14	fugio	(2)

Total: 28

Exercise 15.5

Give the part of speech and meaning of the following Latin words:

1 advenio (2)
2 invenio (2)
3 punio (2)
4 trado (2)
5 vinco (2)
6 autem (2)
7 et ... et ... (2)
8 arma (2)
9 copiae (2)
10 donum (2)
11 frater (2)
12 liberi (2)
13 mater (2)
14 mora (2)

Total: 28

Exercise 15.6

Give the part of speech and meaning of the following Latin words:

1 mors (2)
2 pars (2)
3 pater (2)
4 soror (2)
5 is (2)
6 ante (2)
7 circum (2)
8 inter (2)
9 post (2)
10 pro (2)
11 propter (2)
12 sine (2)
13 sub (2)
14 super (2)

Total: 28

Exercise 15.7

Give the part of speech and meaning of the following Latin words:

1 colligo (2)
2 debeo (2)
3 defendo (2)
4 gero (2)
5 servo (2)
6 vulnero (2)
7 audax (2)
8 crudelis (2)
9 difficilis (2)
10 facilis (2)
11 felix (2)
12 fortis (2)
13 ingens (2)
14 nobilis (2)

Total: 28

Exercise 15.8

Give the part of speech and meaning of the following Latin words:

1 omnis (2)
2 sapiens (2)
3 tristis (2)
4 celeriter (2)
5 nam (2)
6 nunc (2)
7 quam (2)
8 tum (2)
9 postquam (2)
10 se (2)
11 cras (2)
12 forte (2)
13 frustra (2)
14 heri (2)

Total: 28

Exercise 15.9

Give the part of speech and meaning of the following Latin words:

1 hodie	(2)	9 occido	(2)
2 postea	(2)	10 occupo	(2)
3 quoque	(2)	11 possum	(2)
4 antequam	(2)	12 reduco	(2)
5 quamquam	(2)	13 ruo	(2)
6 inquit	(2)	14 saluto	(2)
7 noli/nolite	(2)	**Total: 28**	
8 nuntio	(2)		

Exercise 15.10

Give the case, number and meaning of the following Latin nouns:

1 regis	(3)	6 monte	(3)
2 comitum	(3)	7 senem	(3)
3 mulieris	(3)	8 iuvenum	(3)
4 nominis	(3)	9 itineris	(3)
5 uxorem	(3)	10 milite	(3)
		Total: 30

Exercise 15.11

Give the following forms and translate your answer:

1 3rd singular, future tense of **amo**. (1 + 1)
2 3rd plural, future tense of **moneo**. (1 + 1)
3 1st singular, future tense of **rego**. (1 + 1)
4 1st plural, future tense of **audio**. (1 + 1)
5 2nd singular, future tense of **sum**. (1 + 1)

Total: 10

Exercise 15.12

Give the following forms and translate your answer:

1 3rd singular, pluperfect tense of **amo**. (1 + 1)
2 3rd plural, pluperfect tense of **moneo**. (1 + 1)
3 1st singular, pluperfect tense of **rego**. (1 + 1)
4 1st plural, pluperfect tense of **audio**. (1 + 1)
5 2nd singular, pluperfect tense of **sum**. (1 + 1)

Total: 10

Exercise 15.13

Translate into English:

1 eius domini (2)
2 ad eam puellam (3)
3 cum eis regibus (3)
4 earum matrum (2)
5 sine eis partibus (3)
6 ea bella (2)

Total: 15

Exercise 15.14

Translate into English:

1 ingentes montes (2)
2 ingentium templorum (2)
3 cum matre tristi (3)
4 sine comitibus audacibus (3)
5 post bellum crudele (3)
6 militis felicis (2)

Total: 15

Exercise 15.15

Translate into English:

1 regis audacioris (2)
2 propter dominas crudeliores (3)
3 libertus iratior (2)
4 cum ducibus fortissimis (3)
5 super montes altiores (3)
6 parentes optimi (2)

Total: 15

Exercise 15.16

Translate into English:

1 potest (2)
2 poterant (2)
3 potestis (2)
4 posse (2)
5 possunt (2)
6 potes (2)

Total: 12

Exercise 15.17

Study the passage below (do not write a translation) and answer the questions that follow. Complete sentences are not required.

Acrisius gets a warning.

1   Acrisius rex clarus erat. urbem Argos regebat. filiam unam habebat, nomine <u>Danaen</u>. olim dei Acrisio '<u>cave</u>, Acrisi!' inquit. 'filia tua filium habebit. filius te necabit.' verba deorum Acrisium terruerunt.

5   magnam igitur <u>turrim</u> aedificare constituit. deinde filiam Danaen in turrim posuit. servos autem Danaen <u>custodire</u> iussit. 'sic tutus ero,' inquit. rex miser tamen tutus non erat.

    Iuppiter rex deorum erat. Iuno, regina deorum, uxor
10 eius erat. Iuppiter, quamquam uxorem amabat, plurimas feminas quoque amabat. postquam Danaen pulchram vidit, eam quoque amare constituit. in turrim igitur, ubi puella aderat, intravit. postea Danae filium parvum <u>peperit</u>. nomen pueri Perseus erat.

15 Acrisius, ubi Perseum vidit, <u>perterritus</u> iratusque erat. clamavit: 'quis est pater pueri?' Danae respondit: 'pater pueri est Iuppiter,' inquit, 'rex deorum.' Acrisius et matrem et filium punire constituit.

Danaen = the accusative case of Danae (Greek form)

caveo, -ere (2) = I beware

turrim, f. = tower (accusative)

custodio, -ire, -ivi (4) = I guard

peperit = gave birth to

perterritus, -a, -um = terrified

1   Acrisius rex clarus erat. urbem Argos regebat. (line 1)
    Who was Acrisius?   (2)
2   filiam unam habebat, nomine Danaen. (lines 1–2)
    Who was Danae?   (2)
3   'cave, Acrisi!' inquit. 'filia tua filium habebit. filius te necabit.' (lines 3–4)
    What warning did the gods give to Acrisius?   (2 + 2)
4   verba deorum Acrisium terruerunt. (line 4)
    What effect did this have on Acrisius?   (1)
5   magnam igitur turrim aedificare constituit. deinde filiam Danaen in turrim posuit. servos autem Danaen custodire iussit. (lines 5–7)
    What was Acrisius's plan for dealing with the warning?   (4)
6   rex miser tamen tutus non erat. (lines 7–8)
    What do these words mean?   (2)
7   Iuppiter rex deorum ... Perseus erat. (lines 9–14)
    Translate these lines into good English.   (30)
8   Acrisius ... constituit. (lines 15–18) From these lines give, in Latin, an example of:
    a) a conjunction   (1)
    b) an infinitive   (1)
    c) an adjective   (1)
9   vidit (line 12)
    a) Give the 1st person singular of the present tense of this verb.   (1)
    b) Give the tense of this verb.   (1)
    c) Explain the connection between **vidit** and the English word *vision*. (2)
10 pueri (line 16)
    a) Give the case of this noun.   (1)
    b) Why is this case used?   (1)
    c) What would this word become in the plural?   (1)

                                                                        Total: 55

Exercise 15.18

Study the passage below (do not write a translation) and answer the questions that follow. Complete sentences are not required.

Acrisius tries to dispose of Danae and Perseus.

1	Acrisius <u>Danaen</u> et Perseum in magna <u>cista</u> <u>clausit</u>. deinde servos cistam ad <u>litus</u> portare et in mare iacere iussit. Danae et Perseus <u>perterriti</u> erant. undas timebant. tandem undae cistam ad insulam <u>pepulerunt</u>. ibi senex,
5	Dictys nomine, eos invenit et servavit.

Danae et Perseus in insula laeti diu habitabant. Perseus iuvenis iam erat et mater eius femina <u>adhuc</u> pulchra erat. rex insulae, Polydectes nomine, ubi Danaen conspexit, eam statim amavit et <u>ducere</u>
10   cupiebat. Perseus tamen Polydectem non amabat. ei clamavit: 'numquam matrem meam duces.'

Perseus Polydectem non amabat. Polydectes Perseum non amabat. Perseus fortis erat sed iuvenis. regi igitur, 'Polydectes,' inquit, 'ego te non
15   timeo. ego vir fortis sum.' '<u>si</u> vir fortis es,' respondit Polydectes, '<u>Medusam</u> neca, deinde <u>caput</u> eius cape et ad me porta!'

Danaen = the accusative case of Danae

cista, -ae, f. = chest

claudo, -ere, clausi (3) = I shut

litus, litoris, n. = shore, beach

perterritus, -a, -um = terrified

pello, -ere, pepuli (3) = I drive

adhuc = still

duco, -ere, duxi (3) (here) = I marry

si = if

Medusa, -ae, f. = Medusa (a monstrous Gorgon)

caput, capitis, n. = head

1   Acrisius Danaen et Perseum in magna cista clausit. (line 1)
    What did Acrisius do at the start of this story? **(3)**
2   deinde servos cistam ad litus portare et in mare iacere iussit. (lines 2–3)
    What instructions did he then give? **(2 + 3)**
3   Danae et Perseus perterriti erant. undas timebant. (line 3)
    Why were Danae and Perseus frightened? **(2)**
4   tandem undae cistam ad insulam pepulerunt. (line 4)
    What happened to the chest? **(3)**
5   ibi senex, Dictys nomine, eos invenit et servavit. (lines 4–5)
    How did Dictys come to the rescue? **(2)**
6   Danae ... meam duces. (lines 6–11)
    Translate these lines into good English. **(30)**
7   Perseus ... ad me porta!' (lines 12–17) From these lines, give:
    a) a Latin conjunction. **(1)**
    b) a 3rd declension adjective **(1)**
8   regi (line 14)
    a) In which case is this word.
    b) Why is this case used?
9   vir fortis (line 15) In which case are these words? **1)**
10 respondit (line 15)
a) Give the 1st person singular of the present tense of this verb. **(1)**
b) Give its tense. **(1)**
c) Explain the connection between this Latin word and the English word *response*. **(2)**
11 eius (line 16) Give the gender of this word. **(1)**

Total: 55

Exercise 15.19

Study the passage below (do not write a translation) and answer the questions that follow. Complete sentences are not required.

Perseus receives help from the gods.

1   verba Polydectis Perseum terruerunt. Perseus,
    quamquam iuvenis fortis erat, Medusam saevam
    timebat. di tamen deaeque auxilium Perseo
    dederunt. gladium novum et scutum <u>politum</u> ei   politus, -a, -um = polished
5   dederunt. Perseus, ubi arma accepit, iam laetus erat.
    non iam Medusam timebat. ab insula navigavit et ad
    Medusam iter fecit.

    iter longum erat. Perseus tamen post multa pericula ad
    terram, ubi Medusa habitabat, tandem advenit. 'nonne
10   Medusa adest?' inquit puer. 'ubi est? eam videre cupio.'
    subito Medusa appropinquavit. cum Medusa fortiter   caput, capitis, n. = head
    pugnavit Perseus et auxilio deorum eam occidit. inde   abscido, -ere, abscidi (3) = I cut off
    <u>caput</u> eius <u>abscidit</u> et ad insulam suam iter fecit.

    Perseus Medusam occiderat. ad Graeciam iam   saccus, -i, m. = bag
15   iter faciebat et caput Medusae in <u>sacco</u> portabat.
    in itinere puellam pulchram conspexit, nomine
    Andromedam. di deaeque parentes eius puniebant   monstrum, -i, n. = monster
    et in periculo maximo erat. <u>monstro</u> ei   nocer, -ere, nocui (+ dat.) = I harm

    <u>nocere</u> cupiebat. Perseus tamen eam servavit. caput   saxum, -i, n. = rock
20   Medusae monstro ostendit et in <u>saxum</u> id mutavit.

1 verba Polydectis Perseum terruerunt. (line 1)
  What effect did Polydectes's words have?   **(1)**
2 Perseus, quamquam iuvenis fortis erat, Medusam saevam timebat. (lines 1–3)
  What effect did Medusa have on Perseus?   **(2)**
3 di tamen deaeque auxilium Perseo dederunt. (lines 3–4)
  What outside help did Perseus receive?   **(2)**
4 gladium novum et scutum politum ei dederunt. (lines 4–5)
  What did this help consist of?   **(3)**
5 Perseus, ubi arma accepit, iam laetus erat. (line 5)
  How did Perseus react?   **(2)**
6 non iam Medusam timebat. (line 6)
  How did it make him feel about Medusa?   **(1)**
7 ab insula navigavit et ad Medusam iter fecit. (lines 6–7)
  What did Perseus do at the end of the story?   **(2 + 2)**
8 iter longum ... iter fecit. (lines 8–14)
  Translate these lines into good English.   **(30)**
9 faciebat (line 15)
  a) Give the tense of this verb.   **(1)**
  b) Give its person.   **(1)**
  c) Explain the connection between this word and the English word *factory*.   **(2)**
10 itinere (line 16) What case is this word in and why is this case used?   **(2)**
11 maximo (line 18) This word is a superlative adjective. Give and translate its positive form in the nominative masculine singular.   **(2)**
12 eam (line 19)
  a) What gender is this word?   **(1)**
  b) Give its nominative masculine singular form.   **(1)**

    Total: 55

Exercise 15.20

Translate into good English.

Perseus surprises Polydectes.

1   Perseus, ubi Andromedam servavit, ad Graeciam
     navigavit. Polydectes, ubi Perseum vidit, iratus erat.
     'cur ades?' Perseo clamavit. 'num <u>caput</u> Medusae
     capere poteras?' Perseus respondit: 'Medusam occidi
5   et caput eius hic habeo. specta!' caput Medusae
     Perseus ostendit. Polydectes caput spectavit et in
     <u>saxum</u> statim <u>mutatus</u> <u>est</u>.

     Perseus Polydectem occiderat. Danae, mater pulchra
     Persei, tuta iam erat. diu Perseus et Danae laetissimi
10   habitabant. olim Perseus ad urbem Larissam iter
     fecit. ibi cives <u>ludos</u> spectabant. Perseus <u>discum</u>
     iecit. discus forte <u>spectatorem</u> <u>icit</u> et necavit.
     spectator Acrisius erat. dei verba <u>vera</u> dixerant:
     Perseus <u>avum</u> suum occiderat.

caput, capitis, n. = head

saxum, -i, n. = rock

mutatus est = (he) was turned

ludus, -i, m. = game

discus, -i, m. = discus

spectator, -oris, m. = spectator

icit = (it) struck

verus, -a, -um = true

avus, -i, m. = grandfather

Total: 30

Exercise 15.21

Translate into Latin.

1   The Roman master was praising the boys.   (5)
2   We were walking with the beautiful queen.   (5)
3   Marcus was a good friend.   (4)
4   The famous master is warning the slave-girls with his sword.   (6)

Total: 20

Level 3

Chapter 16: hic, ille, eo

Exercise 16.1

Translate the following into English:

1	hic civis	(2)
2	haec urbs	(2)
3	hoc flumen	(2)
4	hic dux	(2)
5	hae naves	(2)
6	hic libertus	(2)
7	haec mater	(2)
8	hi comites	(2)
9	hae silvae	(2)
10	hoc donum	(2)
11	haec corpora	(2)
12	hi anni	(2)
13	hi fratres	(2)
14	hoc bellum	(2)
15	hic iuvenis	(2)
16	haec uxor	(2)
17	hi homines	(2)
18	hoc mare	(2)
19	haec vulnera	(2)
20	haec pars	(2)

Total: 40

Exercise 16.2

Translate the following into English:

1	huius reginae	(2)
2	huius militis	(2)
3	horum militum	(2)
4	harum navium	(2)
5	ab hoc rege	(2)
6	in hoc bello	(2)
7	propter hanc lucem	(2)
8	huius liberti	(2)
9	horum servorum	(2)
10	his verbis	(2)
11	in hoc flumine	(2)
12	huic dominae	(2)
13	harum uxorum	(2)
14	hoc vulnere	(2)
15	ab hoc iuvene	(2)
16	post haec proelia	(2)
17	ante hanc cenam	(2)
18	huic iuveni	(2)
19	ad hos montes	(2)
20	huius regis	(2)

Total: 40

Exercise 16.3

Translate the following into English:

1	nomen huius pueri Brutus est.	(6)
2	hoc flumen altum est.	(5)
3	hi pueri parvi sunt.	(5)
4	hae puellae tristes sunt.	(5)
5	hanc mulierem laudabam.	(4)
6	aquam huic seni dedit.	(5)
7	hic iuvenis pro patria fortiter pugnabat.	(7)
8	libertus iratus hunc equum e silva duxit.	(8)
9	quis timet hos clamores?	(5)
10	captivus ex oppido cum his viris effugere non poterat.	(10)

Total: 60

Exercise 16.4

Translate the underlined words into Latin*:

1 This soldier was showing the book <u>to the master</u>. (1)
2 These soldiers <u>have eaten</u> the very good dinner. (2)
3 <u>We have built</u> walls in this city. (2)
4 We were not able to destroy these <u>cities</u>. (1)
5 He <u>never</u> praises this unhappy woman. (1)
6 <u>They came</u> to this island and looked at the rivers. (2)
7 He was able to overcome the guards with this <u>sword</u>. (1)
8 The forces of the famous <u>king</u> were able to overcome the enemy. (1)
9 These young men <u>were looking</u> at the bright light. (2)
10 We have never <u>made</u> the journey over these mountains. (2)

Total: 15

* *Your teacher may ask you to translate the whole sentence.*

Exercise 16.5

Translate the following into English:

1 captivi omnes custodes his armis occiderunt. (7)
2 dux horum militum in proelio magno numquam pugnavit. (9)
3 custos captivum miserum in somno hoc gladio necavit. (9)
4 princeps omnes naves ad insulam parvam propter tempestatem duxit. (10)
5 hi cives eum saevum regem magnopere timebant. (8)
6 domina hanc ancillam in eam villam maximam duxerat. (9)
7 propter haec proelia in foro parvo diu manebamus. (9)
8 nonne Romani urbem clarissimam in his septem montibus aedificaverunt? (10)
9 cur hunc senem semper punis? (6)
10 post mortem regis hoc bellum diu gerebamus. (8)

Total: 85

Exercise 16.6

Write down the demonstrative pronouns and then translate the following sentences into English:

1 omnes magistri hunc poetam clarissimum laudabant. (1 + 7)
2 hae mulieres tristissimae principem hostium semper timuerant. (1 + 8)
3 Romani socios nostros in eo proelio superaverunt. (1 + 8)
4 da hanc epistulam dominae meae! (1 + 6)
5 num hostes, o socii, his armis vincere poteritis? (1 + 8)
6 milites trans eos montes dux clarissimus reduxerat. (1 + 8)
7 dominus filios filiasque his verbis laudabat. (1 + 7)
8 novem senes in hoc templo dormiebant. (1 + 7)
9 feminae eos cives nobilissimos laudaverunt. (1 + 6)
10 mulier maritum amabat sed parentes eius gladio necavit. (1 + 10)

Total: 85

Exercise 16.7

Give the case, number and gender of the demonstrative pronouns and then translate the following sentences into English:

1 hic nauta ad insulam parvam navigabat. (3 + 7)
2 eam puellam pulcherrimam heri vidi. (3 + 6)
3 nuntius ad hanc urbem mox adveniet. (3 + 7)
4 hoc corpus ex oppido portare non possumus. (3 + 8)
5 milites omnia haec arma collegerunt. (3 + 6)
6 nomen huius feminae pulchrae Helena est. (3 + 7)
7 muri eius urbis altissimi sunt. (3 + 6)
8 miles hoc gladio bene pugnabat. (3 + 6)
9 dominus donum his iuvenibus dabit. (3 + 6)
10 mulieres vinum horum iuvenum amabant. (3 + 6)

Total: 95

Exercise 16.8

Translate the underlined words into Latin*:

1 This brave woman has sailed to the island. (2)
2 I saw this very beautiful girl yesterday. (2)
3 The messenger gave that letter to the queen. (1)
4 I was carrying this body out of the town. (1)
5 The soldiers have shown all these weapons to me. (2)

Total: 8

* Your teacher may ask you to translate the whole sentence.

Exercise 16.9

Study the passage below (do not write a translation) and answer the questions that follow. Complete sentences are not required.

Menelaus appeals for help from other cities in Greece.

1   Menelaus iratus erat. iratus erat quod Paris uxorem, Helenam nomine, Troiam duxerat. Menelaus hunc virum punire et hanc urbem delere cupiebat. nuntios igitur ad omnes urbes Graeciae misit. hi nuntii haec
5   verba dixerunt: 'audite, omnes! Paris Helenam, uxorem caram Menelai, cepit. Troiam fugit. propter hoc Menelaus iratus est. hanc urbem delere cupit. arma parate! naves et milites colligite! Troiam navigabimus et Troianos puniemus!'
10 Graeci, ubi haec verba audiverunt, multas copias paraverunt. copiae Graecorum ad portum, Aulidem nomine, venerunt. Menelaus, ubi has naves et hos milites vidit, laetissimus erat. omnes salutavit et Troiam navigare statim parabat. bellum autem contra
15 Troianos gerere et Helenam liberare cupivit.

portum = port

Aulidem = accusative case of Aulis (a port in Greece)

1 Menelaus iratus erat. iratus erat quod Paris uxorem, Helenam nomine, Troiam duxerat. (lines 1–2)
Why was Menelaus angry? (2)

2 Menelaus hunc virum punire et hanc urbem delere cupiebat. (lines 2–3)
What two things did he want to do? (2 + 2)

3 nuntios igitur ad omnes urbes Graeciae misit. (lines 3–4)
What action did he take? (3)

4 hi nuntii haec verba dixerunt: 'audite, omnes! Paris Helenam, uxorem caram Menelai, cepit. Troiam fugit. (lines 4–6)
What did the messengers say about Paris's actions? (3)

5 propter hoc Menelaus iratus est. hanc urbem delere cupit. (lines 6–7)
And what effect had this had on Menelaus? (3)

6 arma parate! ... liberare cupivit. (lines 8–15)
Translate these lines into good English. (30)

7 From the passage give, in Latin, one example of each of the following:
   a) an infinitive; (1)
   b) a demonstrative pronoun in the nominative case; (1)
   c) an imperative; (1)
   d) a verb in the future tense. (1)

8 nuntios (line 3) In which case is this noun? Why is this case used? (2)

9 audiverunt (line 10)
   a) Give the tense of this verb. (1)
   b) Give the 1st person singular of the present tense of this verb. (1)
   c) Explain the connection between this word and the English word *audition*. (2)

Total: 55

Exercise 16.10

Translate the following into English:

1	ille libertus	(2)
2	illa navis	(2)
3	illud bellum	(2)
4	illi comites	(2)
5	illae urbes	(2)
6	illa bella	(2)
7	illa mulier	(2)
8	illa arma	(2)
9	illa corpora	(2)
10	illud flumen	(2)
11	illi equi	(2)
12	ille princeps	(2)
13	illa silva	(2)
14	illae copiae	(2)
15	illa verba	(2)
16	illud oppidum	(2)
17	ille iuvenis	(2)
18	illi viri	(2)
19	ille amicus	(2)
20	illi milites	(2)

Total: 40

Exercise 16.11

Translate the following into English:

1	illius custodis	(2)
2	cum illis amicis	(2)
3	illorum senum	(2)
4	illi mulieri	(2)
5	in illa urbe	(2)
6	illarum puellarum	(2)
7	illi deo	(2)
8	illorum iuvenum	(2)
9	in illo itinere	(2)
10	illis armis	(2)
11	ab illis militibus	(2)
12	illi regi	(2)
13	illorum periculorum	(2)
14	illa luce	(2)
15	illis sagittis	(2)
16	illorum hominum	(2)
17	illius amici	(2)
18	illarum mulierum	(2)
19	illius urbis	(2)
20	illi clamores	(2)

Total: 40

Exercise 16.12

Translate the following into English:

1	ille senex felix est.	(5)
2	illa puella crudelis est.	(5)
3	illi milites fessi sunt.	(5)
4	illa navis ingens est.	(5)
5	illud templum magnum et pulchrum est.	(7)
6	illa verba crudelia sunt.	(5)
7	illum regem non laudavi.	(5)
8	princeps illos cives saepe punit.	(6)
9	dux illas mulieres non amat.	(6)
10	nomen illius ducis est Marcus.	(6)

Total: 55

Exercise 16.13

Translate the following into English:

1	hic dominus bonus, ille malus est.	(7)
2	haec insula magna, illa parva est.	(7)
3	ille comes hunc dominum timebat.	(6)
4	hic dominus illum senem terrebat.	(6)
5	illi milites hanc urbem oppugnaverunt.	(6)
6	illi iuvenes has puellas spectabant.	(6)
7	haec femina ad illam insulam navigavit.	(7)
8	illi milites ex hoc oppido fugerunt.	(7)
9	hanc puellam in illa via vidi.	(7)
10	ille dominus hos cives puniverat.	(6)

Total: 65

Exercise 16.14

Translate the following into Latin:

1	I have captured the big city.	(4)
2	He killed his father with a sword.	(4)
3	We shall send letters to the master.	(5)
4	I was throwing a spear.	(3)
5	Consume the wine, citizens!	(4)

Total: 20

Exercise 16.15

Translate the following into Latin:

1	We placed the wine near the large river.	(6)
2	The soldiers were fighting against the Romans.	(5)
3	The leader of the soldiers never sent money to the city.	(8)
4	Tomorrow we shall all run into the town.	(6)
5	Prepare the dinner, wretched slave-girls!	(5)

Total: 30

Exam Practice Questions

Exercise 16.16

Translate the following into Latin:

1 The brave sailors prepared many ships. (6)
2 You (pl.) were carrying the bodies of the citizens into the temple. (6)
3 Today we will make a journey into the mountains. (6)
4 Once the boy and girl loved their father. (7)
5 We have handed over much money to the leader. (5)

Total: 30

Exercise 16.17

Translate the following into English:

1 redibo. (2)
2 perierunt. (2)
3 ibas. (2)
4 ineunt. (2)
5 ii. (2)
6 ibis. (2)
7 periit. (2)
8 exit. (2)
9 ibant. (2)
10 transibunt. (2)
11 itis. (2)
12 rediit. (2)
13 exibo. (2)
14 ierunt. (2)
15 adierunt. (2)

Total: 30

Exercise 16.18

Translate the following into English:

1 pereo. (2)
2 ibitis. (2)
3 exibamus. (2)
4 transit. (2)
5 redii. (2)
6 exibunt. (2)
7 ibamus. (2)
8 periit. (2)
9 redibit. (2)
10 ibat. (2)
11 adit. (2)
12 rediimus. (2)
13 it. (2)
14 exii. (2)
15 iit. (2)

Total: 30

Exercise 16.19

Translate the following into English:

1 transierunt.(2)
2 ibit. (2)
3 imus. (2)
4 transibimus. (2)
5 eunt. (2)
6 peris. (2)
7 exibat. (2)
8 redierunt. (2)
9 adibunt. (2)
10 exibit. (2)
11 transeunt. (2)
12 redibunt. (2)
13 redibimus. (2)
14 pereunt. (2)
15 ibatis. (2)

Total: 15

Exercise 16.20

Translate the following into English:

1 heri flumen transimus. (4)
2 hodie mare transimus. (4)
3 ad urbem eo. (4)
4 i, puer! (3)
5 ad urbem cras adibimus. (5)
6 per viam ibamus. (4)
7 multi iuvenes perierunt. (4)
8 pueri mox redierunt. (4)
9 crasne ad urbem redibis? (5)
10 celeriter exiit. (3)

Total: 40

Exercise 16.21

Study the passage below and answer the questions that follow.

The Greeks assemble at Aulis, but their departure is delayed by contrary winds.

1   Graeci multos milites et multas naves ad Aulidem   Aulis, Aulidis, f. = Aulis
     miserunt. Menelaus autem, ubi illos milites et illas
     naves conspexit, laetissimus erat. Troiam non
     amabat. illam urbem sine mora delere cupiebat.
5   naves tamen navigare non poterant. naves navigare
     non poterant quod venti adversi erant. Graeci prope   adversus, -a, -um = contrary
     naves diu manebant. nihil faciebant. diu ventos
     secundos exspectabant. nemo laetus erat. sed   secundus, -a, -um = favourable
     tandem venti secundi erant.
10   Menelaus comitibus clamavit: 'O amici,' inquit, 'illi
     venti nunc secundi sunt. parate naves! parate arma!
     mare transire debemus!' Graeci, ubi haec verba
     audiverunt, naves celeriter paraverunt et ab Aulide
     abierunt.

1 Translate the passage into good English. (30)
2 From the passage give, in Latin, one example of each of the following:
   a) a demonstrative pronoun; (1)
   b) an imperative; (1)
   c) a verb in the perfect tense. (1)
3 **naves** (line 1)
   a) Give the case of this noun. (1)
   b) Explain the connection between this word and the English word *naval*. (2)
4 **verba** (line 12) Give the gender of this noun. (1)
5 **abierunt** (line 14)
   a) Give the person and number of this verb. (2)
   b) Give the 1st person singular of the present tense of this verb. (1)

Total: 40

Chapter 17: Present passive, numerals 1–1000

Exercise 17.1

Translate the following into English:

1	amamur.	(2)
2	laudatur.	(2)
3	vulnerantur.	(2)
4	vocaris.	(2)
5	portor.	(2)
6	liberamur.	(2)
7	nuntiatur.	(2)
8	laudamini.	(2)
9	necantur.	(2)
10	spectamini.	(2)

Total: 20

Exercise 17.2

Translate the following into English:

1	monetur.	(2)
2	videmini.	(2)
3	movetur.	(2)
4	tenetur.	(2)
5	terreris.	(2)
6	delentur.	(2)
7	videntur.	(2)
8	movemur.	(2)
9	monemini.	(2)
10	iubemur.	(2)

Total: 20

Exercise 17.3

Translate the following into English:

1	regimur.	(2)
2	ponitur.	(2)
3	capimini.	(2)
4	defenditur.	(2)
5	amantur.	(2)
6	mitteris.	(2)
7	traduntur.	(2)
8	occidimini.	(2)
9	vincuntur.	(2)
10	iacitur.	(2)

Total: 20

Exercise 17.4

Translate the following into English:

1	auditur.	(2)
2	inveniuntur.	(2)
3	cogor.	(2)
4	interficitur.	(2)
5	iuvamur.	(2)
6	pelluntur.	(2)
7	relinquitur.	(2)
8	capitur.	(2)
9	ducuntur.	(2)
10	pellimur.	(2)

Total: 20

Exercise 17.5

Translate the following into English:

1	senex militem vulnerat.	(4)
2	miles a sene vulneratur.	(5)
3	iuvenis librum legit.	(4)
4	liber a iuvene legitur.	(5)
5	pueri cibum parant.	(4)
6	cibus a pueris paratur.	(5)
7	magister pueros laudat.	(4)
8	pueri a magistro laudantur.	(5)
9	hostes urbem occupant.	(4)
10	urbs ab hostibus occupatur.	(5)

Total: 45

Exercise 17.6

Translate the following into English:

1	ego puellam amo.	(4)
2	puella a me amatur.	(5)
3	senes vinum bibunt.	(4)
4	vinum a senibus bibitur.	(5)
5	Romani oppidum capiunt.	(4)
6	oppidum a Romanis capitur.	(5)
7	rex terram regit.	(4)
8	terra a rege regitur.	(5)
9	Graeci Romanos vincunt.	(4)
10	Romani a Graecis vincuntur.	(5)

Total: 45

Exercise 17.7

Translate the following into English:

1 Romani Graecos semper vincunt. (5)
2 Graeci a Romanis semper vincuntur. (6)
3 dominus agricolas saepe punit. (5)
4 agricolae a domino saepe puniuntur. (6)
5 poeta libros semper legit. (5)
6 libri a poeta semper leguntur. (6)
7 uxor principis patrem eius amat. (6)
8 senex ab uxore principis amatur. (6)
9 multi milites urbem defendunt. (5)
10 urbs a militibus defenditur. (5)

Total: 55

Exercise 17.8

Translate the following into English:

1 tempestas naves delet. (4)
2 naves tempestate delentur. (4)
3 hostes nos non amant. (5)
4 ab hostibus non amamur. (5)
5 pueri magistrum amant. (4)
6 magister a pueris amatur. (5)
7 cives regem vulnerant. (4)
8 rex a civibus vulneratur. (5)
9 puer urbem videt. (4)
10 urbs a puero videtur. (5)

Total: 45

Exercise 17.9

Translate the following into English:

1 ab hostibus crudelibus spectamur. (5)
2 multi hostium gladiis occiduntur. (5)
3 ad dominam a domino mittor. (6)
4 a patre meo amor. (5)
5 a magistro numquam laudaris. (5)
6 milites sagittis hastisque vulnerantur. (5)
7 aqua in villam a milite portatur. (6)
8 servi felices a domino liberantur. (6)
9 vos a militibus crudelibus capimini. (6)
10 nonne nos a rege defendimur? (6)

Total: 55

Exercise 17.10

Translate the following into English:

1 illi liberti ab hac domina laudantur. (7)
2 hic liber ab illo sene legitur. (7)
3 propter proelia longa, in urbe a custodibus senes defenduntur. (10)
4 hic poeta ab illo iuvene salutatur. (7)
5 viri sapientes ab omnibus semper audiuntur. (7)
6 corpus illius mulieris miserae in templum a filio portatur. (10)
7 duces mali a militibus saepe occiduntur. (7)
8 quis a deis terretur? (5)
9 quis a civibus timetur? (5)
10 quamquam a civibus timemur, nos omnes villas maximas aedificamus. (10)

Total: 75

Exercise 17.11

Write down the passive infinitives and then translate the following into Latin:

1 milites Romani ab hostibus superari non cupiunt. (1 + 8)
2 cives a custodibus saevis capi non cupiebant. (1 + 8)
3 Romani a regibus regi non cupiebant. (1 + 7)
4 puella parva a matre audiri non poterat. (1 + 8)
5 pueri a magistro sapienti moneri debent. (1 + 7)
6 num a senibus montes altissimi videri possunt? (1 + 7)
7 cur a principe crudeli defendi cupitis? (1 + 7)
8 omnes a regina sapienti regi cupiebant. (1 + 7)
9 plurima templa prope flumen magnum aedificari possunt. (1 + 8)
10 femina a marito claro interfici non cupit. (1 + 8)

Total: 85

Exercise 17.12

Translate the following into English:

1 multi viri fortissimi in bello occiduntur. (7)
2 Patroclus ab Hectore occiditur. (5)
3 Hector ab Achille occiditur. (5)
4 corpus Hectoris a Troianis videtur. (6)
5 muri Troiae non delentur. (5)
6 haec urbs a Graecis non capitur. (7)
7 tandem equus maximus a Graecis aedificatur. (7)
8 equus prope urbem ponitur. (5)
9 hic miles a Graecis relinquitur. (6)
10 urbs Troia a Graecis tandem capitur. (7)

Total: 60

Exercise 17.13

Translate the following into Latin:

1 (O) soldiers, carry the bodies of the citizens into the city! (7)
2 Hand over the money, soldier, to the brave citizen! (6)
3 Friends, fight bravely against the Romans! (6)
4 I have shown many books to the master. (5)
5 You (pl.) have run into the river with the horses. (6)
6 Look, boys! The schoolmaster is coming out of the temple. (8)
7 We fear all the sons of the queen. (5)
8 Bad sailors never build good ships. (7)
9 He has thrown a book into the river. (5)
10 They once came to the town. (5)

Total: 60

Exercise 17.14

Translate the following into Latin:

1 The wretched friends look at the happy master. (6)
2 We found the sad girl in the street. (6)
3 Walk slowly towards the master's villa, boys. (7)
4 The boys have always loved the friend's mother. (6)
5 He has come to the temple without a friend. (6)
6 They soon see the beautiful mountains. (5)
7 Look, girls! She has many friends. (7)
8 The king is coming down from the mountains. (5)
9 They all have big swords and spears. (7)
10 The happy citizens enter the town. (5)

Total: 60

Exercise 17.15

Study the passage below (do not write a translation) and answer the questions that follow. Complete sentences are not required.

The Trojan Aeneas urges his friends to abandon Troy.

1 Graeci urbem Troiam delebant. in media urbe aderant
et multos milites Troianos necabant. multa templa
incendebant. multos cives capiebant. Aeneas princeps
Troianus in urbe aderat. hic, ubi milites Graecos vidit,
5 amicos convocavit et haec verba eis dixit: 'o amici,'
inquit, 'urbs nostra a Graecis occupatur. in maximo
periculo sumus. milites nostri necantur. templa nostra
incenduntur. capi non cupio. effugere debemus.
arma capite! domos relinquite! naves parate! statim
10 discedite!' post haec, Aeneas et comites per vias urbis
festinaverunt et e portis celeriter exierunt.

incendo, -ere, incendi (3) = I set on fire, I burn
convoco, -are, -avi (1) = I call together

domos = homes

1 Graeci urbem Troiam delebant. (line 1)
   What were the Greeks doing? (2)
2 in media urbe aderant et multos milites Troianos necabant. (lines 1–2)
   Where were they, and how were they dealing with the Trojan soldiers? (2 + 2)
3 multa templa incendebant. multos cives capiebant. (lines 2–3)
   What else were the Greeks doing? (2 + 2)
4 Aeneas princeps Troianus in urbe aderat. (lines 3–4)
   Who was Aeneas and where was he? (1 + 1)
5 hic, ubi milites Graecos vidit, amicos convocavit et haec verba eis dixit. (lines 4–5)
   Explain what Aeneas did when he saw the Greeks. (1 + 2)
6 'o amici ... e portis exierunt. (lines 5–11)
   Translate these lines into good English. (30)
7 From the passage give an example of:
   a) a verb in the imperfect tense; (1)
   b) a verb in the perfect tense; (1)
   c) a superlative adjective. (1)
8 dixit (line 5)
   a) Give the person of this verb. (1)
   b) Give the 1st person singular of the present tense of this verb. (1)
9 amici (line 5) In which case is this noun? (1)
10 naves (line 9)
   a) In which case is this noun? (1)
   b) Why is this case used? (1)
11 celeriter (line 11) Explain the connection between this word and the English word *accelerate*. (2)

Total: 55

Exercise 17.16

Translate the following into English:

1 dux Romanus centum milites habebat. (6)
2 Graeci mille naves collegerunt. (5)
3 rex crudelis nonaginta captivos occiderunt. (6)
4 incolae octoginta templa aedificaverant. (5)
5 iuvenis quadraginta corpora in silva invenit. (7)
6 princeps quinquaginta milites in forum duxit. (7)
7 num septuaginta naves habetis? (5)
8 post sexaginta annos regina clara periit. (7)
9 cum triginta civibus in forum inierunt. (5)
10 viginti viri in montibus diu manebant. (7)

Total: 60

Exercise 17.17

Translate the following into English:

1 dux captivos collegit et decimum occidit. (8)
2 poeta librum nonum celeriter legebat. (6)
3 senex uxorem octavam magnopere amabat. (6)
4 primus rex urbis Romanae Romulus erat. (7)
5 quartus rex Romae multas naves prope mare collegit. (9)
6 quintus rex, nomine Tarquinius Priscus, servum parvum magnopere laudavit. (10)
7 secundus rex urbis, Numa Pompilius nomine, templum maximum aedificavit. (10)
8 cives septimum regem ex urbe pepulerunt. (7)
9 sextus rex Romae servus fuerat. (6)
10 tertius rex multos incolas superavit. (6)

Total: 75

Chapter 18: Future and imperfect passive, 5th declension, expressions of time

Exercise 18.1

Translate the following into English:

1	portabantur.	(2)	11	capiemur.	(2)
2	mittentur.	(2)	12	non vincar.	(2)
3	audiar.	(2)	13	iubebamur.	(2)
4	vulnerabor.	(2)	14	monebimur.	(2)
5	regebamur.	(2)	15	ducebamini.	(2)
6	occidebantur.	(2)	16	mitteris.	(2)
7	timebor.	(2)	17	mittebantur.	(2)
8	puniar.	(2)	18	ponitur.	(2)
9	conspiciuntur.	(2)	19	superabimini.	(2)
10	interficientur.	(2)	20	occidemini.	(2)

Total: 40

Exercise 18.2

Translate the following into English:

1	legebatur.	(2)	11	oppugnantur.	(2)
2	laudabantur.	(2)	12	dabitur.	(2)
3	vocabor.	(2)	13	nuntiatur.	(2)
4	reducebantur.	(2)	14	videbuntur.	(2)
5	laudor.	(2)	15	regetur.	(2)
6	delebitur.	(2)	16	puniebantur.	(2)
7	necabuntur.	(2)	17	vincemini.	(2)
8	parabantur.	(2)	18	audiuntur.	(2)
9	movebimur.	(2)	19	puniemur.	(2)
10	movemur.	(2)	20	laudamur.	(2)

Total: 40

Exercise 18.3

Translate the following into English:

1	quis a magistro cras laudabitur?	(6)
2	multi a magistro cras laudabuntur.	(6)
3	multi equi ex agris ducebantur.	(6)
4	numquam a Romanis superabimur.	(5)
5	nuntii ad urbem mittebantur.	(5)
6	pueri ab illo magistro saepe puniuntur.	(7)
7	mille naves a Graecis parabantur.	(6)
8	hic liber a me mox legetur.	(7)
9	multa arma militibus a duce dabantur.	(7)
10	laudaris quod fortis es!	(5)

Total: 60

Exercise 18.4

Translate the following into English:

1 Graeci post decem annos urbem Troiam occupaverunt. (8)
2 verba longa a pueris parvis non saepe dicuntur. (9)
3 Graeci in Britannia non saepe videntur. (7)
4 multi captivi a custodibus custodiebantur. (6)
5 dominus crudelis a servis non laudabatur. (7)
6 multi agri ab hostibus delebantur. (6)
7 ille equus a milite hasta vulnerabitur. (7)
8 multae gentes a Romanis superabuntur. (6)
9 Graeci a Romanis tandem vincentur. (6)
10 multa tela a militibus in forum portabuntur. (8)

Total: 70

Exercise 18.5

Translate the following into Latin:

1 The happy men were shouting near the river. (6)
2 I have a famous father and a large villa. (7)
3 The enemy were fighting without spears. (5)
4 The bad master has praised all the brave men. (7)
5 The queen's slave-girl likes money. (5)

Total: 30

Exercise 18.6

Translate the following into Latin:

1 All the soldiers were fighting in the streets. (6)
2 You (sing.) have many friends and big villas. (7)
3 We were eating the dinner with the beautiful girls. (6)
4 Boys, show the book to the schoolmaster! (5)
5 The leader will never drink the citizens' wine. (6)

Total: 30

Exercise 18.7

Study the passage below (do not write a translation) and answer the questions that follow. Complete sentences are not required.

Odysseus deals with three missing sailors.

1	olim Ulixes ad insulam <u>Lotophagorum</u> advenit. nautae eius ibi a Lotophagis tenebantur. Ulixes, ubi eos vidit, <u>attonitus</u> erat. illi enim <u>semisomni</u> erant neque se movere poterant. 'quid facitis?' eos rogavit
5	Ulixes iratus. 'quid fecistis?' nautae ei responderunt: 'noli iratus esse, Ulixes. <u>lotum</u> consumpsimus. lotus optima est. eam amamus. hic manere et dormire cupimus. <u>domum</u> ire non cupimus. nos hic relinque!'
10	Ulixes autem hoc facere non cupiebat. nautis igitur, 'ad naves statim ite.' deinde comitibus clamavit: 'capite <u>funes</u>! hos nautas funibus <u>vincite</u>! deinde eos ad naves ducite!' comites igitur Ulixis nautas ad naves duxerunt. in naves pellebantur et
15	vinciebantur. iratissimi erant.

Lotophagi, -orum, m. pl. = Lotus Eaters

attonitus, -a, -um = amazed
semisomni = half asleep

lotus, -i, f. = the lotus fruit

domum = home

funis, -is, m. = rope
vincio, -ire, vinxi, vinctum (3) = I tie up

1 olim Ulixes ad insulam Lotophagorum advenit. (line 1)
   Where was Ulysses? (2)
2 nautae eius ibi a Lotophagis tenebantur. Ulixes, ubi eos vidit, attonitus erat. (lines 2–3)
   Who did he find there and how did this make him feel? (2 + 1)
3 illi enim semisomni erant neque se movere poterant. (lines 3–4)
   What condition were the sailors in? (3)
4 'quid facitis?' eos rogavit Ulixes iratus. 'quid fecistis?' (lines 4–5)
   What did Ulysses want to know? (2)
5 'noli iratus esse, Ulixes. lotum consumpsimus. lotus optima est. eam amamus. hic manere et dormire cupimus. domum ire non cupimus.' (lines 6–8)
   a) How did the sailors respond to Ulysses' questions? (1)
   b) How might the lotus fruit have contributed to their state of mind? (1)
   c) How did this make them feel about going home? (3)
6 Ulixes autem … iratissimi erant. (lines 10–15) From these lines, give in Latin:
   a) a verb in the imperfect passive; (1)
   b) a conjunction; (1)
   c) an imperative. (1)
7 comitibus (line 11) Give the nominative masculine singular of this word. (1)
8 hos (line 12) In which case is this word? (1)
9 eos (line 13) Give the nominative masculine singular of this word. (1)
10 iratissimi (line 15)
   a) Which part of which adjective is this? (1 + 1)
   b) Explain the connection between this word and the English word *irate*. (2)

Total: 25

Exercise 18.8

Translate the following into English:

1	paucis diebus veniam.	(4)
2	totum diem dormivi.	(4)
3	multas horas currebam; nunc fessus sum.	(8)
4	paucis annis redibo.	(4)
5	septem dies laborabamus.	(4)
6	quarto anno advenerunt.	(4)
7	paucis horis discedemus.	(4)
8	eum tertia hora vidi.	(5)
9	multas horas dormiebat.	(4)
10	multos dies laborabo.	(4)

Total: 45

Exercise 18.9

Translate the following into English:

1	urbs a regibus multos annos regebatur.	(7)
2	liberi dominae crudelis paucas horas dormiebant.	(7)
3	urbs a Graecis multos annos oppugnabatur.	(7)
4	milites paucas horas in equo manebant.	(7)
5	iuvenes quinque horas in villa laborabant.	(7)
6	iter trans montes totum diem faciebatis.	(7)
7	liberti in villa dominae multos dies manebant.	(8)
8	ancillae tristes cenam iuvenibus duas horas parabant.	(8)
9	senex prope flumen altissimum tres dies manebat.	(8)
10	cives Romani sex annos a rege crudeli regebantur.	(9)

Total: 75

Exercise 18.10

Translate the following into English:

1	urbs paucis horis capietur.	(5)
2	senex tertio die periit.	(5)
3	captivi a custodibus decima hora liberabantur.	(7)
4	illo tempore a regibus regebamur.	(6)
5	hostes copias nostras quarto die superaverunt.	(7)
6	rex crudelis illo die occidetur.	(6)
7	Romani auxilium militibus nostris octo diebus dabunt.	(8)
8	mater paterque paucis diebus liberos videbunt.	(7)
9	cives optimi templum quattuor annis aedificaverant.	(7)
10	sexto anno principem ad urbem ducemus.	(7)

Total: 65

Exercise 18.11

Give and translate the following verb parts:

1   The 2nd person plural, present active of **audio**.   (1 + 2)
2   The 3rd person plural, perfect active of **discedo**.   (1 + 2)
3   The 1st person singular, perfect active of **sum**.   (1 + 2)
4   The 3rd person singular, imperfect active of **sum**.   (1 + 2)
5   The 3rd person plural, imperfect passive of **trado**.   (1 + 2)
6   The 1st person plural, present passive of **vulnero**.   (1 + 2)
7   The 3rd person singular, imperfect passive of **punio**.   (1 + 2)
8   The 3rd person plural, imperfect passive of **colligo**.   (1 + 2)
9   The 2nd person singular, future passive of **mitto**.   (1 + 2)
10 The 3rd person plural, future passive of **occido**.   (1 + 2)

Total: 30

Exercise 18.12

Give and explain the case of the underlined words and then translate the sentences into English:

1   illam puellam <u>quinque horas</u> spectabam. eam timeo.   (2 + 9)
2   hic senex uxorem caram <u>septuaginta annos</u> amabat.   (2 + 8)
3   illa tempestas multas naves <u>paucis horis</u> delevit.   (2 + 8)
4   nonne Flavia <u>pulcherrima</u> omnium puellarum est?   (2 + 7)
5   nolite timere, <u>cives!</u> auxilium adveniet.   (2 + 7)
6   <u>septem annos</u> ab illo magistro terrebamur.   (2 + 7)
7   cibus vinumque in villam <u>secundo die</u> portabantur.   (2 + 8)
8   puellae pulchrae ab iuvenibus <u>multas horas</u> spectantur.   (2 + 8)
9   magnae naves ad insulam <u>multos dies</u> tempestate pellebantur. (2 + 9)
10 nonne captivi a domino crudeli <u>secundo die</u> occidentur?   (2 + 9)

Total: 100

Exercise 18.13

1   Translate the passage below into good English: (30)

Odysseus and his men leave the land of the Lotus Eaters.

1   nautae, quod <u>lotum</u> consumpserant, fessi erant. a
    comitibus <u>Ulixis</u> autem ad naves trahebantur et
    iratissimi erant. Ulixes amicis clamavit: 'hi nautae
    in hac terra a <u>Lotophagis</u> manere cogebantur.
5   lotum consumpserunt. eos in naves iacite! celeriter
    discedite!' Graeci, ubi nautas in naves iecerunt,
    omnia celeriter paraverunt. tum trans mare multis
    cum clamoribus transierunt.

lotus, -i, f. = the lotus fruit
Ulixes, Ulixis, m. = Ulysses

Lotophagi, -orum, m. pl. = the Lotus
Eaters

2   consumpserant (line 1)
    a) Give the tense of this verb.   (1)
    b) Give the 1st person singular of its present tense.   (1)
    c) Explain the connection between **consumpserant** and the English word *consumption*. (2)
3   trahebantur (line 2) In which voice is this verb?   (1)
4   iratissimi (line 3)
    a) Which part of the adjective is this?   (1)
    b) Give its positive (nominative masculine singular) form.   (1)
    c) Explain the connection between this word and the English word *irate*. (2)
5   hac (line 4) In which gender is this word?   (1)

Total: 40

Chapter 19: Perfect passive, pluperfect passive, three-termination adjectives (celer)

Exercise 19.1

Translate the following into English:

1 interfectus est. (2)
2 interfecta est. (2)
3 interfecti estis. (2)
4 interfecti sunt. (2)
5 vulnerata es. (2)
6 missus sum. (2)
7 capta est. (2)
8 capti estis. (2)
9 puniti sumus. (2)
10 auditi sunt. (2)
11 visus est. (2)
12 visa est. (2)
13 visi sunt. (2)
14 portatae sumus. (2)
15 victi sunt. (2)
16 pulsus est. (2)
17 relicta est. (2)
18 ducta est. (2)
19 dictum est. (2)
20 moniti estis. (2)

Total: 40

Exercise 19.2

Translate the following into English:

1 puer punitus est. (3)
2 pueri puniti sunt. (3)
3 puella visa est. (3)
4 puellae visae sunt. (3)
5 templum aedificatum est. (3)
6 templa aedificata sunt. (3)
7 Romani victi sunt. (3)
8 miles vulneratus est. (3)
9 tela iacta sunt. (3)
10 senex interfectus est. (3)
11 oppidum oppugnatum est. (3)
12 oppida oppugnata sunt. (3)
13 cives moniti sunt. (3)
14 civis monitus est. (3)
15 pater amatus est. (3)
16 mater amata est. (3)
17 verba audita sunt. (3)
18 voces auditae sunt. (3)
19 urbs deleta est. (3)
20 lux visa est. (3)

Total: 60

Exercise 19.3

Translate the following into English:

1 rex multa verba dixit. (5)
2 multa verba a rege dicta sunt. (6)
3 puellae voces militum audiverunt. (5)
4 voces militum a puellis auditae sunt. (6)
5 amici cibum mox paraverunt. (5)
6 cibus a Romanis mox paratus est. (6)
7 Romani tandem Graecos vicerunt. (5)
8 Graeci a Romanis tandem victi sunt. (6)
9 puer puellam magnopere amavit. (5)
10 puella a puero magnopere amata est. (6)

Total: 55

Exercise 19.4

Translate the following into English:

1 Romani ab hostibus visi sunt. (5)
2 a domino punitus sum. (4)
3 puella a puero visa est. (5)
4 puellae a pueris visae sunt. (5)
5 templum a civibus aedificatum est. (5)
6 muri ab hostibus deleti sunt. (5)
7 multa verba a senibus dicta sunt. (6)
8 sagitta a milite iacta est. (5)
9 servus a domino liberatus est. (5)
10 donum a matre missum est. (5)

Total: 50

Exercise 19.5

Translate the following into English:

1 multae hastae a militibus in proelio iactae sunt. (8)
2 oppidum ab hostibus iam deletum erat. (7)
3 nuntii nostri ab hostibus capti sunt. (7)
4 pecunia militibus a duce data est. (7)
5 pecunia a militibus laetis accepta est. (7)
6 vinum regis boni seni datum est. (7)
7 multae terrae a regina victae erant. (6)
8 multi cives per vias ducti erant. (7)
9 templa urbis mox ab hostibus delebuntur. (7)
10 ille dux a militibus laudatus est. (7)

Total: 70

Exercise 19.6

Translate the following into English:

1 magister a pueris non amatur. (6)
2 miles gladio vulneratus est. (5)
3 multum cibi in flumen ab amicis iacitur. (8)
4 ab hostibus superamur! (4)
5 multa vulnera a militibus accepta erant. (7)
6 hic servus a domino cras punietur. (7)
7 multa verba a duce dicta erant. (7)
8 pecunia civibus a rege data est. (7)
9 arma hostium a Romanis capta sunt. (7)
10 femina pulchra a puero conspecta erat. (7)

Total: 65

Exercise 19.7

Translate the following into English:

1 Helena, ubi ab iuvene visa est, ad urbem Troiam ducta est. (12)
2 multae naves paratae sunt et ad Menelaum missae sunt. (10)
3 Troia a civibus diu defendebatur. (6)
4 equus ingens prope mare relictus erat. (7)
5 equus a Troianis visus est. (6)
6 num equus in urbem trahi potest? (7)
7 urbem Troiam occupari non cupimus. (6)
8 urbs tandem capta est. (5)
9 multi cives, quod ab hostibus vulnerati erant, ex urbe fugerunt. (12)
10 Troiani, quod urbs deleta erat, numquam redierunt. (9)

Total: 80

Exercise 19.8

Translate the following into Latin:

1 Come, citizens! The enemy are capturing the city.   (6)
2 Run, men! The soldiers have destroyed the walls.   (6)
3 We do not like the savage master's father.   (6)
4 They were often walking to the king's villa.   (6)
5 I have seen the town's big temples.   (5)
6 The sad friends were warning the woman's son.   (6)
7 The sailors were shouting to the happy boys.   (5)
8 The gods never come down from the mountains.   (6)
9 I never fight without a big sword.   (6)
10 Brave citizens, you often walk around the walls of the city.   (8)

Total: 60

Exercise 19.9

Translate the following into English:

1 visi eramus.   (2)
2 motum erat.   (2)
3 laudata erat.   (2)
4 necati erant.   (2)
5 ducti eramus.   (2)
6 captus eras.   (2)
7 missus eram.   (2)
8 coactus erat.   (2)
9 defensa erat.   (2)
10 vulnerati eramus.   (2)
11 datum erat.   (2)
12 scriptum erat.   (2)
13 deletum erat.   (2)
14 rogatus eras.   (2)
15 ductus erat.   (2)
16 puniti eratis.   (2)
17 iussi eramus.   (2)
18 visa erat.   (2)
19 nuntiatum erat.   (2)
20 occisus erat.   (2)

Total: 40

Exercise 19.10

Translate the following into English:

1 tandem copiae paratae erant.   (4)
2 hastis vulneratus erat.   (3)
3 hastis vulnerata erat.   (3)
4 a magistro laudati eramus.   (4)
5 omnes muri ab hostibus deleti erant.   (6)
6 ab amicis relictus eram.   (4)
7 a Romanis superati eratis.   (4)
8 a magistro auditi eramus.   (4)
9 a Graecis victi erant.   (4)
10 a domino liberatus eras.   (4)

Total: 40

Exercise 19.11

Translate the following into English:

1	Helena a iuvene forti capta erat.	(6)
2	Helena ad urbem Troiam celeriter ducta erat.	(6)
3	copiae a Graecis paratae erant.	(5)
4	naves ad urbem Troiam mox missae erant.	(6)
5	Troia a Graecis oppugnata erat.	(5)
6	multi viri occisi erant.	(4)
7	equus maximus a Graecis aedificatus erat.	(6)
8	equus in media urbe a Troianis positus erat.	(7)
9	multi Troiani a Graecis interfecti erant.	(6)
10	urbs tandem capta erat.	(4)

Total: 55

Exercise 19.12

Study the passage below (do not write a translation) and answer the questions that follow. Complete sentences are not required.

Ulysses and the end of the war.

1 urbs Troia a Graecis capta erat. Ulixes autem
laetissimus erat. Graecos enim equum <u>ligneum</u>   ligneus, -a, -um = wooden
aedificare iusserat. iam haec verba comitibus
dixit: 'amici, gens Graeca felicissima est. nos a deis
5 amamur. nonne a nobis Troia capta est? a nobis
muri deleti sunt; a nobis templa deleta sunt; paene
omnes principes Troianorum a nobis interfecti sunt.
multa pecunia a nobis capta est. multa praemia
habemus. Helena, uxor Menelai carissima, ad
10 Graeciam nunc reducitur. credite mihi, amici! mox
omnes ad Graeciam redibimus! mox uxores nostras,
mox filios filiasque iterum videbimus!'

diu tamen Ulixes uxorem suam, <u>Penelopen</u> nomine,   Penelopen = the accusative of Penelope
non vidit. neque filium suum, <u>Telemachum</u> nomine,   (Greek form)
15 vidit. multos annos cum comitibus trans maria   Telemachus, -i, m. = Telemachus
errabat et maxima pericula <u>subibat</u>.   subeo, subire, subii = I undergo

1 urbs Troia a Graecis capta erat. Ulixes autem laetissimus erat. (lines 1–2)
Why was Ulysses happy? (2)
2 Graecos enim equum ligneum aedificare iusserat. (lines 2–3)
What had Ulysses done to influence this outcome? (2)
3 amici, gens Graeca felicissima est. nos a deis amamur. (lines 4–5)
Why did Ulysses consider Greece to be lucky? (2)
4 nonne a nobis Troia ... ad Graeciam nunc reducitur. (lines 5–10)
Give the seven points that Ulysses made to support this claim. (7)
5 credite mihi, amici! mox omnes ad Graeciam redibimus! (lines 10–11)
What was the first promise he gave his men? (2)
6 mox uxores nostras, mox filios filiasque iterum videbimus! (lines 11–12)
What was the second promise? (2)
7 diu tamen Ulixes uxorem suam, Penelopen nomine, non vidit. neque filium suum,
Telemachum nomine, vidit. (lines 13–15)
Did these promises come true for Ulysses himself? Explain your answer. (4)
8 multos annos cum comitibus trans maria errabat et maxima pericula subibat. (lines 15–16)
What accounted for the delay in Ulysses's return home? (4)

Total: 25

Exercise 19.13

Give the 1st person singular (masculine), perfect passive of each of the following verbs and translate your answer:

1 moneo, monere, monui, monitum (2)
2 rego, regere, rexi, rectum (2)
3 audio, audire, audivi, auditum (2)
4 porto, portare, portavi, portatum (2)
5 interficio, interficere, interfeci, interfectum (2)
6 duco, ducere, duxi, ductum (2)
7 deleo, delere, delevi, deletum (2)
8 capio, capere, cepi, captum (2)
9 vulnero, vulnerare, vulneravi, vulneratum (2)
10 mitto, mittere, misi, missum (2)
11 video, videre, vidi, visum (2)
12 vinco, vincere, vici, victum (2)
13 iacio, iacere, ieci, iactum (2)
14 amo, amare, amavi, amatum (2)
15 punio, punire, punivi, punitum (2)

Total: 30

Exercise 19.14

Give the 1st person plural (feminine), pluperfect passive of each of the following verbs and translate your answer:

1 punio, punire, punivi, punitum (2)
2 peto, petere, petivi, petitum (2)
3 custodio, custodire, custodivi, custoditum (2)
4 libero, liberare, liberavi, liberatum (2)
5 porto, portare, portavi, portatum (2)
6 saluto, salutare, salutavi, salutatum (2)
7 colligo, colligere, collegi, collectum (2)
8 trado, tradere, tradidi, traditum (2)
9 vulnero, vulnerare, vulneravi, vulneratum (2)
10 mitto, mittere, misi, missum (2)
11 video, videre, vidi, visum (2)
12 vinco, vincere, vici, victum (2)
13 iacio, iacere, ieci, iactum (2)
14 duco, ducere, duxi, ductum (2)
15 cogo, cogere, coegi, coactum (2)

Total: 30

Exercise 19.15

Give the case of the underlined words* and translate the following sentences.

1 The book has been written by a wise <u>man</u>. (1)
2 The gifts have been given to the <u>good</u> slave-girl. (1)
3 The old man has been killed with a <u>spear</u>. (1)
4 <u>Brave</u> boys are loved by their parents. (1)
5 The temples were being built near the walls of the <u>city</u>. (1)
6 <u>Come</u> quickly, girls! Your villa has been destroyed. (2)
7 A huge ship had been built by the wise <u>sailors</u>. (1)
8 The girl was ordered to flee by the <u>queen</u>. (1)
9 We have <u>sent</u> the other citizens into the mountains. (2)
10 The sailor was killed <u>near</u> the forum. (1)

Total: 12

* Your teacher may ask you to translate the whole sentence.

Exercise 19.16

Give the person, number and tense of the underlined verbs and then translate the sentences into English.

1 mulieres a maritis crudelibus non <u>laudantur</u>. (3 + 8)
2 naves celeres ex insula minima cras <u>pellentur</u>. (3 + 8)
3 omnes milites celeres in proelium <u>currebant</u>. (3 + 7)
4 a domino crudeli saepe <u>puniti sumus</u>. (3 + 6)
5 num haec puella celeris <u>erit</u>? (3 + 6)
6 tempestates naves celeres saepe <u>delent</u>. (3 + 6)
7 cives sapientes regibus pessimis numquam <u>credunt</u>. (3 + 7)
8 Romani multis gentibus <u>persuaserunt</u>. (3 + 6)
9 multa animalia a viris crudelibus iam <u>occisa erant</u>. (3 + 8)
10 multi cives celeres ex oppido iam <u>fugerant</u>. (3 + 8)

Total: 100

Exercise 19.17

Give and explain the case of the underlined words and then translate the sentences into English.

1 o domine, noli credere illi <u>militi</u>!   (2 + 6)
2 num omnes naves celeres illa <u>tempestate</u> delebuntur?   (2 + 9)
3 senes sapientissimi <u>hoc</u> facere numquam poterunt.   (2 + 7)
4 <u>praemia</u> magna his iuvenibus saepe data sunt.   (2 + 7)
5 Romani igitur hanc totam <u>urbem</u> deleverunt.   (2 + 7)
6 dux virtutem omnium <u>civium</u> laudavit.   (2 + 6)
7 femina laetissima <u>puellis</u> sapientibus credidit.   (2 + 6)
8 illa <u>femina</u> celeris ab hoc domino cras monebitur.   (2 + 9)
9 pauci senes <u>celeres</u> fuerunt.   (2 + 5)
10 nautae tempestatem saeviorem quam <u>illam</u> numquam viderant.   (2 + 8)

Total: 90

Exercise 19.18

Study the passage below (do not write a translation) and answer the questions that follow. Complete sentences are not required.

Ulysses comes to the land of the Lotus Eaters.

1   post decem annos tota urbs Troia a Graecis capta
       erat. muri deleti erant et templa <u>incensa</u> erant,   incendo, -ere, incendi, incensum = I set
       neque multi Troiani effugere potuerant. <u>Ulixes</u>   alight, burn
       comitesque Troia discesserant et ad Graeciam   Ulixes = Ulysses
5   navibus celeribus redibant. multos dies trans mare
       navigabant. tandem naves Graecorum ad terram
       <u>Lotophagorum</u> tempestate pulsae sunt. ibi incolae,   Lotophagi, -orum, m. pl. = Lotus Eaters
       quod <u>lotum</u> consumebant, semper dormire et in hac   lotus, -i, f. = the fruit of the lotus
       terra manere cupiebant.

1 post decem annos tota urbs Troia a Graecis capta erat. (lines 1–2)
   How long did it take to capture Troy?   (2)
2 muri deleti erant et templa incensa erant. (line 2)
   What happened to the city?   (2)
3 neque multi Troiani effugere potuerant. (line 3)
   What about the Trojans themselves?   (2)
4 Ulixes comitesque Troia discesserant et ad Graeciam navibus celeribus redibant. (lines 3–5)
   What did Ulysses do after this?   (4)
5 multos dies trans mare navigabant. (lines 5–6)
   For how long were they at sea?   (1)
6 tandem naves Graecorum ad terram Lotophagorum tempestate pulsae sunt. (lines 6–7)
   How did Ulysses come to be at the land of the Lotus Eaters?   (2)
7 ibi incolae, quod lotum consumebant, semper dormire et in hac terra manere cupiebant. (lines 7–9)
   What effect did the lotus plant have on the inhabitants?   (2)

Total: 15

Exercise 19.19

Translate the passage below into good English.

Ulysses loses some of his crew.

1 Ulixes tres nautas ad oppidum <u>Lotophagorum</u> misit. hos
nautas cibum aquamque petere et ad naves paucis horis
redire iussit. <u>ipse</u> interea cum ceteris comitibus prope naves
manebat. multas horas ibi manebant. post septem horas
5 tamen tres nautae non redierant. a Lotophagis tenebantur. res
<u>Ulixem</u> terrebat. <u>sollicitus</u> erat. tandem dux sollicitus nautas
petere constituit. haec verba comitibus dixit: 'sollicitus sum.
amici nostri non redierunt. diu absunt. fortasse a Lotophagis
capti sunt. ego eos petam. quis mecum venire potest?'

Lotophagi, -orum, m.
pl. = Lotus Eaters
ipse = he himself

Ulixes, Ulixis, m. = Ulysses
sollicitus, -a, -um = worried

Total: 30

Exercise 19.20

Study the passage below (do not write a translation) and answer the questions that follow. Complete
sentences are not required.

Odysseus finds his three missing sailors.

1 comites <u>Ulixis</u>, quod amicos invenire magnopere cupiebant,
duci voce magna clamaverunt, 'amici nostri in periculo sunt.
hic manere non cupimus. eos inveniemus. amici a nobis mox
liberabuntur.' Ulixes, ubi haec verba audivit, laetus erat. paucos
5 comites prope naves reliquit atque illis 'naves bene custodite!'
inquit. 'ego ceterique paucis horis redibimus. nautas mox
inveniemus.' Ulixes comitesque ad oppidum <u>Lotophagorum</u>
contenderunt. nautas, qui a Lotophagis superati erant, mox
invenerunt. sed ubi eos viderunt, attoniti erant.

Ulixes, Ulixis, m. = Ulysses

Lotophagi, -orum, m.
pl. = Lotus Eaters

1 Give from the passage an example in Latin of:
   a) a pluperfect passive;   (1)
   b) an imperative;   (1)
   c) a verb in the future passive.   (1)
2 **haec** (line 4) Give the gender of this pronoun.   (1)
3 **reliquit** (line 5)
   a) In which tense is this verb?   (1)
   b) Give its 1st person singular, present tense.   (1)
4 **paucis horis** (line 6)
   a) In which case are these words?   (1)
   b) Why is this case used?   (1)
5 **invenerunt** (line 9)
   a) This word means *they found*. How would you say in Latin, *they find*?   (1)
   b) Explain the connection between this word and the English word *invention*. (1)

Total: 10

Exercise 19.21

Translate the following sentences into Latin.

1 You (sing.) always lead the soldiers bravely.   (5)
2 We were showing the villa to all the citizens.   (5)
3 Run, women! The savage men are coming.   (7)
4 They will shout to the gods.   (3)

Total: 20

Chapter 20: Relative clauses

Exercise 20.1

Translate the following sentences into English:

1   puer, qui in villa laborat, fessus est.   (9)
2   puella, quae in foro ambulabat, irata erat.   (9)
3   milites, qui in proelio victi sunt, in montes contenderunt.   (10)
4   puellae, quae in silva ludebant, magistro non crediderunt.   (10)
5   nonne ducem, qui bene pugnabat, laudabis?   (8)
6   mulier, quae maritum amat, cum liberis cantat.   (9)
7   pueri mali magistrum, qui librum legebat, conspexerunt.   (9)
8   custodes captivos, qui in bello capti erant, liberaverunt.   (9)
9   nautae mare, quod* altissimum erat, timebant.   (8 + 1)
10 bella, quae longissima erant, cives audaces semper terrebant.   (10)

This word could mean two things in this sentence. Put both.

Total: 90 + 1

Exercise 20.2

Translate the following sentences into English:

1   rex cives, quos puniverat, in oppidum duxit.   (9)
2   puella, quam omnes amant, in templo cum amicis cantabat.   (11)
3   vinum, quod dominus consumebat, omnes laudant.   (8)
4   flumen altissimum, quod transire non poterimus, subito conspeximus.   (10)
5   vir clarus, quem in foro vidisti, mortuus est.   (9)
6   opus, quod* difficile est, non amamus.   (8 + 1)
7   feminae, quas rex crudelis puniverat, ex urbe exierunt.   (10)
8   num ille est dux quem in proelio vulneravisti?   (10)
9   nonne hae sunt ancillae quas dominus heri liberavit?   (10)
10 templa maxima, quae rex clarus aedificaverat, omnes laudabant.   (10)

This word could mean two things in this sentence. Put both.

Total: 95 + 1

Exercise 20.3

Translate the following sentences into English:

1   hic est magister bonus cui pecuniam dedi.   (8)
2   hi sunt amici quibus vinum dabis.   (7)
3   haec est puella cuius pater clarus et nobilis est.   (10)
4   hi sunt cives quorum dominus crudelis est.   (8)
5   villa in qua habito minima est.   (7)
6   hi sunt pueri quibuscum saepe ludo.   (7)
7   puer quocum ludo amicus meus est.   (8)
8   verba quae dixit magister mala erant.   (8)
9   ibi est villa ex qua multi servi effugerunt.   (9)
10 femina nobilis quam vides audacissima est.   (8)

Total: 80

Exercise 20.4

Identify and give the case and number of the relative pronoun and then translate the following sentences into English:

1	Menelaus, cuius uxor Helena erat, clarissimus erat.	(3 + 9)
2	Paris, qui princeps Troianus erat, ad Menelaum venit.	(3 + 10)
3	Paris Helenam, quae pulcherrima erat, capere statim constituit.	(3 + 10)
4	Paris Helenam ad urbem Troiam in nave, quae celerrima erat, duxit.	(3 + 13)
5	Menelaus, qui iratissimus erat, multos nuntios ad omnes urbes Graeciae misit.	(3 + 13)
6	copiae quas Menelaus collegit magnae erant.	(3 + 8)
7	Troia erat oppidum cuius muri validissimi erant.	(3 + 8)
8	Menelaus Troiam, quae magna urbs erat, delere cupiebat.	(3 + 10)
9	milites quos laudavit Menelaus fortissimi erant.	(3 + 8)
10	Helena, quam Menelaus magnopere amabat, ad Graeciam tandem reducta est.	(3 + 11)

Total: 130

Exercise 20.5

Translate the underlined words* into Latin.

1	I love the man who <u>is walking</u> in the forum.	(2)
2	We watch the citizens who <u>are standing</u> near the walls.	(2)
3	The father gave money to his <u>daughter</u>, whom he loved.	(1)
4	He is walking to the forum <u>without</u> the friends whom he likes.	(1)
5	They <u>all</u> loved the queen who ruled the city for a long time.	(1)
6	Marcus, <u>I was consuming</u> the food which you had prepared for me.	(1)
7	<u>Today</u> my teacher will read the book which you gave to me.	(1)
8	Many <u>sad</u> old men were sitting in the temple which you (sing.) had built.	(1)
9	I have been praised, Marcus, by the <u>schoolmaster</u> whom you like.	(1)
10	We have been warned by the <u>citizens</u> who guard the city.	(1)

Total: 12

* Your teacher may ask you to translate the whole sentence.

Exercise 20.6

Study the passage below (do not write a translation) and answer the questions that follow. Complete sentences are not required.

> *Ulysses leaves the land of the Lotus Eaters.*
>
> 1 tres nautae, qui <u>lotum</u> consumpserant, ex oppido <u>Lotophagorum</u> ad naves a comitibus ducebantur. ei qui naves custodiebant, ubi hos viderunt, laetissimi erant. <u>Ulixes</u> ipse magna voce custodibus clamavit:
> 5 'hi nautae in hac terra a Lotophagis manere cogebantur. lotum consumpserunt. ad patriam nostram, quam nos omnes amamus, redire non cupiebant. eos in naves iacite! celeriter discedite!'
>
> Graeci, ubi nautas in naves iecerunt, omnia celeriter
> 10 paraverunt. inde in navibus – quae celerrimae erant – e terra Lotophagorum discedere poterant.

lotus, -i, f. = the lotus fruit
Lotophagi, -orum, m. pl. = the Lotus Eaters
Ulixes, Ulixis, m. = Ulysses

→

1 tres nautae, qui lotum consumpserant. (line 1)
What had the three sailors done? (1)
2 ex oppido Lotophagorum ad naves a comitibus ducebantur. (lines 1–2)
What then happened to them? (3)
3 ei qui naves custodiebant, ubi hos viderunt, laetissimi erant. (lines 2–4)
What effect did this have on those guarding the ships? (2)
4 Ulixes ipse magna voce custodibus clamavit. (line 4)
What did Ulysses do? (3)
5 'hi nautae in hac terra a Lotophagis manere cogebantur. (lines 5–6)
What reason did Ulysses give for their disappearance? (2)
6 ad patriam nostram, quam nos omnes amamus, redire non cupiebant. (lines 6–8)
What effect did the lotus fruit have on the sailors? (4)
7 From the passage, give an example in Latin of:
    a) a relative pronoun in the accusative;
    b) a present infinitive;
    c) an imperative. (3)
8 iecerunt (line 9)
    a) Give the tense of this verb. (1)
    b) Give its person and number. (2)
    c) Give its 1st person singular, present tense. (1)
9 navibus (line 10)
    a) In which case is this noun? (1)
    b) Why is this case used? (1)
10 poterant (line 11) Give the 1st person singular, present tense of this verb. (1)

Total: 25

Exercise 20.7

Translate the following sentences into Latin:

1 Romans are often good soldiers. (6)
2 They were running to the villa. (4)
3 The citizens have carried the bodies out of the city. (6)
4 Walk slowly, boys. (4)

Total: 20

Exercise 20.8

Study the following sentences (do not write a translation*). Give and explain the case of the underlined words.

1 Paris ex urbe Troia discessit et ad Menelaum adiit. (1 + 1)
2 Paris Helenam cepit et eam ad urbem Troiam duxit. (1 + 1)
3 Menelaus auxilium amicorum rogavit et magnas copias collegit. (1 + 1)
4 Menelaus magnas copias collegit quod Troiam oppugnare cupiebat. (1 + 1)
5 Graeci Troiam oppugnaverunt et Paridem, qui filius regis erat, puniverunt. (1 + 1)
6 Graeci multis armis et copiis audacibus urbem quam Troiani defendebant occupaverunt. (1 + 1)
7 Troiani fortiter pugnaverunt nec tamen urbem servaverunt. (1 + 1)
8 Troiani Graecos qui urbem oppugnabant magnopere timebant. (1 + 1)
9 tandem Graeci equum ingentem aedificaverunt et prope mare reliquerunt. (1 + 1)
10 multi milites ex equo cucurrerunt et templa deleverunt. (1 + 1)

Total: 20

Your teacher may ask you to translate the sentences.

Exercise 20.9

Study the following sentences (do not write a translation*). From each of the underlined words, give an English word that is derived from the Latin one and explain the connection between the two.

1 tu, propter opus difficile, <u>somno</u> superatus es. (1 + 1)
2 magnam turbam <u>feminarum</u>, quae in via clamabant, vidimus. (1 + 1)
3 quod sapiens esse cupio, <u>libros</u> semper lego. (1 + 1)
4 multam pecuniam militi <u>audaci</u> heri dedi. (1 + 1)
5 multi <u>viri</u> in proeliis saevis saepe occiduntur. (1 + 1)
6 quinto die princeps <u>cives</u> ex oppido pepulit. (1 + 1)
7 <u>custodes</u> captivos miseros in villis eorum tenebant. (1 + 1)
8 omnes incolae in forum <u>convenerunt</u>. (1 + 1)
9 nemo fidei ducis, quem <u>laudabas</u>, credidit. (1 + 1)
10 princeps superbus filios <u>senis</u> semper puniebat. (1 + 1)

Total: 20

* Your teacher may ask you to translate the sentences.

Exercise 20.10

Give and explain the case of the underlined words, and then translate the following sentences into English:

1 multae gentes, <u>quae</u> Romanos non amabant, auxilium rogaverunt. (2 + 10)
2 hic agricola, qui plures equos quam <u>ille</u> habet, laetissimus est. (2 + 12)
3 illa urbs, quae ab <u>hostibus</u> diu oppugnabatur, tandem occupata est. (2 + 11)
4 urbs Troia, quam Graeci diu oppugnabant, decimo <u>anno</u> capta est. (2 + 11)
5 nautae, <u>quibus</u> naves celerrimas dedimus, ab insula hodie navigabunt. (2 + 11)

Total: 65

Exercise 20.11

Give the tense of the underlined verbs, and then translate the following sentences into English:

1 agricolae, qui in agris diu <u>laboraverant</u>, effugere coacti sunt. (1 + 10)
2 animalia, quae in silvis <u>aderant</u>, cibum frustra petebant. (1 + 10)
3 multae naves, quas Romani ad insulam pepulerant, tempestate <u>deletae sunt</u>. (1 + 11)
4 nonne dominus illum puerum punire <u>cupiebat</u>? (1 + 7)
5 senex, qui filiam videre <u>cupit</u>, per montes multos dies ambulabat. (1 + 12)

Total: 55

Exercise 20.12

Write down and give the case of the relative pronoun, and then translate the following into English:

1 aqua in villam, quam regina clara aedificaverat, a servo portabatur. (2 + 12)
2 domini civibus miseris, qui praemia amant, non saepe credunt. (2 + 11)
3 urbs parva ab hostibus, quos timemus, multos annos oppugnabatur. (2 + 11)
4 senes, quorum liberi in bello pugnabant, a duce laudati sunt. (2 + 11)
5 cur vinum agricolae irato, quem omnes timemus, dedisti? (2 + 10)

Total: 65

Exercise 20.13

Write down the adverbs and then translate the following into English:

1 milites multa animalia sagittis quas habebamus celeriter interfecerunt.   (1 + 9)
2 multa animalia a militibus hastis tandem interfecta sunt.   (1 + 8)
3 cur Graeci urbem Troiam multos annos oppugnabant?   (1 + 8)
4 noli hoc iterum facere, iuvenis!   (1 + 6)
5 milites, quorum corpora invenimus, fortiter pro patria pugnaverant.   (1 + 9)

Total: 45

Chapter 21: fero, alius, ipse, idem, volo, nolo; indirect statement

Exercise 21.1

Translate the following into English:

1	fers.	(1)	9	fert.	(1)
2	feretur.	(1)	10	feremus.	(1)
3	tulit.	(1)	11	ferebat.	(1)
4	ferre.	(1)	12	ferebatur.	(1)
5	tuli.	(1)	13	ferent.	(1)
6	tulerunt.	(1)	14	ferunt.	(1)
7	lati sunt.	(1)	15	tuleramus.	(1)
8	latus est.	(1)			

Total: 15

Exercise 21.2

Translate the following into English:

1 vir multum cibi tulerat. (5)
2 multam pecuniam cras feram. (5)
3 quid fers? (3)
4 milites arma ferunt. (4)
5 arma a militibus ferebantur. (5)
6 quid a militibus cras feretur? (6)
7 cibus in villam ab iuvenibus cras feretur. (8)
8 gladii a militibus lati sunt. (5)
9 quid miles audax ferebat? (5)
10 senex corpus ferebat. (4)

Total: 50

Exercise 21.3

Translate the following into English:

1 cras vinum optimum in villam domini feremus. (8)
2 copiae nostrae aliam urbem occupaverant. (6)
3 princeps alios milites in proelium ducere cupiebat. (8)
4 dux ipse copias fortiter in proelium duxit. (8)
5 magister eosdem pueros semper laudabat. (6)
6 post bellum alii in urbe manebant, alii trans montes redierunt. (12)
7 rex custodes ipsos in foro custodiebat. (7)
8 rex ipse custodes in foro custodiebat. (7)
9 eundem poetam saepe audiebamus. (5)
10 mulier dona eadem marito carissimo semper dedit. (8)

Total: 75

Exercise 21.4

Give and explain the case of the underlined words and then translate the following sentences into English:

1 nemo regem <u>eundem</u> laudare cupiebat.   (2 + 6)
2 num princeps <u>ipse</u> incolas miseros occidet?   (2 + 7)
3 quis reginam <u>ipsam</u> in templum ducet?   (2 + 7)
4 nos omnes corpora <u>alia</u> e proelio tulimus.   (2 + 8)
5 propter moram longam, cives <u>mortui</u> in oppidum lati erant.   (2 + 9)
6 <u>eidem</u> milites sine armis optimis semper pugnabant.   (2 + 8)
7 ei iuvenes alios amicos in silva <u>eadem</u> exspectabant.   (2 + 9)
8 hi homines illa animalia gladiis <u>eisdem</u> vulneraverant.   (2 + 8)
9 nonne uxor regis ipsa post mortem <u>eius</u> reget?   (2 + 9)
10 num uxor regis <u>ipsius</u> post mortem suam reget?   (2 + 9)

Total: 100

Exercise 21.5

Study the passage below (do not write a translation) and answer the questions that follow. Complete sentences are not required.

Odysseus and his men continue their voyage.

1   <u>Ulixes</u> ipse comitesque a <u>Lotophagis</u> effugerant.
     multos dies multasque noctes trans mare
     navigaverunt. tandem, postquam ventis et undis
     pulsi sunt, ad aliam terram advenerunt. in ea
5   terra gens <u>gigantum</u> habitabat. Graeci e navibus
     <u>descenderunt</u> et cenam in <u>litore</u> paraverunt. deinde
     omnem noctem dormiverunt.

> Ulixes, Ulixis, m. = Ulysses
> Lotophagi, -orum, m. pl. = the Lotus Eaters
> gigas, gigantis, m. = giant
> descendo, -ere, descendi = I come down
> litus, litoris, n. = the shore

1 Ulixes ipse comitesque a Lotophagis effugerant. (line 1)
   What has just happened?   (2)
2 multos dies multasque noctes trans mare navigaverunt. (lines 2–3)
   What did they then do?   (4)
3 postquam ventis et undis pulsi sunt (lines 3–4)
   What had affected their voyage?   (2)
4 ad aliam terram advenerunt. (line 4)
   Where did they end up?   (2)
5 in ea terra gens gigantum habitabat. (lines 4–5)
   What was unusual about this place?   (2)
6 Graeci e navibus descenderunt et cenam in litore paraverunt. (lines 5–6)
   What did they do when they had disembarked from their ships?   (2)
7 deinde omnem noctem dormiverunt. (lines 6–7)
   For how long did they sleep?   (1)

Total: 15

Exercise 21.6

Translate the following passage into English:

The Greeks come face to face with a monster.

1   prima luce e somno <u>surrexerunt</u>. <u>Ulixes</u> ipse et
     duodecim amici, ubi gladios et tela collegerunt,
     a <u>litore</u> discesserunt et cibum aquamque
     petebant. mox ad <u>antrum</u>, in quo multum cibi erat,
5   advenerunt. Graeci, ubi cibum viderunt, laetissimi
     erant. cibum autem, quod <u>fame</u> perire nolebant, ad
     naves ferre constituerunt. Ulixes amicos festinare
     iussit. Graeci tamen, dum cibum ad naves ferunt,
     <u>gigantem</u> ingentem viderunt.

surgo, -ere, surrexi, surrectum = I rise
Ulixes, Ulixis, m. = Ulysses
litus, litoris, n. = shore
antrum, -i, n. = cave

fames, famis, f. = hunger

gigas, gigantis, m. = giant

Total: 30

Exercise 21.7

Translate the following into Latin:

1   The little girls were not afraid of the Romans.   (6)
2   The women carried the bodies of the soldiers into the temple.   (7)
3   I have never seen the famous king.   (5)
4   The savage master frightens the girl with a sword.   (6)
5   The man is carrying a body out of the town.   (6)

Total: 30

Exercise 21.8

Translate the following into Latin:

1   Many boys and girls often run in the street.   (9)
2   The sad Roman was watching the queen.   (5)
3   They have found a body in the temple.   (5)
4   I have handed over the money to the sailor.   (4)
5   The master's son has made a journey into the mountains.   (7)

Total: 30

Exercise 21.9

Translate the following into Latin:

1   We all like the good wine.   (5)
2   Teachers always carry books and wine into the ships.   (9)
3   The men do not like the difficult journey.   (6)
4   I have captured the leader's son.   (4)
5   Run, boys! The schoolmaster is coming.   (6)

Total: 30

Exercise 21.10

Translate the following into English:

1 volumus.	(1)	6 nolebant.	(1)	11 noles.	(1)	16 non vis.	(1)
2 non vult.	(1)	7 non vultis.	(1)	12 velle.	(1)	17 nolle.	(1)
3 volebat.	(1)	8 voluit.	(1)	13 volent.	(1)	18 nolunt.	(1)
4 volebant.	(1)	9 voluerunt.	(1)	14 noluit.	(1)	19 volet.	(1)
5 nolebat.	(1)	10 vis.	(1)	15 volebatis.	(1)	20 noluerunt.	(1)

Total: 20

Exercise 21.11

Give the case and number of the underlined words and translate the sentences into English:

1 Graeci Troiam ipsam oppugnare volebant.   (2 + 6)
2 ceteri Graeci laborare numquam volunt.   (2 + 6)
3 Ulixes ipse ad Graeciam redire volebat.   (2 + 7)
4 hic puer cantare non vult.   (2 + 6)
5 milites autem hoc facere nolebant.   (2 + 6)
6 puer magistrum alium audire nolebat.   (2 + 6)
7 Helena ipsa ad urbem Troiam ire nolebat.   (2 + 8)
8 omnes cives sapientes esse volunt.   (2 + 6)
9 Romani multas alias gentes vincere volebant.   (2 + 7)
10 magister pueros eosdem terrere non vult.   (2 + 7)

Total: 85

Exercise 21.12

Translate the following into English:

1 dicit puerum currere.   (4)
2 dicit pueros clamare.   (4)
3 dicunt fabrum¹ laborare.   (4)
4 dicunt milites pugnare.   (4)
5 audio avem² cantare.   (4)
6 audio senes dormire.   (4)
7 credo matrem miseram esse.   (4)
8 credimus patrem fessum esse.   (4)
9 audio milites venire.   (4)
10 audit generum³ mortuum esse.   (4)

Total: 40

1 faber, fabri, m. = builder   2 avis, avis, f. = bird   3 gener, generi, m. = son-in-law

Exercise 21.13

Translate the following into English:

1 custos dicit hunc captivum effugere.   (6)
2 custos dixit hos incolas effugere.   (6)
3 dominus audit hunc poetam appropinquare.   (6)
4 audivit hos iuvenes appropinquare.   (5)
5 vidi omnes agricolas laborare.   (5)
6 video omnes ancillas laborare.   (5)
7 magister non credit puerum laborare.   (6)
8 princeps non credebat cives bonos esse.   (7)
9 pater dicit filium suum pecuniam amare.   (7)
10 puellae dixerunt hunc magistrum bonum esse.   (7)

Total: 60

Exercice 21.14

Translate the following into English:

1	credimus omnes magistros sapientes esse.	(6)
2	video te tandem bene laborare.	(6)
3	audio puellam venire.	(4)
4	dicunt Romanos oppidum oppugnare.	(5)
5	nautae dixerunt nimbum¹ maximum appropinquare.	(6)
6	dux clamavit se militem fortem esse.	(6)
7	magistri credunt puellas bene laborare.	(6)
8	audimus illum virum vocem magnam habere.	(7)
9	audio regem ipsum cum praeda² effugere.	(7)
10	Marcus dicit matrem cenas bonas parare.	(7)

Total: 60

1 nimbus, -i, m. = storm-cloud
2 praeda, -ae, f. = plunder

Exercice 21.15

Study the passage below (do not write a translation) and answer the questions that follow. Complete sentences are not required.

Trapped by Polyphemus.

1	Ulixes hunc gigantem vidit et magnopere timuit. credidit comites in magno periculo iam esse. credidit se ipsum quoque in magno periculo esse. comitibus clamavit gigantem appropinquare.	gigas, gigantis, m. = giant
5	dixit eum saevum esse, et unum oculum in medio capite habere. 'festinate, comites!' inquit. 'ad antrum redite! Polyphemus venit!'	oculus, -i, m. = eye
		caput, capitis, n. = head
		antrum, -i, n. = cave
	Ulixes comitibus facile persuasit et mox in antrum omnes inierunt. deinde exitum antri saxo ingenti	exitus
10	clausit et in antro se celabant. gigantem, quem iratissimum esse crediderunt, in antro exspectabant.	saxum, -i, n. = rock
		claudo, -ere, clausi, clausum = I shut
		celo, -are, -avi, -atum = I hide

1 Ulixes hunc gigantem vidit et magnopere timuit. (line 1)
How did Ulysses react to what he saw? (2)

2 credidit comites in magno periculo iam esse. (line 2)
How did he think it affected his companions? (3)

3 credidit se ipsum quoque in magno periculo esse. (line 3)
How did he think it affected himself? (2)

4 comitibus clamavit gigantem appropinquare. (line 4)
What did he tell his companions? (2)

5 dixit eum saevum esse, et unum oculum in medio capite habere. (lines 5–6)
How did he describe the monster? (4)

6 'festinate, comites!' inquit. 'ad antrum redite! (lines 6–7)
What instructions did he give? (2)

7 From the passage give an example in Latin of:
  a) a reflexive pronoun. (1)
  b) an adverb. (1)
  c) a superlative adjective. (1)

8 comitibus (line 8)
  a) In which case is this noun? (1)
  b) Why is this case used? (1)

→

9 **esse** (line 11) What part of the verb **sum** is this? (1)
10 **crediderunt** (line 11)
    a) Give the tense of this verb. (1)
    b) Give the 1st person singular of the present tense of this verb. (1)
11 **exspectabant** (line 11)
    a) This verb means *they were waiting*. How would you say in Latin *they are waiting*? (1)
    b) Explain the connection between this word and the English word *expectation*. (1)

Total: 25

Exercise 21.16

Translate the following into Latin:

1 We were walking near the big horses. (5)
2 The Romans have built many ships. (5)
3 The enemy killed the citizens with their spears. (5)
4 Run, farmers! He is coming. (5)

Total: 20

Exercise 21.17

Translate the following passage into good English:

Polyphemus and the stake.

1   omnes Graeci magnopere timebant. iam
      viderant Polyphemum animal crudelissimum
      esse. Ulixes, qui audacissimus Graecorum erat,
      Polyphemum dolo superare constituit. poculum
5   vino plenum cepit et ad gigantem appropinquavit.
      'bibe hoc vinum, Polypheme,' inquit. 'dulcissimum
      est.' gigas vinum cepit et statim bibit. deinde Ulixi
      clamavit: 'hoc vinum optimum est. da mihi plus
      vini!' Ulixes ei poculum alterum, deinde tertium,
10   deinde quartum dedit. Polyphemus mox ebrius
      erat. ad terram subito cecidit et obdormivit.
      Graeci, ubi viderunt Polyphemum dormire,
      palum ceperunt et in oculum gigantis truserunt.
      ille statim surrexit et magna voce clamavit:
15   'quis es? quis mihi nocet?' caecus et iratissimus
      erat. Graeci ex antro effugere volebant.

Ulixes, Ulixis, m. = Ulysses
dolus, -i, m. = trickery
poculum, -i, n. = cup
plenus, -a, -um, + ablative = full of
gigas, gigantis, m. = giant
dulcis, -is, -e = sweet
ebrius, -a, -um = drunk
cado, -ere, cecidi, casum = I fall
obdormio, -ire, obdormivi,
-itum = I fall asleep
palus, -i, m. = a stake
oculus, -i, m. = eye
trudo, -ere, trusi, trusum = I thrust
surgo, -ere, surrexi, surrectum = I get up
noceo, nocere, nocui (+ dat.) = I harm
caecus, -a, -um = blind
antrum, -i, n. = cave

Total: 100

Chapter 22: Revision of Level 3

Exercise 22.1

Give the part of speech and meaning of the following Latin words:

1	superbus	(2)
2	eo	(2)
3	exeo	(2)
4	hic	(2)
5	ille	(2)
6	ineo	(2)
7	pereo	(2)
8	redeo	(2)
9	transeo	(2)
10	civis	(2)
11	corpus	(2)
12	dux	(2)
13	flumen	(2)
14	hostes	(2)

Total: 28

Exercise 22.2

Give the part of speech and meaning of the following Latin words:

1	iter	(2)
2	miles	(2)
3	mons	(2)
4	navis	(2)
5	pater	(2)
6	rex	(2)
7	urbs	(2)
8	centum	(2)
9	decimus	(2)
10	mille	(2)
11	nonaginta	(2)
12	nonus	(2)
13	octavus	(2)
14	triginta	(2)

Total: 28

Exercise 22.3

Give the part of speech and meaning of the following Latin words:

1	annus	(2)
2	custodio	(2)
3	custos	(2)
4	dies	(2)
5	fides	(2)
6	hora	(2)
7	impero	(2)
8	persuadeo	(2)
9	octoginta	(2)
10	secundus	(2)
11	peto	(2)
12	res	(2)
13	spes	(2)
14	tempestas	(2)

Total: 28

Exercise 22.4

Give the part of speech and meaning of the following Latin words:

1	circum	(2)
2	contra	(2)
3	de	(2)
4	pro	(2)
5	sine	(2)
6	animal	(2)
7	celer	(2)
8	cogo	(2)
9	volo	(2)
10	interficio	(2)
11	labor	(2)
12	nec	(2)
13	nox	(2)
14	opus	(2)

Total: 28

Exercise 22.5

Give the part of speech and meaning of the following Latin words:

1 pello   (2)
2 princeps   (2)
3 relinquo   (2)
4 difficilis   (2)
5 fortis   (2)
6 facilis   (2)
7 omnis   (2)
8 tristis   (2)
9 contendo   (2)
10 credo   (2)
11 gens   (2)
12 interea   (2)
13 lente   (2)
14 paene   (2)

Total: 28

Exercise 22.6

Give the part of speech and meaning of the following Latin words:

1 qui   (2)
2 somnus   (2)
3 invenio   (2)
4 mitto   (2)
5 ostendo   (2)
6 pono   (2)
7 trado   (2)
8 venio   (2)
9 fero   (2)
10 alius   (2)
11 idem   (2)
12 ipse   (2)
13 iuvo   (2)
14 nolo   (2)

Total: 28

Exercise 22.7

Give the person, number, tense, voice and the 1st person singular of the present active of the following verbs, and then translate:

1 coactus est.   (6)
2 ferimur.   (6)
3 missus sum.   (6)
4 posuerunt.   (6)
5 rexerunt.   (6)
6 potuerunt.   (6)
7 laudaveramus.   (6)
8 videbimur.   (6)
9 voluerunt.   (6)
10 currebant.   (6)

Total: 60

Exercise 22.8

Translate the following into English:

1 equi a puellis amantur.   (5)
2 a magistro saepe laudantur.   (5)
3 senex in foro spectatur.   (5)
4 terra a regina regitur.   (5)
5 captivi a custodibus monentur.   (5)
6 nemo a domina amatur.   (5)
7 cives in oppido custodiuntur.   (5)
8 animalia in silvis occiduntur.   (5)
9 milites in bello superantur.   (5)
10 navis a nautis aedificatur.   (5)

Total: 50

Exercise 22.9

Translate the following into English:

1 multos annos regebat.   (4)
2 quinque dies manebat.   (4)
3 sexto anno discessit.   (4)
4 sex diebus peribit.   (4)
5 septima hora aderant.   (4)

Total: 20

Exercise 22.10

Translate the following into English:

1 in urbem ducentur.   (4)
2 ex oppido pellentur.   (4)
3 a custodibus occidetur.   (4)
4 liber non legebatur.   (4)
5 cena lente consumebatur.   (4)

Total: 20

Exam Practice Questions

Exercise 22.11

Translate the following into English:

1 iuvenes quinque dies custoditi sunt. (5)
2 milites secundo die occisi sunt. (5)
3 incolae contra muros pulsi sunt. (5)
4 labor difficilis tandem factus est. (5)
5 naves celeres iam aedificatae erant. (5)

Total: 25

Exercise 22.12

Translate the following into English:

1 mater quae liberos non amabat in villa aderat. (10)
2 principes qui copias in proelium duxerunt optimi erant. (10)
3 senex qui in montibus inventus est mox periit. (9)
4 feminas quas omnes amabant laudabas. (7)
5 nonne rex cui pecuniam dedisti optimus est? (9)

Total: 45

Exercise 22.13

Translate the following into English:

1 dicit cibum bonum esse. (5)
2 audimus hostes ad urbem venire. (6)
3 dixerunt ducem oppidum occupare. (5)
4 clamavit se pugnare velle. (5)
5 audio mulierem cantare. (4)

Total: 25

Exercise 22.14

Translate the following into Latin:

1 You (sing.) were calling the daughter of the sad woman. (5)
2 He has placed the wine near the wall. (5)
3 Friends never hand over money to the enemy. (6)
4 They threw the letter into the river. (5)
5 Walk slowly, boys! (4)

Total: 25

Exercise 22.15

Translate the following into Latin:

1 The good friends always find money in the temple. (8)
2 The soldiers led the unhappy schoolmaster out of the villa. (7)
3 Run, Romans! The master has sent bad men into the city. (10)
4 I was always calling the sailors. (4)
5 The brave citizens were fighting against the enemy. (6)

Total: 35

Exercise 22.16

Study the passage below (do not write a translation) and answer the questions that follow. Complete sentences are not required.

The Greeks escape from Polyphemus and reach the island of Aeolia.

1	in insula aderant alii <u>gigantes</u>, amici Polyphemi. hi, ubi vocem Polyphemi audiverunt, celeriter ad <u>antrum</u> eius festinaverunt. 'cur clamas?' inquiunt. 'quis tibi <u>nocet</u>?'
5	'Nemo mihi nocet!' respondit gigas miser. Ulixes enim nomen Neminem esse dixerat. ceteri gigantes <u>attoniti</u> erant nec iam ibi manebant. crediderunt Polyphemum <u>ebrium</u> esse.

gigas, gigantis, m. = giant

antrum, -i, n. = cave
noceo, -ere, nocui (+ dat.) = I harm

attonitus, -a, -um = astonished
ebrius, -a, -um = drunk

1 in insula aderant alii gigantes, amici Polyphemi. (line 1)
   Who else was on the island?   (2)
2 hi, ubi vocem Polyphemi audiverunt, celeriter ad antrum eius festinaverunt. (lines 2–3)
   What did they hear and what did they then do?   (1 + 2)
3 'cur clamas?' inquiunt. 'quis tibi nocet?' (lines 3–4)
   What two questions did they ask?   (2)
4 'Nemo mihi nocet!' respondit gigas miser. (line 5)
   What was his reply?   (1)
5 Ulixes enim nomen Neminem esse dixerat. (lines 5–6)
   Why did he reply in that way?   (2)
6 ceteri gigantes attoniti erant nec iam ibi manebant. (lines 6–7)
   What effect did his reply have on Polyphemus's friends?   (3)
7 crediderunt Polyphemum ebrium esse. (lines 7–8)
   Why did it have this effect?   (2)

Total: 15

Exercise 22.17

Translate the passage below into good English:

The Greeks are blocked.

1	Graeci, quamquam Polyphemus vulneratus erat, timebant. Polyphemus ipse iratissimus erat. credidit autem Graecos ex <u>antro</u> effugere velle. <u>saxum</u> ingens igitur pro <u>ianua</u> posuit. propter hoc, nemo
5	exire poterat. inde <u>gigas</u> saevus <u>obdormivit</u>. in antro cum Polyphemo aderant <u>oves</u>. hae totam noctem ibi manebant nec effugere poterant.

antrum, -i, n. = cave
saxum, -i, n. = rock
ianua, -ae, f. = opening, way in
gigas, gigantis, m. = giant
obdormio, -ire, -ivi, -itum = I fall asleep
ovis, ovis, f. = sheep

Total: 30

Exercise 22.18

Study the passage below (do not write a translation) and answer the questions that follow. Complete sentences are not required.

Saved by the sheep.

1	Ulixes igitur comites sub <u>ventribus</u> <u>ovium</u> <u>celabat</u>.	venter, ventris, m. = stomach
	se ipsum quoque ibi celabat. prima luce, ubi	ovis, ovis, f. = sheep
	Polyphemum oves liberavit, Graeci sub animalibus	celo, -are, -avi, -atum = I hide
	ex <u>antro</u> exierunt. ad navem celeriter cucurrerunt.	antrum, -i, n. = cave
5	crediderunt se tutos iam esse.	

1 **comites** (line 1) Give the case of this noun. (1)
2 **se** (line 2) What part of speech is this word and what does it mean? (1 + 1)
3 **luce** (line 2) Give and explain the case of this word. (1 + 1)
4 **liberavit** (line 3) This word means he *freed*. How would you say in Latin, *he frees*? (1)
5 From the passage, give in Latin an example of a preposition followed by the ablative. (1)
6 **exierunt** (line 4)
   a) Give the tense of this verb. (1)
   b) Give the 1st person singular of the present tense of this verb. (1)
   c) Explain the connection between this word and the English word *exit*. (1)

Total: 10

Exercise 22.19

Translate into Latin:

1 The men always walked slowly. (5)
2 At last the citizens came down from the mountains. (6)
3 I have given money to my father. (4)
4 All the citizens fear the gods. (5)

Total: 20

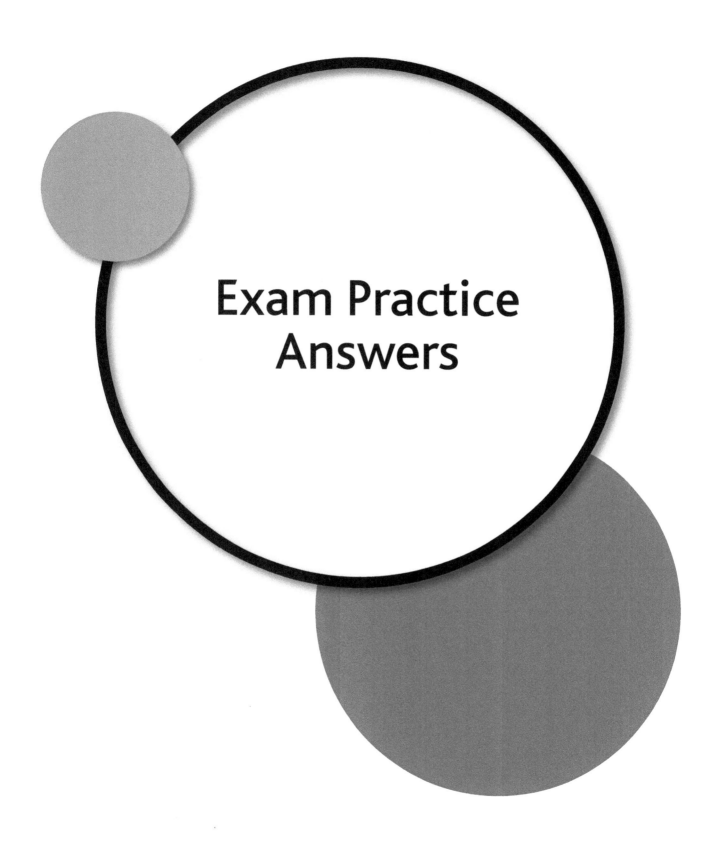

Exam Practice
Answers

Level 1
Chapter 1

Reminder to pupils

Remember: some Latin to English translation questions will use a verb in 3rd person singular, but without a nominative.

For example:

aquam reginae dat.

In the following answer section, 'he' is given as the default answer in such cases:

He gives water to the queen.

But, you can also translate this sentence as:

She gives water to the queen.

Either option would obviously be correct. Indeed, in some cases it might be possible to translate the sentence with the pronoun 'it':

It gives water to the queen.

If in doubt, check with your teacher!

Exercise 1.1

1   The woman does not watch the daughters.   (5)
2   The poet overcomes the farmer.   (4)
3   The sailor loves the island.   (4)
4   The queen watches the poets and the farmers.   (6)
5   You prepare the arrows and the money.   (5)
6   You do not call the girls and farmers.   (6)

Total: 30

Exercise 1.2

1   feminam non amamus.   (4)
2   nauta reginam spectat.   (4)
3   puella et femina epistulam parant.   (6)
4   nautae puellam non vocant.   (5)
5   puellae hastas amant.   (4)
6   puella et femina nautam non amant.   (7)

Total: 30

Exercise 1.3

1   The sailors love the islands.   (4)
2   The poets overcome the farmer.   (4)
3   The queen watches the poet and the farmer.   (6)
4   The girls and the farmers prepare the water.   (6)
5   The women do not watch the daughter.   (5)
6   We prepare water and money.   (5)

Total: 30

Exercise 1.4

1   regina cenam non parat.   (5)
2   nauta pecuniam spectat.   (4)
3   puella cenam non parat.   (5)
4   nautae hastas non amant.   (5)
5   reginam non spectamus.   (4)
6   reginae et nautae feminam non amant.   (7)

Total: 30

Exercise 1.5

1   The women and the farmer are hurrying.   (5)
2   The queen loves the poets and farmers.   (6)
3   We look at the island.   (4)
4   The inhabitants prepare the road.   (4)
5   I love the country of the inhabitants.   (5)
6   Flavia and the farmer call the sailor.   (6)

Total: 30

Exercise 1.6

1   nautae pecuniam et cenas amant.   (6)
2   puellae pecuniam non spectant.   (5)
3   nautae viam parant.   (4)
4   regina nautam non amat.   (5)
5   feminam non vocas.   (4)
6   regina et femina nautas amant.   (6)

Total: 30

Exercise 1.7

1 She is walking and singing. (2)
2 He is walking and singing. (2)
3 He is not sailing. (1)
4 He loves her. (2)
5 Yes. (1)
6 They shout and call to each other. (3)
7 They prepare dinner, they sing, they don't fight, they love each other. (4)

Total: 15

Exercise 1.8

Marcus is a farmer. The farmer is working. Flavia is a girl. Flavia loves the farmer. Marcus watches Flavia. He loves Flavia. Flavia is preparing dinner. The farmer loves dinners. Flavia watches the farmer. The farmer is singing and working. The farmer is preparing the land and building a villa. He is building a villa and preparing the road. Flavia loves villas. Flavia loves farmers.

Minerva is a goddess. The goddess watches the farmer and the girl. The goddess does not love the farmer. The goddess does not love the country. She does not love the inhabitants. The inhabitants do not love the goddess.

The goddess calls the girl and the farmer. 'I am a goddess,' she says. 'I am the goddess Minerva.'

Marcus and Flavia are not singing. They are not working. Flavia is not preparing the dinner. Marcus is not preparing the water. The farmer does not love the goddess. The girl does not love the goddess. They do not love the goddess Minerva.

Total: 100

Exercise 1.9

1

Latin word from passage	Meaning of the Latin word	An English word which comes from the Latin word
vocat (line 3)	calls	vocation, vocal
aquam (line 6)	water	aquatic, aqueous, aqua-sports, etc.

(4)

2 B accusative (1)
3 D spectant (1)
4 laboras (line 5)
  a) B 2nd (1)
  b) A singular (1)
5 D villam (1)
6 A dea (1)

Total: 10

Exercise 1.10

1 nautae viam aedificant. (4)
2 feminae epistulam spectant. (4)
3 puella reginam non amat. (5)
4 puella et femina cenam parant. (6)
5 feminam et nautam vocatis. (5)
6 regina puellam et feminam amat. (6)

Total: 30

Chapter 2

Exercise 2.1

1. The woman was praising the country. (4)
2. The poet was killing the farmer. (4)
3. The sailor was not carrying water. (5)
4. The queen was giving money to the woman. (5)
5. The farmer was standing in the road. (5)
6. The women and the farmer were living in the villa. (7)

Total: 30

Exercise 2.2

1. feminae pecuniam portabant. (4)
2. nauta reginam non laudabat. (5)
3. puella viam intrabat. (4)
4. nautae et feminae hastas non portant. (6)
5. puellas non necabamus. (4)
6. puella et femina nautas non laudabant. (7)

Total: 30

Exercise 2.3

1. Nominative plural; The sailors were sailing to the island. (1 + 6)
2. Accusative plural; The poets were fighting against the farmers. (1 + 5)
3. Ablative singular; You were walking with the poet and the farmer. (1 + 6)
4. Accusative singular; They were carrying water to the farmer. (1 + 5)
5. Dative singular; The daughter was singing to the woman.
   or
   Genitive singular; The daughter of the woman was singing. (1 + 4)
6. Dative singular; We were giving money to the queen. (1 + 4)

Total: 36

Exercise 2.4

1. Nominative singular; **Flavia cenam parabat.** (1 + 4)
2. Accusative singular; **nauta pecuniam spectabat.** (1 + 4)
3. Nominative singular; **puellae et femina cenam parabant.** (1 + 6)
4. Nominative plural; **nautae et reginae hastas non laudant.** (1 + 6)
5. Accusative singular; **reginam non laudabamus.** (1 + 4)
6. Nominative plural; **puellae et nautae pecuniam portabant.** (1 + 6)

Total: 36

Exercise 2.5

1. 3rd person plural; The women were hurrying into the villa. (1 + 5)
2. 3rd person plural; The inhabitants were working near the villa. (1 + 5)
3. 3rd person plural; The sailors were sailing from the island. (1 + 5)
4. 3rd person plural; The inhabitants were hurrying through the streets. (1 + 5)
5. 3rd person singular; The farmer was hurrying across the island. (1 + 5)
6. 3rd person singular; He was carrying money and arrows. (1 + 5)

Total: 30

Exercise 2.6

1 1st person plural; **reginam amabamus et laudabamus.** (1 + 6)
2 3rd person plural; **pecuniam non portabant.** (1 + 4)
3 3rd person plural; **nautae feminam non necabant.** (1 + 5)
4 3rd person singular; **regina nautas non laudat.** (1 + 5)
5 2nd person plural; **feminas non laudabatis.** (1 + 4)
6 3rd person singular; **regina nautam et puellas laudabat.** (1 + 6)

Total: 36

Exercise 2.7

1   a) He was walking to Flavia's villa. (2)
    b) He was carrying water. (1)
    c) Flavia was preparing dinner and Marcus was singing. (2)
    d) Flavia worked near Marcus and Marcus stood near Flavia. (2)
    e) Marcus praised the dinner, praised Flavia, they both loved the dinner and they sang. (3)
    f) They hurry out of the villa and stand in the street. (2)
    g) The farmer loves the girl and the dinner. (2)
    h) The girl loves the dinner. (1)

Total: 15

2 Marcus was a farmer. Flavia was a girl. Marcus was hurrying to the villa of Flavia. Marcus was carrying water. The farmer walked into the villa. Flavia was working in the villa. She was preparing dinner. Flavia was preparing dinner and Marcus was singing.

Flavia was working near the farmer. The farmer was standing near Flavia. Flavia was singing with the farmer. The farmer was working with the girl. The girl was preparing the dinner and the farmer was preparing the water.

Marcus praises the dinner. Marcus praises Flavia. The farmer and the girl love the dinner and they sing. The farmer and the girl hurry out of the villa and they stand in the road. They hurry through (along) the road. The farmer loves the girl. The farmer loves the dinner. The girl loves the farmer. The girl loves the dinner. (30)

3 a)

Latin word from passage	Meaning of the Latin word	An English word which comes from the Latin word
laborabat (line 4)	was working	labour, laboratory, laborious
viam (line 7)	road	viaduct, via

(4)

    b) D accusative, because it is after the preposition **ad** (1)
    c) B imperfect (1)
    d) B cenam
       D aquam (2)
    e) B puella (1)
    f) C amabat (1)

Total: 10

4   a) pecuniam portabant. (3)
    b) femina reginam laudabat. (4)
    c) puellas spectant. (3)
    d) hastas portabamus. (3)
    e) regina clamabat et puellas vocabat. (7)

Total: 20

Chapter 3

Exercise 3.1

1 The woman was afraid of the master. (4)
2 The poet does not have a horse. (5)
3 The sailor saw you. (4)
4 The freedman was giving a sword to the master. (5)
5 Marcus was standing in the temple. (5)
6 The boys and girls were laughing in the villa. (7)

Total: 30

Exercise 3.2

1 dominus gladium non portabat. (5)
2 Romanos non monebant. (4)
3 puer templum intrabat. (4)
4 nautae et feminae magistrum non timent. (7)
5 oppida non delebamus. (4)
6 amici vinum et libros laudabant. (6)

Total: 30

Exercise 3.3

1 The Romans were not hurrying to the field. (6)
2 The boys were fighting with (against) the master. (5)
3 Many freedmen were laughing with the good poet. (7)
4 The tired boy was walking to the big temple. (7)
5 The women were not afraid of the dangers of war. (6)
6 We saw your money. (4)

Total: 35

Exercise 3.4

1 pueri et puellae libros non habent. (7)
2 magister pueros monebat. (4)
3 Romani oppidum aedificabant. (4)
4 equi aquam non timent. (5)
5 templa non delebant. (4)
6 servi et ancillae dominum timebant. (6)

Total: 30

Exercise 3.5

1 The Greeks feared the shields of the Romans. (5)
2 The inhabitants were singing near the sacred temple. (6)
3 The bad sailors were sailing from the big island. (7)
4 Many inhabitants feared our goddess. (6)
5 The savage master was hurrying across the field. (6)
6 The beautiful queen was watching us. (5)

Total: 35

Exercise 3.6

1	libros et equos habemus.	(5)
2	Romanos non timebant.	(4)
3	Romani pueros non necabant.	(5)
4	magister puerum non timet.	(5)
5	templum non delebatis.	(4)
6	reginam laudabamus sed dominum timebamus.	(7)

Total: 30

Exercise 3.7

1	He was a farmer.	(2)
2	She was a beautiful girl.	(2)
3	She was a savage goddess.	(1)
4	They were afraid of her.	(2)
5	She prepared lots of wine.	(1)
6	He said he loved the dinner, the wine and Flavia.	(3)
7	Marcus went into the villa and praised the good dinner, praised Flavia and laughed.	(4)

Total: 15

Exercise 3.8

Marcus is sitting near Flavia. Flavia is a beautiful girl. Marcus watches Flavia. Marcus loves Flavia. Marcus is a farmer. Marcus is a handsome farmer. Flavia is sitting near Marcus. Flavia is watching Marcus. She loves the handsome farmer.

Flavia gives a lot of wine to Marcus. She gives food and lots of wine to the handsome farmer. Marcus loves wine and good food. Flavia kisses Marcus. Marcus blushes and hurries out of the villa. He hurries across the big field and along the road but he laughs and sings. He loves Flavia.

Total: 30

Exercise 3.9

1

Latin word from passage	Meaning of the Latin word	An English word which comes from the Latin word
videbat (line 2)	saw	visible, video
miser (line 9)	unhappy	miserable, miser

(4)

2	D accusative, because it is after the preposition **per**	(1)
3	C adjective	(1)
4	a) B librum	
	b) B accusative	(2)
5	C malos	(1)
6	B non timetis	(1)

Total: 10

Exercise 3.10

1	Romani equum timent.	(4)
2	dominus/magister librum spectabat.	(4)
3	gladios parabant.	(3)
4	libros non portabam.	(4)
5	vinum et equos habetis.	(5)

Total: 20

Chapter 4

Exercise 4.1

1	lego; The good boy was reading the book.	(1 + 5)
2	discedo; We shall depart from the temple.	(1 + 4)
3	curro; The Romans were running through the field.	(1 + 5)
4	lego; The good freedman was reading a letter to the master.	(1 + 6)
5	rego; The savage queen was ruling the inhabitants.	(1 + 5)
6	duco; You were leading the friends to the temple.	(1 + 5)

Total: 36

Exercise 4.2

1	dormio; The tired girls are sleeping.	(1 + 4)
2	venio; The Romans are coming to the big temple.	(1 + 6)
3	audio; We listen to the beautiful poet.	(1 + 4)
4	dormio; He is sleeping near the wall of the big town.	(1 + 6)
5	venio; You come across the water with the sailor.	(1 + 6)
6	audio; You listen to the words of the master.	(1 + 4)

Total: 36

Exercise 4.3

1	timeo; Why are you afraid of the words of the master?	(1 + 5)
2	sum; Where is the good friend of the farmer?	(1 + 6)
3	rego; Who is ruling in the new town?	(1 + 6)
4	laboro; Was Marcus working in your villa?	(1 + 7)
5	timeo; Were the women afraid of the horse?	(1 + 5)
6	do; Why was he/she giving money to the boys?	(1 + 5)

Total: 40

Exercise 4.4

1	Amicable; The friends were drinking wine in the villa.	(1 + 6)
2	Dominate, dominant; The Romans were very much afraid of the master.	(1 + 5)
3	Agriculture; The farmers therefore depart from the fields.	(1 + 6)
4	Dormitory, dormant; Why is the poet sleeping in the temple?	(1 + 6)
5	Puerile; Savage masters never love boys.	(1 + 6)
6	Duct, duke, viaduct, aqueduct; What are you leading to the villa?	(1 + 5)

Total: 40

Exercise 4.5

1	Adjective; Do you like the sacred books?	(1 + 5)
2	Verb; Why did the sailor fear the deep water?	(1 + 6)
3	Adjective; The inhabitants feared the new queen.	(1 + 5)
4	Verb; Where are the arrows and shields?	(1 + 6)
5	Adverb; Marcus was praising the food and wine very much.	(1 + 7)
6	Noun; Therefore the master was moving the money.	(1 + 5)

Total: 40

Exercise 4.6

1	equos non habent.	(4)
2	nautas non timetis.	(4)
3	Romani puellas et feminas necabant.	(6)
4	pueri magistrum non timent.	(5)
5	cenam non amas.	(4)
6	gladios habemus sed Romanos timemus.	(7)

Total: 30

Exercise 4.7

1	They are friends.	(2)
2	They are working and writing.	(2)
3	Because she is an arrogant girl.	(1)
4	She chastises him (i.e. tells him to stop).	(2)
5	He asks them what they are doing and why they are fighting.	(2)
6	He is angry with Sextus and punishes him. Sextus cries.	(3)
7	They are not happy. They do not like him.	(3)

Total: 15

Exercise 4.8

Flavia has a friend. Flavia's friend is Marcus. Marcus has a (girl)friend. Marcus's (girl)friend is Flavia. Marcus is walking along the road. Flavia is also walking along the road. Flavia is hurrying to school. She is crying. She is crying because Sextus always annoys her in school. She does not like Sextus because he is a bad boy. Marcus sees Flavia. 'Flavia,' Marcus immediately asks, 'why are you crying?' Flavia replies to Marcus, 'O Marcus, I am crying because Sextus annoys me in school. Then the master punishes me. He is a bad man. He never punishes Sextus. I do not like Sextus. He is a bad boy.' Marcus is angry because Flavia is crying. He kisses Flavia. Flavia is now happy because Marcus kisses her. The friends laugh. Marcus and Flavia walk to school. They are happy.

Total: 30

Exercise 4.9

1

Latin word from passage	Meaning of the Latin word	An English word which comes from the Latin word
videt (line 3)	sees	vision, visible, video
libros (line 4)	books	library

(4)

2	D accusative, because it is after the preposition **ad**	(1)
3	A nominative	(1)
4	C 3rd	(1)
5	C adjective	(1)
6	D **sum**	(1)
7	C **respondebat**	(1)

Total: 10

Chapter 5

Exercise 5.1

1	The Trojans were always afraid of the Greeks.	(5)
2	For a long time the Greeks wanted to capture Troy.	(6)
3	The Trojans do not fear the Greeks' plan.	(6)
4	'What are you doing, Greeks?' they say. 'Why are you throwing the horse into the water?'	(10)
5	The savage goddess never loved the country of the Trojans.	(7)
6	The Trojans wanted to build a new town.	(6)
		Total: 40

Exercise 5.2

1	The famous master had four sons.	(6)
2	They were building seven temples in the big town.	(7)
3	The beautiful queen had nine daughters.	(6)
4	The small boy was carrying eight books into the villa.	(8)
5	Therefore the sailors sailed to Greece.	(6)
6	'Do you want to capture Troy?' asked (said) the master.	(7)
		Total: 40

Exercise 5.3

1	**timebas.** 'Why were you afraid of the bad man?'	(1 + 5)
2	**tres Troiani.** Three Trojans were sailing from the small island.	(1 + 7)
3	**dominus tuus.** Your master never adopts a new plan.	(1 + 7)
4	**amici vestri.** Your friends adopted many plans.	(1 + 6)
5	**cupiebat .** He wanted to build five temples in the town.	(1 + 7)
6	**nauta fessus.** The tired sailor was throwing the new spears into the road.	(1 + 8)
		Total: 46

Exercise 5.4

1	**filios.** The savage god wants to kill the sons of the goddess.	(7)
2	**none.** The tired master was sleeping in the big villa.	(7)
3	**none.** He was not writing in the book of the unhappy boy.	(7)
4	**agros.** The Roman farmer had six fields.	(6)
5	**none.** The unhappy boys were not writing in the book.	
	or	
	none. They were not writing in the book of the unhappy boy.	(7)
6	**nos.** The savage men feared us greatly.	(6)
		Total: 46

Exercise 5.5

1	**in.** The sailor was drinking in the villa with nine friends.	(1 + 8)
2	**trans.** The master's slave was leading ten horses across the field.	
	or	
	trans. The slave was leading the master's ten horses across the field.	(1 + 8)
3	**in.** The Romans were building a sacred temple in the new town.	(1 + 8)
4	**in.** The master's three daughters were singing in the street.	(1 + 7)
5	**none.** The new master was giving books to the boys.	(1 + 6)
6	**none.** Where is the famous son of the savage Trojan?	(1 + 7)

Total: 50

Exercise 5.6

1	filius virum timet.	(4)
2	Romanos audiunt.	(3)
3	Romani deos amant.	(4)
4	Romanus equos videt.	(4)
5	viros non amatis.	(4)
6	deus filium et feminam amat.	(6)

Total: 25

Exercise 5.7

1	They are in a town, entering an inn.	(2)
2	They want to eat food and drink wine.	(2)
3	Because the food and wine are good.	(1)
4	Four sailors. They stand near Marcus and Flavia.	(3)
5	They get drunk.	(2)
6	She gets scared.	(2)
7	He is angry with them. He leads Flavia out of the inn.	(3)

Total: 15

Exercise 5.8

Marcus and Flavia walk out of the inn because Flavia is afraid of the four drunken sailors. The sailors also walk out of the inn. 'Marcus! I am afraid of the sailors,' shouts Flavia. They decide to hurry. The sailors also now hurry along the road. 'I am afraid of the sailors, Marcus,' shouts Flavia. They run. The sailors also run. Thus the sailors soon catch Marcus and Flavia.

A sailor shouts, 'What are you doing here?' Marcus replies, 'We are walking home.' The sailor asks, 'Who is the girl?' Marcus angrily replies, 'The girl is Flavia. She is my girlfriend.'

The sailor shouts, 'Your girlfriend? Flavia is beautiful. Do you love me, Flavia?'

The sailors laugh. 'Where is your money?' a sailor shouts. Marcus is now very angry. 'We do not have any money,' he replies. The sailors suddenly depart.

Total: 30

Exam Practice Answers

Exercise 5.9

1 This question tests your knowledge of the origins of English words. Complete the table below. One example has been completed for you.

Latin word from passage	Meaning of the Latin word	An English word which comes from the Latin word
nautae (line 4)	sailors	nautical
amici (line 5)	of a friend	amicable

(4)

2 C accusative, because it agrees with the object (1)
3 C adjective (1)
4   a) B 2nd (1)
    b) A singular (1)
5 C saevum (1)
6 B timebant (1)

Total: 10

Exercise 5.10

1 domini vinum spectant. (4)
2 murum delebatis. (3)
3 puellam non monebam. (4)
4 Romani vinum amant. (4)
5 deum et viros times. (5)

Total: 20

Chapter 6

Exercise 6.1

1	**timeo.** The Trojans have not feared/did not fear the Greeks.	(1 + 5)
2	**oppugno.** The Greeks have attacked Troy.	(1 + 4)
3	**audio.** The Trojans have heard the plan of the Greeks.	(1 + 5)
4	**facio, pono.** 'What have you done?' they asked. 'Why have you placed the horse near the water?'	(2 + 9)
5	**amo.** The god loved the country of the Trojans.	(1 + 5)
6	**aedifico.** The Trojans have built a new town.	(1 + 5)

Total: 40

Exercise 6.2

1	**specto.** The master watched his four sons.	(1 + 5)
2	**aedifico.** I have built seven temples in the new town.	(1 + 7)
3	**amo.** The new queen loved her nine daughters.	(1 + 6)
4	**duco.** The small boy has led six horses into the field.	(1 + 8)
5	**navigo.** The Trojans have not sailed into Greece.	(1 + 6)
6	**mitto.** The husband of the mistress sent a letter to her friend.	(1 + 7)

Total: 45

Exercise 6.3

1	3rd singular. The freedman has prepared the mistress's garden.	(1 + 5)
2	3rd plural. The angry masters have departed out of the big villa.	(1 + 7)
3	3rd singular. The savage mistress has not terrified the good freedman.	(1 + 7)
4	2nd singular. O master, why have you led the tired prisoners into the garden?	(1 + 8)
5	3rd singular. The son of the master led the freedmen into the crowd.	
	or	
	The son led the master's freedmen into the crowd.	(1 + 7)
6	3rd plural. The prisoners have not remained in the wood.	(1 + 6)

Total: 46

Exercise 6.4

1	perfect. The Romans have decided to remain near the wood.	(1 + 6)
2	perfect. The freedmen have not eaten the mistress's food.	(1 + 6)
3	imperfect. The man's sons were playing in the garden.	(1 + 6)
4	perfect. Have you shown the letter to the freedman?	(1 + 5)
5	imperfect. Your master was holding a long letter.	(1 + 6)
6	perfect. The mistress ordered the freedmen to remain.	(1 + 5)

Total: 40

Exercise 6.5

1	**consumo.** Have you eaten the dinner?	(1 + 3)
2	**duco.** Why have you led the crowd of freedmen into the garden?	(1 + 7)
3	**pono.** My husband has placed the book in a new place.	(1 + 8)
4	**porto.** We have carried the money into the temple.	(1 + 5)
5	**do.** The mistress has given the letter to the freedmen.	(1 + 5)
6	**timeo.** You have never feared the anger of your husband.	(1 + 6)

Total: 40

Exercise 6.6

1	cenam semper laudabamus.	(4)
2	equos non timeo.	(4)
3	Romanus non est nauta.	(5)
4	villam intrabat.	(3)
5	dominum/magistrum non times.	(4)
6	feminae vinum saepe portabant.	(5)

Total: 25

Exercise 6.7

1	She ran out of the inn.	(2)
2	She was crying and very cross.	(2)
3	They remained in the inn.	(2)
4	'Who was that beautiful girl?'	(2)
5	He says it was Flavia who is, or rather was, his girlfriend.	(2)
6	It makes her angry.	(2)
7	She doesn't love him. He is a bad boy. He is not her friend.	(3)
8	However Marcus did not want to reply to Valeria. He blushed. 'I do not love you, Marcus,' said Valeria. 'You are a bad boy. You are not my friend. Goodbye!' The unhappy girl hit Marcus and angrily hurried out of the inn. Marcus stayed in the inn, astonished. He was alone.	(30)

Total: 45

Exercise 6.8

Flavia and Valeria were friends. Flavia loved Valeria and Valeria loved Flavia. The girls did not love Marcus.

Flavia and Valeria were walking along the road. Flavia was telling a long story. 'The Greeks wanted to capture a big town,' she said. 'They attacked the town of Troy and fought with many Trojans. They killed many Trojans and captured many.'

'Why did the Greeks want to capture Troy?' asked Valeria.

'The Greeks did not like the Trojans. They did not like the master of Troy. They did not like the master's son.'

'Why did they not like the master?' asked Valeria. 'Why did they not like his son? I do not understand.

'The Trojan master's son loved a girl.The girl was the daughter of a Greek lord. The girl was Helena. Many Greeks loved Helena. Many Greeks promised to protect Helena.'

Total: 30

Exercise 6.9

1

Latin word from passage	Meaning of the Latin word	An English word which comes from the Latin word
insulam (line 2)	island	insulate, insular, peninsula
notus (line 5)	famous	noted, notable

(4)

2	D genitive, because it means *of*	(1)
3	D ablative, because it is after a preposition	(1)
4	C preposition	(1)
5	B imperfect	(1)
6	B present infinitive	(1)
7	C perfect	(1)

Total: 10

Exercise 6.10

1	Romani templa aedificant.	(4)
2	puella reginam non vocat.	(5)
3	villam intrabant.	(3)
4	deus nautas saepe monebat.	(5)
5	muros non aedificabant.	(4)
6	feminas semper spectas.	(4)
		Total: 25

Chapter 7

Exercise 7.1

1	I am absent	(1)
2	He is present	(1)
3	He was present	(1)
4	They were present	(1)
5	I was absent	(1)
6	I was present	(1)
7	They are present	(1)
8	They are absent	(1)
9	We are present	(1)
10	You were absent	(1)

Total: 10

Exercise 7.2

1	I am (present) in the garden.	(4)
2	You are (present) in the villa.	(4)
3	We are (present) in the temple.	(4)
4	They are (present) in the forum.	(4)
5	They were (present) on the island.	(4)
6	The queen is (present) in the villa.	(5)
7	I am (present) in the forum.	(5)
8	The slave-girls were (present) in the villa.	(5)
9	The Trojans were (present) in the town.	(5)
10	We are (present) in the villa.	(5)

Total: 45

Exercise 7.3

1	Once, the freedmen decided to destroy the garden when the mistress was absent.	(10)
2	Because the war was long and savage, the Greeks were present near the town for a long time.	(13)
3	They were attacking Troy because they did not like the Trojans.	(7)
4	'Why are you remaining here?' asked the freedman. 'Why is your mistress absent?'	(11)
5	The god praised the inhabitants because he loved the country of the Trojans.	(9)
6	The savage master was absent. The Trojans therefore built a new town.	(10)

Total: 60

Exercise 7.4

1	When she saw the farmer, Lucia hurried into the villa.	(8)
2	Because she saw the farmer, Flavia hurried into the villa.	(8)
3	When the mistress caught Julia, she called her husband.	(7)
4	The freedman showed the book to his son because he liked to read.	(8)
5	Because he was tired, the Greek master was present in the villa for a long time.	(10)
6	The savage Romans always carried big spears into battle.	(9)

Total: 50

Exercise 7.5

1	Many happy boys were always present in the garden.	(8)
2	The boys were very much afraid because the savage master was present.	(8)
3	For a long time the inhabitants were not afraid because our queen was absent.	(9)
4	Who is in the garden? Why is the mistress absent?	(8)
5	Because they fought bravely, the Romans often terrified the Greeks.	(8)
6	Again and again, the freedman ordered the slave-girl to prepare the food.	(9)

Total: 50

Exercise 7.6

1	'Hurry into the garden, Marcus! the master is there.'	(9)
2	'Listen to the master, boy, because he is fierce.'	(8)
3	'Listen to the master's words, freedmen, and write the letters.'	(9)
4	'Lead your husband into the villa, o unhappy woman.'	(7)
5	'Hold the money, Marcus, and prepare the food for the master.'	(9)
6	'Reply to the master, girls, because he is angry.'	(8)

Total: 50

Exercise 7.7

1	**ducite.** 'Lead the horses into the big fields, farmers!'	(1 + 7)
2	**pugnate.** 'Fight bravely, Romans, near the walls of the big town!'	(1 + 9)
3	**cantate.** 'Because the angry queen is coming into the temple, sing well!'	(1 + 10)
4	**da.** 'Give the money to the master, o unhappy freedman, because he is angry!'	(1 + 9)
5	**date.** 'Because you are fighting with the Greeks, give help to the allies!'	(1 + 9)
6	**manete, consumite.** 'Remain in the wood, allies, and eat the food!'	(2 + 9)

Total: 60

Exercise 7.8

1	magister libros saepe laudabat.	(5)
2	pecuniam et epistulas portabat.	(5)
3	amicos non specto.	(4)
4	regina cenam et vinum videt.	(6)
5	deos non timetis.	(4)
6	gladios et hastas semper portabant.	(6)

Total: 30

Exercise 7.9

1	Marcus, Flavia and four sailors.	(2)
2	He orders them to leave.	(2)
3	Because they are not afraid of Marcus.	(1)
4	The sailors shout at Marcus and Flavia, telling them to hand over their money because they want to buy wine.	(2)
5	He takes his sword and runs at them.	(2)
6	He has a sword, they don't.	(2)
7	'Our money is safe, we are safe.'	(4)

Total: 15

Exercise 7.10

Marcus and Flavia were safe. Flavia was no longer terrified. Flavia praised Marcus. 'Marcus, you are a strong, brave man. I am happy because we are safe. The sailors were afraid of you. I was also afraid of you. The sailors did not want to fight because they were afraid of you.'

Marcus said to Flavia, 'Flavia, I am also happy because we are safe.'

'Marcus, come to my villa. I have some food. I have prepared a good dinner. You are my hero.'

Marcus was happy. He loved food. He also loved Flavia's dinners. Marcus and Flavia therefore hurried to Flavia's villa.

Total: 30

Exercise 7.11

1

Latin word from passage	Meaning of the Latin word	An English word which comes from the Latin word
constituit (line 7)	she decided	constitution
vidit (line 8)	she saw	vision, visible, video

(4)

2   C accusative, because it is the object (1)
3   B imperfect (1)
4   C preposition (1)
5   B present infinitive (1)
6   a)   A present tense (1)
    b)   C sum (1)

Total: 10

Exercise 7.12

1   clamabamus et templum delebamus. (6)
2   magister libros et epistulam portat. (6)
3   gladium videt. (3)
4   puellae dominum non amant. (5)
5   reginam spectabam et vocabam. (6)
6   reginam saepe laudatis. (4)

Total: 30

Chapter 8

Exercise 8.1

1	They have loved.	(2)
2	They run.	(2)
3	We see.	(2)
4	You were writing.	(2)
5	I fight.	(2)
6	He replies.	(2)
7	He has replied.	(2)
8	We were remaining.	(2)
9	You have been/you were.	(2)
10	They shout.	(2)
	Total: 20	

Exercise 8.2

1	You lead.	(2)
2	You say.	(2)
3	They have played.	(2)
4	We send.	(2)
5	We have moved.	(2)
6	You have departed.	(2)
7	You were attacking.	(2)
8	You show.	(2)
9	He has prepared.	(2)
10	I have placed.	(2)
	Total: 20	

Exercise 8.3

1	We see.	(2)
2	They have overcome.	(2)
3	You were.	(2)
4	You were carrying.	(2)
5	They hear.	(2)
6	He has killed.	(2)
7	They kill.	(2)
8	He has moved.	(2)
9	He has ordered.	(2)
10	He gives.	(2)
	Total: 20	

Exercise 8.4

1	They have decided.	(2)
2	He has captured.	(2)
3	I wanted.	(2)
4	He was leading.	(2)
5	We have thrown.	(2)
6	You praise.	(2)
7	They have stood.	(2)
8	You have carried.	(2)
9	You send.	(2)
10	We were hurrying.	(2)
	Total: 20	

Exercise 8.5

1	We were running quickly.	(3)
2	He was fighting bravely.	(3)
3	They have sailed for a long time.	(3)
4	I never play.	(3)
5	You write well.	(3)
6	They often cried.	(3)
7	I have slept for a long time.	(3)
8	At last they departed.	(3)
9	He suddenly entered.	(3)
10	He is always drinking.	(3)
	Total: 30	

Exercise 8.6

1	The Romans built a big town.	(5)
2	The sailor did not fear the dangers.	(5)
3	A crowd of women was standing in the street.	(6)
4	You said many words.	(4)
5	The Romans destroyed many temples.	(5)
	Total: 25	

Exercise 8.7

1	The new town has high walls.	(6)
2	Many sailors are approaching quickly.	(5)
3	Today I am working. Yesterday however I did nothing.	(7)
4	The Romans were carrying many shields.	(5)
5	Many good men fought in the battle.	(7)
	Total: 30	

Exam Practice Answers

Exercise 8.8

1 The freedmen hurried into the sacred temple. (6)
2 Once there were many famous Romans. (6)
3 The bad master does not praise the unhappy slave. (6)
4 The beautiful women were preparing good food. (6)
5 The bad boys never listen to the schoolmasters. (6)

Total: 30

Exercise 8.9

1 The master terrified the boy with angry words. (6)
2 We always fight with swords and shields. (6)
3 The master gave much money to Marcus. (6)
4 I killed the bad man with my spear. (6)
5 The famous poet was reading a good book. (6)

Total: 30

Exercise 8.10

1 The sailors' words were bad. (5)
2 Crowds of Romans are coming. (4)
3 The walls of the temple are high and strong. (7)
4 The boy's friend was singing. (4)
5 We never listen to the master's words. (5)

Total: 25

Exercise 8.11

1 They love to play. (3)
2 Flavia wanted to fight. (4)
3 The master ordered Brutus to fight. (5)
4 I never want to work. (4)
5 The freedman decided to run. (4)

Total: 20

Exercise 8.12

1 Walk slowly, boys! (4)
2 Write a book, poet! (4)
3 Move the horses, farmers! (4)
4 Drink the wine, friend! (4)
5 Leave your weapons, sailors! (4)

Total: 20

Exercise 8.13

1 The boy was standing in the street. (5)
2 The inhabitants fought against the barbarians. (5)
3 We are in great danger. (5)
4 The freedman ran through the gate. (5)
5 The girl is playing with her friends. (5)

Total: 25

Exercise 8.14

1 Was the farmer looking at the sky for a long time? (6)
2 Did the master say bad words? (6)
3 Are the inhabitants destroying the walls? (5)
4 Do the boys have shields? (5)
5 Did the Briton have many fields and meadows? (8)

Total: 30

Exercise 8.15

1 3rd plural, present, **rideo**, they laugh. (5)
2 3rd singular, imperfect, **oppugno**, he was attacking. (5)
3 1st plural, imperfect, **pono**, we were placing. (5)
4 2nd plural, perfect, **do**, you have given. (5)
5 3rd plural, perfect, **sto**, they have stood. (5)
6 3rd plural, perfect, **laboro**, they have worked. (5)
7 3rd plural, present, **constituo**, they decide. (5)
8 2nd plural, perfect, **curro**, you have run. (5)
9 3rd plural, perfect, **scribo**, they have written. (5)
10 1st plural, imperfect, **paro**, we were preparing. (5)

Total: 50

Exercise 8.16

1. 3rd plural, present, **venio**, they come. (5)
2. 3rd singular, imperfect, **sum**, he was. (5)
3. 2nd singular, imperfect, **porto**, you were carrying. (5)
4. 2nd singular, present, **neco**, you are killing. (5)
5. 3rd plural, perfect, **bibo**, they have drunk. (5)
6. 2nd singular, imperfect, **dormio**, you were sleeping. (5)
7. 3rd singular, perfect, **iubeo**, he has ordered. (5)
8. 3rd singular, present, **moneo**, he warns. (5)
9. 2nd singular, perfect, **capio**, you have captured. (5)
10. 3rd plural, imperfect, **dico**, they were saying. (5)

Total: 50

Exercise 8.17

1. **amabam**, I was loving. (2)
2. **estis**, you are. (2)
3. **vidisti**, you have seen. (2)
4. **portaverunt**, they have carried. (2)
5. **timebamus**, we were fearing. (2)

Total: 10

Exercise 8.18

1. **videt**, he sees. (2)
2. **delebatis**, you were destroying. (2)
3. **laudavimus**, we have praised. (2)
4. **festinant**, they hurry. (2)
5. **monuisti**, you have warned. (2)

Total: 10

Exercise 8.19

1. **fuit**, he has been. (2)
2. **tenebam**, I was holding. (2)
3. **regis**, you rule. (2)
4. **capit**, he takes. (2)
5. **audiebas**. (2)

Total: 10

Exercise 8.20

1. accusative. The sailors were not afraid of the women. (1 + 5)
2. nominative. The farmers love the fields. (1 + 4)
3. accusative. The towns have walls. (1 + 4)
4. accusative. The masters were punishing the boys. (1 + 4)
5. nominative. The girls were praising the gods. (1 + 4)

Total: 26

Exercise 8.21

1. The boys always run and shout. (6)
2. Julia and Valeria are girls. (6)
3. The farmers love silver and gold. (6)
4. We often run and play. (6)
5. The friends laugh and play. (6)
6. The ambassador is tired but happy. (6)
7. The boy has food and water. (6)
8. We are fighting against the Romans and Greeks. (6)
9. The farmers have spears and arrows. (6)
10. The boys enter and work. (6)

Total: 60

Exercise 8.22

1. Marcus and Sextus are boys. (6)
2. I laugh and play. (5)
3. The boy and girl run. (5)
4. The pirate departs from the province. (5)
5. They are running and playing. (5)
6. The sailor fears the wind and the waves. (6)
7. The master warns the boys and girls. (6)
8. The master enters and calls (his) uncle. (7)
9. The girl enters and sees her friend. (7)
10. The boys and girls laugh and play. (8)

Total: 60

Exercise 8.23

1 Romulus and Remus were Romans. (6)
2 We always laugh and play. (6)
3 Valeria and Aurelia are Romans. (6)
4 The master calls Sextus and Marcus. (6)
5 Sextus and Marcus listen to the master. (6)
6 The master was watching the boy and girl. (6)
7 The boy was afraid of the farmers
   and sailors. (6)
8 The Latins had food and water. (6)
9 The pupils were tired and unhappy. (6)
10 The temple was sacred and beautiful. (6)

Total: 60

Exercise 8.24

1 You have frightend. (2)
2 They have asked. (2)
3 They have destroyed. (2)
4 We have sent. (2)
5 He has seen. (2)
6 You have heard. (2)
7 They have decided. (2)
8 You have shouted. (2)
9 We have ruled. (2)
10 He has come (2)
   or
   He comes. (2)

Total: 20

Exercise 8.25

1 He has said. (2)
2 He has ordered. (2)
3 We have run. (2)
4 He captures. (2)
5 You have done/made. (2)
6 We have remained. (2)
7 You have captured. (2)
8 They have approached. (2)
9 I have drunk. (2)
10 He has been/he was. (2)

Total: 20

Exercise 8.26

1 imperfect. I was approaching. (1 + 2)
2 present. The slave is working. (1 + 3)
3 imperfect. The friend was fighting. (1 + 3)
4 present. The boy is good. (1 + 4)
5 perfect. The sailor has sailed. (1 + 3)

Total: 20

Exercise 8.27

1 nominative. The books are good. (1 + 4)
2 accusative. You were carrying the swords. (1 + 3)
3 accusative. We fear the wars. (1 + 3)
4 accusative. The sailors threw the big spears. (1 + 5)
5 accusative. The Romans were building high walls. (1 + 5)

Total: 25

Exercise 8.28

1 **manebam**. I was remaining. (2 + 2)
2 **navigavistis**. You have sailed. (2 + 2)
3 **aedificat**. He builds. (2 + 2)
4 **steti**. I have stood. (2 + 2)
5 **fuerunt**. They have been/they were. (2 + 2)

Total: 20

Exercise 8.29

1 nominative. The girls are not singing. (1 + 4)
2 nominative. The gifts are beautiful. (1 + 4)
3 accusative. The inhabitants were building the walls. (1 + 4)
4 accusative. The boys carried the shields. (1 + 4)
5 nominative. The girls fear the masters. (1 + 4)

Total: 25

Exercise 8.30

1 3rd singular, perfect, **voco**. He has called. (4 + 2)
2 3rd plural, imperfect, **appropinquo**. They were approaching. (4 + 2)
3 2nd singular, perfect, **iacio**. You have thrown. (4 + 2)
4 1st plural, present, **oppugno**. We attack. (4 + 2)
5 3rd singular, perfect, **iubeo**. He has ordered. (4 + 2)

Total: 30

Exercise 8.31

1 **appropinquabant**. They were approaching. (1 + 2)
2 **vocabat**. He was calling. (1 + 2)
3 **navigabam**. I was sailing. (1 + 2)
4 **oppugnabas**. You were attacking. (1 + 2)
5 **iubebat**. He was ordering. (1 + 2)
6 **iubebant**. They were ordering. (1 + 2)
7 **superabamus**. We were overcoming. (1 + 2)
8 **stabat**. He was standing. (1 + 2)
9 **delebant**. They were destroying. (1 + 2)
10 **dabamus**. We were giving. (1 + 2)

Total: 30

Exercise 8.32

Once the gods and goddesses were holding a celebration on Mount Olympus. They were eating food and drinking wine. They were holding the celebration because Peleus was marrying Thetis. Thetis was a goddess. Peleus was a mortal man. The gods and goddesses were happy. They were laughing. Suddenly however Discordia, a bad goddess, came in. When they saw Discordia, the other gods were not happy. They were no longer laughing. They were not laughing because they did not like Discordia. They shouted, 'What do you want, Discordia? Why are you here? We don't like you. Leave immediately!' Discordia replied, 'Listen gods! Listen goddesses! I have a gift. I have a beautiful gift. Here it is.' Then Discordia put an apple down near the food. She laughed and went away. The gods and goddesses approached the apple. They looked at the apple.

Total: 30

Exercise 8.33

1   He was working in the school. (2)
2   Many pupils and Marcus. (2)
3   A wasp suddenly entered the school. (1)
4   Because the pupils stopped working. (2)
5   Kill the wasp immediately. (2)
6   He took the wasp and showed it to the pupils. (3)
7   He said he had killed the wasp and told them to get on with their work. (3)

Total: 15

Exercise 8.34

Marcus was a good boy. The pupils liked Marcus because he was good but they were very much afraid of the master. The master did not like the pupils because he was savage. He did not like Marcus because Marcus was lazy. Marcus did not like working.

Once the master was shouting in the school about wasps. The master was afraid of wasps and was always killing them. Marcus very much liked wasps and decided to obstruct the master. He therefore took a big book and rushed towards the angry master.

'Go away, bad man!' he shouted. 'The wasp is terrified. Why are you frightening it?'

The pupils, Marcus's friends, were laughing and rushed towards the master. The astonished master hurried out of the school and ran into the street.

Total: 30

Exercise 8.35

1

Latin word from passage	Meaning of the Latin word	An English word which comes from the Latin word
iratus (line 1)	angry	irate
constituit (line 6)	decided	constitution

(4)

2   C ablative, because it is after a preposition (1)
3   B imperfect (1)
4   D adverb (1)
5   C 3rd (1)
6   C numeral (1)
7   C risit (1)

Total: 10

Exercise 8.36

1   amici vinum et cenam parant. (6)
2   deus puellas et pueros spectabat. (6)
3   Romanos non timebamus. (3)
4   hastam et gladium portas. (5)

Total: 20

Level 2
Chapter 9

Exercise 9.1

1	I have seen the companion.	(3)
2	The leader is running.	(3)
3	I love my wife.	(4)
4	The king is ruling.	(3)
5	We love the woman.	(3)
6	I have a brother and sister.	(5)
7	The king has a beautiful wife.	(5)
8	We saw many soldiers.	(4)
9	We were approaching the high mountain.	(5)
10	My parents are coming now.	(5)

Total: 40

Exercise 9.2

1	Marcus is the brother of Aurelia.	(5)
2	Aurelia is the sister of Marcus.	(5)
3	The girl was preparing food for (her) father.	(5)
4	The girl does not love (her) sister.	(5)
5	The slaves are hurrying to the mountain.	(5)
6	There are many roads in the mountains.	(6)
7	The king loved (his) mother and father.	(5)
8	The king had a beautiful wife.	(5)
9	I have a good father.	(4)
10	My sister is bad.	(5)

Total: 50

Exercise 9.3

1	The prisoner is always fighting with the soldier.	(6)
2	The man often sings with (his) companion.	(6)
3	The mistress's brother is angry.	(5)
4	The king rules the land well.	(5)
5	The king gives money to the soldier.	(5)
6	The freedman takes the king's money.	(5)
7	My wife has a famous brother.	(6)
8	My mother's brother was famous.	(6)
9	The Roman gave many gifts to the woman.	(6)
10	The king's wife is beautiful.	(5)

Total: 55

Exercise 9.4

1	reges	(1)
2	comitis	(1)
3	ducibus	(1)
4	homine	(1)
5	militum	(1)
6	luci	(1)
7	mulieribus	(1)
8	parentem	(1)
9	clamores	(1)
10	uxor	(1)

Total: 10

Exercise 9.5

1	corporis	(1)
2	flumina	(1)
3	itineri	(1)
4	rex	(1)
5	nominibus	(1)
6	flumen	(1)
7	corpore	(1)
8	itinera	(1)
9	parentibus	(1)
10	comitum	(1)

Total: 10

Exercise 9.6

1	accusative singular	(1)
2	genitive plural	(1)
3	genitive singular	(1)
4	dative or ablative plural	(2)
5	nominative, vocative or accusative plural	(3)
6	genitive singular	(1)
7	nominative or vocative singular	(2)
8	accusative singular	(1)
9	dative or ablative plural	(2)
10	genitive singular	(1)

Total: 15

Exercise 9.7

1 The strong leader has a big body. (6)
2 The man was looking at the deep river for a long time. (6)
3 The soldiers made long journeys. (5)
4 The king's name was Tarquinius. (5)
5 The shouts of the Trojans terrified the horses. (5)
6 The soldiers threw the miserable man into the river. (7)
7 The mistress's freedmen feared the king.
   or
   The freedman's mistresses feared the king. (5)
8 The Roman soldiers praised (their) companions. (5)
9 We made many journeys across the mountains. (6)
10 You were looking at the bodies of many men. (5)

Total: 55

Exercise 9.8

1 cenam bonam paro. (4)
2 puerum parvum videmus. (4)
3 dominum/magistrum saevum habeo. (4)
4 Romanum clarum spectabant. (4)
5 multos libros portabat. (4)
6 villa pulchra erat. (4)
7 feminas bonas amo. (4)
8 regina pulchra est. (4)
9 puellae miserae sunt. (4)
10 Romani gladios portabant. (4)

Total: 40

Exercise 9.9

1 e villa ambulabant. (4)
2 nautae cum Romanis pugnabant. (5)
3 villam prope templum aedificabant. (5)
4 multos libros in villam portabant. (6)
5 gladios magnos et hastas habent. (6)
6 Romani gladiis pugnabant. (4)
7 ad ancillam miseram ambulabas. (5)
8 nautae deos non timent. (5)
9 cum viro misero ambulabamus. (5)
10 pueri amici semper erant. (5)

Total: 50

Exercise 9.10

1 magistrum malum spectabamus. (4)
2 puella cum femina ambulat. (5)
3 magistrum saevum timebam. (4)
4 Romani templum magnum delebant. (5)
5 ad templum cum pecunia ambulabamus. (6)
6 e templo magno ambulabant. (5)
7 puella misera in villam ambulat. (6)
8 gladiis et hastis pugnant. (4)
9 puellae semper miserae erant. (5)
10 amici cenas magnas non amant. (6)

Total: 50

Exercise 9.11

1 Marcus and Sextus were Roman soldiers. (5)
2 Valeria and Aurelia are Roman women. (5)
3 I have a beautiful mother and an angry father. (7)
4 My sister did not like our parents. (7)
5 The sailors were looking at the bright light for a long time. (6)
6 The soldiers did not want to sail across the river. (6)
7 Why was the king terrifying the horse? (5)
8 The Roman soldiers attacked the city with spears and arrows. (7)
9 The king's mother and father were angry. (6)
10 My brother was capturing the Trojan prisoners. (6)

Total: 60

Exercise 9.12

1 nominative plural. The soldiers were hurrying to the river. (1 + 5)
2 accusative plural. The freedman no longer had (his) parents. (1 + 5)
3 accusative singular. The girls suddenly approached the woman. (1 + 5)
4 accusative plural. You have always loved beautiful gifts. (1 + 5)
5 nominative plural. The men praised the famous women. (1 + 5)
6 nominative singular. The high mountain is beautiful. (1 + 5)
7 accusative plural. The boy loves (his) famous parents. (1 + 5)
8 ablative singular. The king lived with his wife. (1 + 5)
9 genitive singular. The leader's wife fears the war. (1 + 5)
10 dative plural. The leader's mother was singing to the soldiers. (1 + 5)

Total: 60

Exercise 9.13

1 nomina (1)
2 iter (1)
3 corporis (1)
4 fluminibus (1)
5 hominibus (1)
6 itineri (1)
7 nomine (1)
8 corpora (1)
9 parens (1)
10 flumen (1)

Total: 10

Exercise 9.14

1 accusative singular. The sailor does not fear the sea. (1 + 5)
2 nominative singular. The soldiers' journey was long. (1 + 5)
3 accusative singular. The soldiers were carrying the king's body. (1 + 5)
4 accusative plural. We made many long journeys. (1 + 5)
5 genitive singular. The water of the river was deep. (1 + 5)
6 ablative singular. There are many temples in the city. (1 + 6)
7 accusative plural. I love towns and cities. (1 + 5)
8 genitive singular. The king's name was Sextus. (1 + 5)
9 accusative singular. My father often sails alone across the sea. (1 + 8)
10 ablative singular. The friends were tired from (their) long journey. (1 + 6)

Total: 65

Exercise 9.15

1 imperfect. We were carrying many bodies out of the temple. (1 + 6)
2 imperfect. The young men's journey was both long and miserable. (1 + 7)
3 perfect. The king saw a bright light and the high mountains. (1 + 7)
4 imperfect. The name of the city was Rome. (1 + 5)
5 present. Girls often love handsome young men. (1 + 6)
6 perfect. The father gave a lot of money to the young man. (1 + 6)
7 imperfect. I was watching my mother and father in the city yesterday. (1 + 7)
8 imperfect. The sailor had a big body. (1 + 5)
9 present. We are soon coming to the deep river.
   or
   perfect. We soon came to the deep river. (1 + 6)
10 perfect. Tired from the journey, we slept for a long time. (1 + 5)

Total: 70

Exercise 9.16

1 cum viro malo pugnatis. (5)
2 magistrum saevum timemus. (4)
3 templum magnum est. (4)
4 Romani in templo pugnabant. (5)
5 puerum miserum vocabat. (4)
6 amicum non habeo. (4)
7 multas feminas et puellas videbam. (6)
8 cenam saepe paramus. (4)
9 equum parvum habes. (4)
10 regina misera deos timet. (5)

Total: 45

Exercise 9.17

1 puer miser dominum timebat. (5)
2 nautae miseri pecuniam numquam habent. (6)
3 viri clari cum gladiis saepe pugnant. (6)
4 feminas pulchras saepe videbamus. (5)
5 femina cenam cum amico parat. (6)
6 pueri magistrum saevum semper timent. (6)
7 ad villam magnam ambulabat. (5)
8 tandem vinum et pecuniam habebant. (6)
9 deus nautas miseros monebat. (5)
10 amici in templo clamabant. (5)

Total: 55

Exercise 9.18

1 vocative plural. O kings! (1 + 1)
2 ablative singular. With the wife (1 + 1)
3 accusative singular. To the river (1 + 1)
4 ablative singular. On the journey (1 + 1)
5 ablative singular. With the companion (1 + 1)
6 accusative singular. Into the light (1 + 1)
7 dative singular. To/for the wife (1 + 1)
8 genitive plural. Of the soldiers (1 + 1)
9 dative singular. To/for the leader (1 + 1)
10 ablative singular. In the river (1 + 1)

Total: 20

Exercise 9.19

1 regis (1)
2 uxores (1)
3 matri (1)
4 pater (1)
5 fratribus (1)
6 montem (1)
7 sorore (1)
8 matres (1)
9 fratribus (1)
10 patrum (1)

Total: 10

Exercise 9.20

1	I saw the high mountain.	(4)
2	The angry father is running.	(4)
3	I love my wife.	(4)
4	The famous king was ruling well.	(5)
5	We love our mother.	(4)
6	I have both a brother and a sister.	(5)
7	The king has a beautiful sister.	(5)
8	We saw many mountains.	(4)
9	We were approaching the high mountain.	(5)
10	My wife is sleeping now.	(5)

Total: 45

Exercise 9.21

1	nominative singular. Marcus is Aurelia's brother.	(1 + 5)
2	genitive singular. Aurelia is Marcus's sister.	(1 + 5)
3	dative singular. The girl was preparing food for (her) father.	(1 + 5)
4	accusative singular. The girl does not like (her) sister.	(1 + 5)
5	accusative singular. The slaves hurry to the moutain.	(1 + 5)
6	ablative plural. There are many roads in the mountains.	(1 + 6)
7	nominative singular. The king loved (his) mother and father.	(1 + 5)
8	accusative singular. The king had a beautiful wife.	(1 + 5)
9	accusative singular. I have a good father.	(1 + 4)
10	nominativ singular. My sister is bad.	(1 + 5)

Total: 60

Exercise 9.22

1	verb. The boy was always fighting with (his) sister.	(1 + 6)
2	preposition. The girl often fights with (her) brother.	(1 + 6)
3	adjective. The father of the bad boy is angry.	(1 + 6)
4	adverb. The good king rules the land well.	(1 + 6)
5	noun. The king gives a lot of money to (his) sister.	(1 + 6)
6	verb. The freedman takes the famous king's money.	(1 + 6)
7	adjective. My mother has a famous brother.	(1 + 6)
8	noun. My mother's brother was famous.	(1 + 6)
9	verb. The boy gave (his) mother many gifts.	(1 + 6)
10	adjective. The new wife of the king is beautiful.	(1 + 6)

Total: 70

Exercise 9.23

1	The son. **filius**	(1 + 1)
2	The women. **feminae**	(1 + 1)
3	The men. **viri**	(1 + 1)
4	The man. **vir**	(1 + 1)
5	The horses. **equi**	(1 + 1)
6	The swords. **gladii**	(1 + 1)
7	The walls. **muri**	(1 + 1)
8	Sailors. **nautae**	(1 + 1)
9	The Romans. **Romani**	(1 + 1)
10	The queen. **regina**	(1 + 1)

Total: 20

Exercise 9.24

1	1st person singular, present. **habeo**	(2 + 2)
2	3rd person singular, present. **est**	(2 + 2)
3	3rd person singular, imperfect. **parabat**	(2 + 2)
4	1st person plural, present. **videmus**	(2 + 2)
5	3rd person plural, present. **amant**	(2 + 2)
6	3rd person plural, present. **sunt**	(2 + 2)
7	3rd person singular, perfect. **paravit**	(2 + 2)
8	3rd person plural, imperfect. **clamabant**	(2 + 2)
9	1st person singular, present. **intro**	(2 + 2)
10	1st person plural, imperfect. **monebamus**	(2 + 2)

Total: 40

Exercise 9.25

1	towards. ad muros	(1 + 2)
2	with. cum magistro	(1 + 2)
3	to. ad villam	(1 + 2)
4	in. in via	(1 + 2)
5	from. ab/ex oppido	(1 + 2)
6	near. prope templum	(1 + 2)
7	out of. e villa	(1 + 2)
8	in. in oppido	(1 + 2)
9	out of. e templo	(1 + 2)
10	into. in villam	(1 + 2)
		Total: 30

Exercise 9.26

1	nominative plural. Marcus and Sextus are Roman boys.	(1 + 7)
2	genitive singular. Brutus and Aurelia are the parents of the boy.	(1 + 7)
3	vocative singular. O leader, you have a good mother and a famous father.	(1 + 9)
4	accusative singular. My sister was often afraid of the savage mistress.	(1 + 7)
5	accusative plural. The leader often warned both (his) companions and (his) soldiers.	(1 + 8)
6	genitive plural. The man saw a big crowd of soldiers.	(1 + 6)
7	accusative singular. The soldiers watched the light for a long time.	(1 + 5)
8	nominative plural. The Roman soldiers attacked the town with spears and arrows.	(1 + 8)
9	genitive singular. The mother and father of the king were angry.	(1 + 7)
10	accusative singular. My brother has a big body.	(1 + 6)
		Total: 80

Exercise 9.27

1	rex festinabat. The king was hurrying.	(2 + 3)
2	puella fratrem habebat. The girl had a brother.	(3 + 4)
3	puella non appropinquabat. The girl was not approaching.	(2 + 4)
4	donum amavisti. You loved the gift.	(2 + 3)
5	vir feminam laudavit. The man praised the woman.	(3 + 4)
		Total: 30

Exercise 9.28

1	montes alti sunt pulchri. The high mountains are beautiful.	(4 + 5)
2	pueri patres amant. The boys love (their) fathers.	(3 + 4)
3	reges sorores habebant. The kings had sisters.	(3 + 4)
4	uxores bella timent. The wives are afraid of the wars.	(3 + 4)
5	matres discesserunt. The mothers departed.	(2 + 3)
		Total: 35

Exercise 9.29

1	On Mount Olympus.	(2)
2	Looking at the apple.	(3)
3	'The golden apple is for the most beautiful woman.'	(4)
4	She was both his sister and his wife.	(4)
5	That she was the most beautiful.	(2)
6	The goddess Athena looked at the apple. She read the words. 'You are wrong, Juno,' she said. 'The apple is mine. The apple is mine because I am the most beautiful.' The goddess Venus looked at the apple. She read the words. 'You are wrong, goddesses,' she said. 'I am the most beautiful. Therefore the apple is mine. Hand over the apple to me!'	(30)
7	a) they decided. Constitution.	(2)
	b) father. Paternal.	(2)
8	imperfect	(1)
9	habeo	(1)
10	a) sum	(1)
	b) imperfect	(1)
	c) 3rd	(1)
	d) singular	(1)

Total: 55

Exercise 9.30

1	amici pecuniam amant.	(4)
2	vir vinum et librum portabat.	(6)
3	amici dominum/magistrum non monent.	(5)
4	clamabant et vinum laudabant.	(5)

Total: 20

Chapter 10

Exercise 10.1

1 The king ruled the Roman citizens for a long time. (6)
2 The leader was fighting with the enemy. (5)
3 The Roman sailors carried (their) ships into the sea. (7)
4 We were waiting for the old Roman man in the temple. (6)
5 The Romans often praised the strong young men. (6)
6 Where are the companions of the enemy? (5)
7 The young man was very much afraid of the other citizens. (6)
8 The master loved his dear wife for a long time. (6)
9 The unhappy old man threw the young man into the middle of the sea. (8)
10 The queen freed the other prisoners. (5)

Total: 60

Exercise 10.2

1 The young men were approaching the sea. (5)
2 We were looking at the big cities for a long time. (5)
3 The young man was waiting for the ships of the enemy for a long time. (6)
4 Why are you carrying the bodies of the enemy into the middle of the city? (8)
5 We hurried into the middle of the enemy. (5)
6 We were making a long journey to our* sea. (7)
7 The mistress killed her dear husband near the mountains. (7)
8 I was telling long stories to the young men. (5)
9 For a long time the Roman soldiers wandered through the hight mountains. (8)
10 They have freed the other citizens. (4)

* It lay at the heart of their empire.

Total: 60

Exercise 10.3

1 iuvenes (1)
2 civis (1)
3 hostibus (1)
4 mari (1)
5 militum (1)
6 senum (1)
7 urbibus (1)
8 iuvenum (1)
9 hostes (1)
10 civium (1)

Total: 10

Exercise 10.4

1 iuvenis (1)
2 maria (1)
3 militi (1)
4 civis (1)
5 navibus (1)
6 montem (1)
7 urbe (1)
8 cives (1)
9 urbium (1)
10 senis (1)

Total: 10

Exercise 10.5

1 genitive plural. The young Roman men hurried into the enemy's temple.   (1 + 7)
2 ablative plural. The Romans built (their) city on seven mountains.   (1 + 7)
3 accusative singular. The Romans fought with the enemy near the sea.   (1 + 7)
4 accusative plural. The queen did not like the names of the citizens.   (1 + 6)
5 ablative singular. The old man lived in the city with the woman.   (1 + 7)
6 genitive plural. We were looking at the enemy's big ships.   (1 + 5)
7 accusative singular. The Roman sailors wandered over the sea for a long time.   (1 + 7)
8 ablative singular. The freedman was approaching with the strong young man.   (1 + 6)
9 ablative plural. You lived in the mountains with (your) companions.   (1 + 6)
10 genitive plural. The mistress decided to free (her) parents' dear slave.   (1 + 7)

Total: 75

Exercise 10.6

1 **flumen longum est**. The river is long.   (3 + 3)
2 **urbem diu oppugnabas**. You were attacking the city for a long time.   (2 + 3)
3 **donum spectavi**. I looked at the present.   (2 + 2)
4 **puer montem vidit**. The boy saw the mountain.   (3 + 3)
5 **poeta cantabat**. The poet was singing.   (2 + 2)

Total: 25

Exercise 10.7

1 **iuvenes currunt**. The young men are running.   (2 + 2)
2 **itinera longa sunt**. The journeys are long.   (3 + 3)
3 **iam advenimus**. We are now arriving.   (1 + 2)
4 **reges urbes ceperunt**. The kings captured the cities.   (3 + 3)
5 **urbes pulchrae erant**. The cities were beautiful.   (3 + 3)

Total: 25

Exercise 10.8

1 epistulas amat.   (3)
2 regina multos filios habet.   (5)
3 villam pulchram habet.   (4)
4 Romani oppidum hastis oppugnabant.   (5)
5 deus saevus oppidum delebat.   (5)
6 filii reginae deos timebant.   (5)
7 viri puellam in oppido videbant.   (6)
8 templum cum gladiis intrabamus.   (5)
9 nautae equos non timent.   (5)
10 puella mala equos prope muros spectat.   (7)

Total: 50

Exercise 10.9

1 They came to Jupiter. (2)
2 Who is the most beautiful? They want the apple. (2 + 2)
3 He was afraid of the goddesses' anger (2)
4 They are all beautiful and all have beautiful bodies. (4)
5 A young man who lives near Troy. (1 + 2)
6 'He loves beautiful women. Paris will choose the most beautiful (woman). Ask Paris!' The three goddesses were angry. However they decided to question Paris. Therefore they made the journey to the city. It was not a long journey. They therefore soon found Paris. When Paris saw a bright light, he was afraid. The goddesses told the young man the story about the golden apple. 'Jupiter has sent us to you, Paris. He orders you to choose the most beautiful goddess. Now, choose!' (30)
7 a) anger; irate (2)
   b) young man; juvenile (2)
8 imperative (1)
9 ablative (singular) (1)
10 feminine (1)
11 timebant (1)
12 Iuppiter (1)
13 adverb (1)
14 a) deos numquam timemus. (4)
   b) puer bonus servum malum vocabat. (6)
   c) multae feminae reginam spectant. (5)
   d) Romani muros magnos aedificabant. (5)

Total: 75

Exercise 10.11

1 We shall carry. (2)
2 He will destroy. (2)
3 You will sit. (2)
4 They will kill. (2)
5 I shall approach. (2)
6 You will overcome. (2)
7 He will wander. (2)
8 They will hold. (2)
9 You will enter. (2)
10 We shall shout. (2)
11 They will free. (2)
12 We shall give. (2)
13 You will tell. (2)
14 You will wait. (2)
15 They will tell. (2)
16 You will laugh. (2)
17 He will see. (2)
18 We shall work. (2)
19 You will sing. (2)
20 We shall warn. (2)

Total: 40

Exercise 10.12

1 They will build. (2)
2 I shall order. (2)
3 You will reply. (2)
4 They will stand. (2)
5 We shall fight. (2)
6 They will attack. (2)
7 He will shout. (2)
8 You will frighten. (2)
9 They will destroy. (2)
10 You will give. (2)
11 We shall approach. (2)
12 He will destroy. (2)
13 I shall remain. (2)
14 I shall ask. (2)
15 We shall laugh. (2)
16 I shall see. (2)
17 We shall sit. (2)
18 He will stand. (2)
19 You will warn. (2)
20 They will live. (2)

Total: 40

Exercise 10.13

1	aedificamus.	(1)
2	ambulant.	(1)
3	amabam.	(1)
4	clamat.	(1)
5	delemus.	(1)
6	habes.	(1)
7	intro.	(1)
8	laudabant.	(1)
9	monemus.	(1)
10	necat.	(1)
11	parabam.	(1)
12	portas.	(1)
13	pugnabant.	(1)
14	spectat.	(1)
15	estis.	(1)
16	timemus.	(1)
17	vides.	(1)
18.	vocabamus.	(1)
19.	est.	(1)
20	delet.	(1)

Total: 20

Exercise 10.14

1	3rd person singular. He will remain.	(1 + 2)
2	2nd person plural. You will attack.	(1 + 2)
3	1st person plural. We shall remain.	(1 + 2)
4	2nd person singular. You will kill.	(1 + 2)
5	1st person singular. I shall hold.	(1 + 2)
6	1st person plural. We shall see.	(1 + 2)
7	3rd person plural. They will watch.	(1 + 2)
8	3rd person plural. They will call.	(1 + 2)
9	3rd person singular. He will frighten.	(1 + 2)
10	2nd person plural. You will hurry.	(1 + 2)
11	1st person singular. I shall warn.	(1 + 2)
12	2nd person plural. You will approach.	(1 + 2)
13	2nd person plural. You will hold.	(1 + 2)
14	2nd person singular. You will enter.	(1 + 2)
15	3rd person plural. They will ask.	(1 + 2)
16	1st person singular. I shall destroy.	(1 + 2)
17	2nd person singular. You will call.	(1 + 2)
18	3rd person plural. They will have.	(1 + 2)
19	3rd person plural. They will build.	(1 + 2)
20	1st person plural. We shall prepare.	(1 + 2)

Total: 60

Exercise 10.15

1	1st person plural. We shall rule.	(1 + 2)
2	3rd person singular. He will consume.	(1 + 2)
3	1st person singular. I shall read.	(1 + 2)
4	3rd person plural. They will be.	(1 + 2)
5	2nd person plural. You will arrive.	(1 + 2)
6	1st person plural. We shall drink.	(1 + 2)
7	1st person singular. I shall run.	(1 + 2)
8	1st person plural. We shall run.	(1 + 2)
9	2nd person singular. You will hand over.	(1 + 2)
10	3rd person singular. He will send.	(1 + 2)
11	1st person plural. We shall decide.	(1 + 2)
12	1st person plural. We shall play.	(1 + 2)
13	2nd person singular. You will be.	(1 + 2)
14	2nd person singular. You will read.	(1 + 2)
15	1st person singular. I shall flee.	(1 + 2)
16	2nd person plural. You will decide.	(1 + 2)
17	3rd person plural. They will send.	(1 + 2)
18	3rd person plural. They will play.	(1 + 2)
19	2nd person plural. You will want.	(1 + 2)
20	1st person singular. I shall depart.	(1 + 2)

Total: 60

Exercise 10.16

1	He will flee.	(1)
2	We shall show.	(1)
3	You will be.	(1)
4	You will sleep.	(1)
5	We shall write.	(1)
6	They will run.	(1)
7	They will accept.	(1)
8	We shall capture.	(1)
9	He will sleep.	(1)
10	He will be.	(1)
11	We shall depart.	(1)
12	I shall sleep.	(1)
13	They will punish.	(1)
14	I shall come.	(1)
15	I shall be.	(1)
16	You will capture.	(1)
17	I shall throw.	(1)
18	You will accept.	(1)
19	You will place.	(1)
20	He will say.	(1)

Total: 20

Exercise 10.17

1	He runs.	(1)
2	He will run.	(1)
3	We rule.	(1)
4	We shall rule.	(1)
5	He will hurry.	(1)
6	We hurry.	(1)
7	He is.	(1)
8	He will be.	(1)
9	He will shout.	(1)
10	He will drink.	(1)
11	He drinks.	(1)
12	They will show.	(1)
13	They show.	(1)
14	He will punish.	(1)
15	He punishes.	(1)
16	We see.	(1)
17	We shall see.	(1)
18	They will remain.	(1)
19	They remain.	(1)
20	They will be.	(1)

Total: 20

Exercise 10.18

1	You will carry.	(1)	11	We sleep.	(1)
2	They prepare.	(1)	12	We enter.	(1)
3	I shall give.	(1)	13	You will laugh.	(1)
4	We destroy.	(1)	14	You will read.	(1)
5	We shall call.	(1)	15	I shall have.	(1)
6	You will destroy.	(1)	16	They will arrive.	(1)
7	We shall sleep.	(1)	17	He will flee.	(1)
8	He will tell.	(1)	18	He flees.	(1)
9	They have.	(1)	19	They capture.	(1)
10	You read.	(1)	20	You will have.	(1)

Total: 20

Exercise 10.19

1	imperfect. Yesterday the pupil was working.	(1 + 4)
2	present. Today the allies are fighting.	(1 + 4)
3	future. Tomorrow the priest will flee.	(1 + 4)
4	imperfect. Yesterday we were attacking the town.	(1 + 4)
5	present. Today we are attacking the town.	(1 + 4)
6	future. Tomorrow we shall capture the town.	(1 + 4)
7	imperfect. The boys were often running.	(1 + 4)
8	present. The boys never run.	(1 + 4)
9	future. The boys will run tomorrow.	(1 + 4)
10	imperfect. Once I watched the beautiful girls.	(1 + 5)
11	present. Today I am watching many beautiful girls.	(1 + 6)
12	future. Tomorrow I shall watch many beautiful girls.	(1 + 6)
13	imperfect. Yesterday the Romans were carrying shields.	(1 + 5)
14	present. Today the Romans are carrying shields.	(1 + 5)
15	future. Tomorrow the Romans will carry shields.	(1 + 5)
16	imperfect. Once a queen ruled the country.	(1 + 5)
17	present. The master praises the piety of the Romans.	(1 + 5)
18	future. Who will consume the new wine?	(1 + 5)
19	imperfect. Why were the young men fighting in the temple?	(1 + 6)
20	imperfect. Nine old men were approaching the mountain.	(1 + 6)

Total: 115

Exercise 10.20

1	imperfect. ambulabant.	(1 + 2)
2	imperfect. clamabat.	(1 + 2)
3	imperfect. laudabat.	(1 + 2)
4	imperfect. oppugnabant.	(1 + 2)
5	present. festinant.	(1 + 2)

Total: 15

Exercise 10.21

1	wine; vinum.	(1 + 1)
2	teachers; magistros.	(1 + 1)
3	the books; libros.	(1 + 1)
4	dinner; cenam.	(1 + 1)
5	the horses; equos.	(1 + 1)

Total: 10

Exercise 10.22

1	I shall approach the city.	(4)
2	The king has a beautiful wife.	(5)
3	The woman has a strong husband.	(5)
4	The old man was carrying wine and books to the sea.	(8)
5	We shall soon make a journey into the moutains.	(6)
6	The other soldiers were waiting for the tired young man for a long time.	(7)
7	The leader of the citizens was defending the famous city.	(6)
8	The old man will soon free the unhappy slave-girl.	(6)
9	Citizens, you will look at the mountains and the sea for a long time.	(7)
10	We shall lead nine young men into the sea.	(6)

Total: 60

Exercise 10.23

1	3rd person singular. **est**.	(1+2)
2	3rd person singular. **habebit**.	(1+2)
3	1st person plural. **ambulabamus**.	(1+2)
4	2nd person plural. **portabatis**.	(1+2)
5	3rd person plural. **pugnabunt**.	(1+2)

Total: 15

Exercise 10.24

1	You are indeed beautiful.	(2)
2	He does not want to choose.	(2)
3	Come back tomorrow.	(3)
4	He will decide who is the most beautiful.	(2)
5	It makes them angry.	(2)
6	She secretly offers to make him very powerful if he gives her the apple.	(4)
7	Athena also approached Paris in secret. She said to Paris, 'If you (will) choose me, I shall make you a very wise man.' Then the goddess went away. Afterwards, Venus approached Paris in secret. She said to Paris, 'If you (will) choose me, I shall give you a very beautiful woman. The woman will be your wife.' Then she went away. Paris was now alone.	(30)
8	a) woman; feminine	(2)
	b) alone; sole, solo, solitary	(2)
9	future	(1)
10	accusative (singular)	(1)
11	**dabant**	(1)
12	**discedo**	(1)
13	adverb	(1)
14	imperfect	(1)
15	a) **pueri semper laeti sunt**.	(5)
	b) **domini/magistri servos numquam laudant**.	(5)
	c) **multos libros ad magistrum portamus**.	(6)
	d) **Romani templa aedificabant**.	(4)

Total: 75

Chapter 11

Exercise 11.1

1 He plays.	(2)
2 He is not afraid, is he?	(2)
3 He is laughing, isn't he?	(2)
4 They were fighting.	(2)
5 Were they walking?	(2)
6 You were not working, were you?	(2)
7 They escaped.	(2)
8 Shall we sail?	(2)
9 You fled, didn't you?	(2)
10 They didn't arrive, did they?	(2)

Total: 20

Exercise 11.2

1 Achilles was fighting well.	(4)
2 Achilles was fighting well, wasn't he?	(5)
3 The Greeks were not fighting well, were they?	(5)
4 The soldier is strong/He is a strong soldier.	(4)
5 The soldier is strong/He is a strong soldier, isn't he?	(5)
6 The soldier is not strong/He is not a strong soldier, is he?	(5)
7 Hector was a famous soldier.	(5)
8 Hector was famous, wasn't he?	(5)
9 Hector was not a famous soldier, was he?	(6)
10 Hector was the leader of the Trojans, wasn't he?	(6)

Total: 50

Exercise 11.3

1 The citizens were defending (their) city well, weren't they?	(6)
2 The boy did not catch sight of the Trojan, did he?	(5)
3 The Greeks did not conquer the Romans, did they?	(5)
4 Strong/Brave citizens don't fear death, do they?	(6)
5 You caught sight of the woman in the city yesterday, didn't you?	(7)
6 You love your mother, don't you?	(5)
7 The Greeks collected many weapons, didn't they?	(6)
8 The woman did not want to kill (her) husband, did she?	(5)
9 The Roman soldiers fought well in the battle, didn't they?	(8)
10 The Trojans were not fleeing from the great city, were they?	(7)

Total: 60

Exercise 11.4

1 cum nautis clamabamus.	(4)
2 reginam timetis.	(3)
3 cenam cum puero parat.	(5)
4 femina clara pecuniam in villa parabat.	(7)
5 dominus/magister tamen Romanos non timet.	(6)

Total: 25

Exercise 11.5

1 pueri cum puellis bonis saepe pugnant. (7)
2 Romani in oppido numquam pugnant. (6)
3 deos in templo laudabas. (5)
4 muros prope villam non aedificabam. (6)
5 puer parvus hasta magna pugnabat. (6)

Total: 30

Exercise 11.6

1 You are playing; I am working. (4)
2 We are Romans; you are Greeks. (6)
3 We do not love you. (4)
4 You do not love us. (4)
5 I do not love you. (4)
6 You do not love me. (4)
7 No one saw me. (3)
8 I love the girl. (3)
9 The girl does not love me. (4)
10 I saw you in the city. (4)

Total: 40

Exercise 11.7

1 The enemy are watching us. (4)
2 The Romans do not like us. (5)
3 My father likes you. (5)
4 I shall punish you, slave! (4)
5 Who is calling me? (4)
6 The master is calling you. (4)
7 The woman was watching you. (4)
8 Who will give me money? (5)
9 I will give you a lot of money. (6)
10 The girls will play with us. (4)

Total: 45

Exercise 11.8

1 Why was Paris standing near me? (6)
2 The enemy were often fighting against us. (6)
3 My father will give you money. (6)
4 Ambassadors, the master will give you silver. (6)
5 The Carthaginians won't hurry to me, will they? (6)
6 My friends will play with me, won't they? (5)
7 A few companions were singing with us. (5)
8 The master never gives us presents. (6)
9 The old man gave me a present and you (some) money. (7)
10 Why does the master like you, not me? (7)

Total: 60

Exercise 11.9

1 3rd person plural, imperfect. **pugnabant**. (3 + 2)
2 3rd person plural, imperfect. **spectabant**. (3 + 2)
3 1st person singular, present. **porto**. (3 + 2)
4 3rd person singular, present. **parat**. (3 + 2)
5 3rd person plural, imperfect. **delebant**. (3 + 2)
6 1st person plural, present. **ambulamus**. (3 + 2)
7 3rd person singular, imperfect. **vocabat**. (3 + 2)
8 3rd person singular, present. **intrat**. (3 + 2)
9 3rd person singular, imperfect. **laudabat**. (3 + 2)
10 3rd person singular, imperfect. **monebat**. (3 + 2)

Total: 50

Exercise 11.10

1	I saw the blood-stained beard of wretched Hector.	(6)
2	He wounded wretched Hector with a big spear.	(6)
3	The priest warned the stupid Trojans again.	(6)
4	The charioteer seized the big and swift horse.	(6)
5	The famous king collected (his) cavalry immediately.	(6)
		Total: 30

Exercise 11.11

1	We break through the walls and throw open the city's fortifications.	(8)
2	First before everyone Laocoon runs down from the citadel.	(8)
3	Then he hurled a big spear into the side of the horse.	(8)
4	The shepherds were dragging the young man with loud shouting to the king.	(8)
5	The priest Laocoon was sacrificing a big bull at the altar.	(8)
		Total: 40

Exercise 11.12

1	ablative singular. The soldiers fought bravely in the battle.	(1 + 6)
2	ablative singular. I caught sight of the citizen in the city yesterday.	(1 + 6)
3	accusative plural. Many ships were defending the island against the enemy.	(1 + 7)
4	nominative plural. The soldiers were fighting well in the battle.	(1 + 6)
5	accusative plural. The Romans were often waging war against the Greeks.	(1 + 7)
6	genitive plural. The weapons of the Roman soldiers were new.	(1 + 6)
7	ablative singular. The companions departed from the island in (their) ships without delay.	(1 + 9)
8	ablative plural. The enemy wounded many citizens with (their) weapons.	(1 + 6)
9	accusative singular. The master did not like me because I was never working.	(1 + 9)
10	accusative plural. The enemy forces received many wounds from us.	(1 + 8)
		Total: 80

Exercise 11.13

1	future. The Roman citizens will never fear the enemy.	(1 + 6)
2	imperfect. The leader was fighting well against the Trojan soldiers.	(1 + 7)
3	future. They will defend the city with big walls.	(1 + 5)
4	imperfect. The soldiers were attacking the city with spears and arrows.	(1 + 6)
5	present. The old men and the parents of the girls are very much afraid of the leader of the enemy.	(1 + 9)
6	future. At last we will make a journey into the city.	(1 + 6)
7	perfect. The leader's companions greeted the the woman's sons.	(1 + 6)
8	present. You are afraid of death, aren't you?	(1 + 4)
9	perfect. The Trojans killed seven soldiers.	(1 + 5)
10	imperfect. The wounds of the enemy were not bad, were they?	(1 + 6)
		Total: 70

Exercise 11.14

1   Protesilaus was dead. The Greeks had rushed against the walls of Troy. They had fought bravely and for
    a long time beneath the walls, but in vain. They had wounded many Trojans, they had killed many Trojans,
    but they had not captured the city.
    Agamemnon, Menelaus's brother, was the leader of the Greeks. He was not happy. He said to (his)
    soldiers, 'Companions, we shall not capture Troy today. The walls of Troy are high and strong. The citizens
    of Troy are also strong. They defend (their) walls well. I order you to pitch camp. Sleep well! Tomorrow we
    will fight against the enemy again.'
    After the Greek soldiers had listened to Agamemnon's words, they pitched camp.
    They were tired and soon they slept.   (30)
2   **muros** = walls. A mural is a painting on a wall.   (2)
3   a) nominative;   (1)
    b) because it refers to the subject of the sentence (he);

    or
    because it is the complement of the verb **erat**.   (1)
4   **capio**.   (1)
5   a) 3rd person plural;   (1)
    b) present.   (1)
6   a) accusative;   (1)
    b) it is the object.   (1)
7   adjective.   (1)

                                                                                          Total: 40

Exercise 11.15

1   <u>templum</u> aedificaverant.   (1)
2   <u>reginam</u> viderat.   (1)
3   <u>muros</u> deleveras.   (1)
4   <u>ad</u> oppidum ambulaveramus.   (1)
5   <u>saepe</u> cum amicis pugno.   (1)
6   puerum <u>malum</u> puniveratis   (1)
7   in <u>oppidum</u> iter fecerat.   (1)
8   <u>epistulam</u> ad amicum meum miserat.   (1)
9   magistrum <u>semper</u> audimus.   (1)
10 in villam <u>vinum</u> portaverant.   (1)

                                        Total: 10

Exercise 11.16

1   We had loved.   (2)
2   They had captured.   (2)
3   You had heard.   (2)
4   He had ruled.   (2)
5   I had given.   (2)
6   He had led.   (2)
7   We had warned.   (2)
8   He had terrified.   (2)
9   They had replied.   (2)
10 I had sent.   (2)

                    Total: 20

Exercise 11.17

1   He had placed.   (2)
2   They had run.   (2)
3   You had departed.   (2)
4   I had read.   (2)
5   We had slept.   (2)
6   We had walked.   (2)
7   He had fled.   (2)
8   You had made/done.   (2)
9   We had laughed.   (2)
10 You had destroyed.   (2)

                    Total: 20

Exercise 11.18

1   We had remained.   (2)
2   They had seen.   (2)
3   He had fought.   (2)
4   They had entered.   (2)
5   He had captured.   (2)
6   You had warned.   (2)
7   He had drunk.   (2)
8   He had said.   (2)
9   We had played.   (2)
10 You had killed.   (2)

                    Total: 20

Exercise 11.19

1 The master was angry because we had laughed. (7)
2 The boy had not read the book. (5)
3 The boys had been bad. (4)
4 The girl had wounded the boy. (4)
5 We had not heard the words. (4)
6 The master was happy because he had slept well. (8)
7 The young men had worked well. (4)
8 At last the wife had departed. (4)
9 The mistress had prepared the food. (4)
10 The friend had given a lot of money to you. (6)

Total: 50

Exercise 11.20

1 The enemy were happy because we had gone away. (7)
2 The gods had conquered the Romans. (4)
3 They had never destroyed the city. (4)
4 We had arrived quickly. (3)
5 They had captured many towns. (4)
6 The boy was running quickly because he had seen the master. (8)
7 The angry master had caught sight of the freedman. (5)
8 The strong soldiers had terrified the citizens. (5)
9 At last the man had killed the leader. (5)
10 The bad soldier had wounded (his) sister. (5)

Total: 50

Exercise 11.21

1 The boy had worked for a long time. (4)
2 The leader had been angry. (4)
3 The soldiers had fought well. (4)
4 I had slept well. (3)
5 The unhappy boy had not laughed. (5)
6 The battle had been long;
   or
   It had been a long battle. (4)
7 The enemy had overcome many lands. (5)
8 The master had freed many slaves. (5)
9 The king of the enemy had hurried to the river. (6)
10 The soldiers had attacked the town bravely. (5)

Total: 45

Exercise 11.22

1	Twelve young men had run out of the town.	(6)
2	No one had read (the) sixteen books.	(5)
3	The tired messenger had said nothing.	(5)
4	The old man had drunk a lot of water.	(5)
5	The woman had received eleven wounds.	(5)
6	He had sent fourteen presents to (his) father.	(6)
7	Twenty soldiers had hurried into the river.	(6)
8	We had not caught sight of (the) seventeen girls.	(5)
9	(The) eighteen soldiers had not fought well.	(6)
10	Eleven citizens had defended the town bravely.	(6)

Total: 55

Exercise 11.23

1	hostes <u>numquam</u> superaveramus.	(1)
2	urbem <u>saepe</u> occupaverant.	(1)
3	regem <u>miserum</u> vulneraverat.	(1)
4	oppidum <u>magnum</u> defenderamus.	(1)
5	puellam <u>pulchram</u> videram.	(1)

Total: 5

Exercise 11.24

1	<u>multa</u> templa dux deleverat.	(1)
2	miles amicum <u>hasta</u> vulneraverat.	(1)
3	hostes contra <u>oppidum</u> ruerant.	(1)
4	<u>nautae</u> navem diu exspectaverant.	(1)
5	Graeci <u>multos</u> Romanos occiderant.	(1)

Total: 5

Exercise 11.25

1	**vocant**; they call.	(2)
2	**habebamus**; we had.	(2)
3	**deletis**; you destroy.	(2)
4	**videbas**; you saw.	(2)
5	**parat**; he prepares.	(2)

Total: 10

Exercise 11.26

1	1st person plural, future tense of **defendo**; we shall defend.	(4 + 2)
2	3rd person singular, imperfect tense of **trado**; he was handing over.	(4 + 2)
3	3rd person singular, pluperfect tense of **vinco**; he had conquered.	(4 + 2)
4	2nd person plural, future tense of **sum**; you will be.	(4 + 2)
5	3rd person singular, perfect tense of **accipio**; he has received.	(4 + 2)

Total: 30

Exercise 11.27

1	virtutem non <u>habeo</u>.	(2)
2	hostes saevi <u>erant</u>.	(2)
3	<u>Romanos</u> <u>numquam</u> superabimus.	(2)
4	<u>oppidum</u> <u>magnum</u> cras occupabunt.	(2)
5	<u>Romani</u> Graecos <u>non</u> superaverunt.	(2)

Total: 10

Exercise 11.28

1	vir virtutem magnam <u>habet</u>.	(2)
2	virtus militum clara <u>erat</u>.	(2)
3	cives muros oppidi <u>delebant</u>.	(2)
4	milites urbem <u>hastis</u> <u>et</u> sagittis oppugnabant	(2)
5	<u>amicos</u> meos in urbe <u>saepe</u> video.	(2)

Total: 10

Exercise 11.29

1	**parabant**; they were preparing.	(1 + 2)
2	**vocabat**; he was calling.	(1 + 2)
3	**monebamus**; we were warning.	(1 + 2)
4	**timebamus**; we were fearing.	(1 + 2)
5	**aedificabatis**; you were building.	(1 + 2)
6	**delebat**; he was destroying.	(1 + 2)
7	**videbant**; they saw.	(1 + 2)
8	**clamabat**; he was shouting.	(1 + 2)
9	**amabat**; he was loving.	(1 + 2)
10	**portabam**; I was carrying.	(1 + 2)

Total: 30

Exercise 11.30

1 The Greeks had not yet captured Troy. (2)
2 They had pitched camp near the city. (2)
3 **diu**; for a long time. (2)
4 They were unable to destroy the walls. (2)
5 It made them angry. (2)
6 Priam was the king of Troy. The king had many strong children. One of his sons, called Hector, was a man of great courage. Hector always fought bravely for the Trojans. There were also many brave soldiers among the Greeks. Achilles however was the strongest (of them). Achilles had a friend called Patroclus. Because Hector had killed Patroclus in battle, Achilles greatly hated the Trojans. (30)
7 Preposition. (1)
8 Imperfect. (1)
9 Accusative (plural). (1)
10 Genitive (singular). (1)
11 **pugnabant**. (2)
12 a) 3rd; (1)
   b) nominative (plural). (1)
13 a) **prope urbem, inter Graecos**; (1)
   b) **virtutis**; (1)
   c) **pro Troianis, in proelio**. (1)
14 The Latin word **urbem** means *city*. Urban affairs are those to do with a city. (2)
14 The Latin word **nomine** means by *name*. To nominate someone is to name them. (2)

Total: 55

Exercise 11.31

1	**regina deos claros timebat**.	(5)
2	**pueri miseri equum gladio monebant**.	(6)
3	**feminae ad templum ambulant**.	(5)
4	**Augustus dominus bonus erat**.	(4)

Total: 20

Chapter 12

Exercise 12.1

1 Menelaus was a Greek soldier. He was a good man/That man was good.	(10)
2 Helen was Menelaus's wife. She was a beautiful woman/That woman was beautiful.	(10)
3 There is a forum in the city. It is a big forum.	(10)
4 Marcus has a son. He loves him.	(7)
5 Marcus has a daughter. He loves her.	(7)
6 Marcus has a son and a daughter. He loves them.	(9)
7 Marcus has a son. He gives him money.	(8)
8 It is a big island/The island is big. Many inhabitants live in it.	(10)
9 Marcus received many books. He is always reading them.	(9)
10 Marcus has a beautiful wife. Her name is Aurelia.	(10)
	Total: 90

Exercise 12.2

1 Aurelia has fifteen friends. Her friends are famous.	(10)
2 Marcus and Aurelia have seventeen slaves. Their slaves are good.	(12)
3 Marcus often gives them money.	(6)
4 Marcus is reading a long book. There are many words in it.	(10)
5 Marcus sent good wine to Aurelia. She is now drinking it.	(12)
6 Marcus has many weapons. His weapons are new.	(10)
7 The master had built twelve temples. He likes them.	(8)
8 The king likes (his) children. He often gives them lots of money.	(10)
9 The boy had asked for water. The master gave it to him.	(9)
10 The forum is new. We are now looking at it.	(8)
	Total: 95

Exercise 12.3

1 The master did not like the bad boy. He was therefore punishing him.	(10)
2 Protesilaus was fighting bravely. However the Trojans soon killed him.	(10)
3 The Greeks rushed against the Trojans. They killed sixteen of them.	(10)
4 The brave soldier had received seven wounds. His wounds were bad.	(11)
5 The master had a good slave, called Sextus. He freed him yesterday.	(11)
6 The ship was big. There were nineteen sailors in it.	(10)
7 The master said many words. However no one was listening to them.	(10)
8 Many girls were approaching. We soon caught sight of them.	(8)
9 The Roman soldiers were good. The Greeks had not overcome them.	(10)
10 The farmers had twenty fields. Their fields were big.	(10)
	Total: 100

Exercise 12.4

1 When the friend came, the man greeted him.	(8)
2 My master has a beautiful wife. I often see her.	(10)
3 The woman was beautiful. Many men loved her.	(9)
4 The city was big. The Romans decided to seize it.	(9)
5 The master's wine is good. I often drink it.	(9)
6 The Greeks had collected many weapons. They put them in (their) ships.	(10)
7 Menelaus and Helen were Greeks. He was famous, she was beautiful.	(12)
8 Because the citizens were good, the master gave them lots of money.	(11)
9 Because he loved the girl, the boy gave her many presents.	(10)
10 We shall soon capture the city with their help, shan't we?	(7)
	Total: 95

Exercise 12.5

1 fratrem <u>habeo.</u> eum amo. (2)
2 sororem <u>habet.</u> eam amo. (2)
3 nomen novum <u>habes.</u> id non amo. (2)
4 multos <u>equos</u> habetis. eos amo. (1)
5 <u>multas</u> filias habemus. eas amo. (2)
6 <u>dominus/magister</u> viginti dona ei dedit. (1)
7 fratrem eius non <u>amo.</u> (2)
8 puellas <u>spectabam;</u> matrem earum non amabam. (2)
9 arma eorum nova erant. <u>prope</u> muros ea posuerunt. (1)
10 undeviginti amicos habeo. <u>pecuniam</u> eis dedi. (1)

Total: 16

Exercise 12.6

1 ambulabamus. We were walking. (1 + 2)
2 nautae clamabant. The sailors were shouting. (2 + 3)
3 deos laudamus. We praise the gods. (2 + 3)
4 pueros monebatis. You were warning the boys. (2 + 3)
5 pueri amicos habent. The boys have friends. (3 + 4)

Total: 25

Exercise 12.7

1 reginae spectant. The queens are watching. (2 + 3)
2 puellas videtis. You see the girls. (2 + 3)
3 amicos vocabatis. You were calling the friends. (2 + 3)
4 cum amicis ambulatis. You are walking with (your) friends. (3 + 4)
5 Romani gladiis non pugnant. The Romans are not fighting with swords. (3 + 5)

Total: 30

Exercise 12.8

1 amicum laudabat. He praised (his) friend. (2 + 2)
2 reginam monebat. He warned the queen. (2 + 2)
3 amicum laudas. You praise the friend. (2 + 2)
4 puella librum non portabat. The girl was not carrying the book. (3 + 4)
5 epistulam spectabat. He was looking at the letter. (3 + 3)

Total: 25

Exercise 12.9

1 Romanus erat. He was a Roman. (2 + 3)
2 templum magnum est. The temple is big. (3 + 4)
3 nauta pugnabat. The sailor was fighting. (2 + 3)
4 agricola ambulat. The farmer is walking. (2 + 3)
5 mones. You are warning. (1 + 2)

Total: 25

Exercise 12.10

1	exspectabant. They were waiting for.	(1 + 2)
2	conspexit. He caught sight of.	(1 + 2)
3	ruam. I shall rush.	(1 + 2)
4	occidebatis. You were killing.	(1 + 2)
5	es. You are.	(1 + 2)

Total: 15

Exercise 12.11

1	3rd person plural, pluperfect, **conspicio**; they had caught sight of.	(4 + 2)
2	2nd person singular, perfect, **fugio**; you have fled.	(4 + 2)
3	3rd person singular, future, **ruo**; he will rush.	(4 + 2)
4	2nd person plural, pluperfect, **occido**; you had killed.	(4 + 2)
5	1st person plural, perfect, **accipio**; I have received.	(4 + 2)

Total: 30

Exercise 12.12

1	Because the winds were favourable, they prepared their ships.	(3)
2	They quickly sailed in them across the sea.	(3)
3	No one wanted to disembark from the ships.	(3)
4	a) The gods.	(1)
	b) The first one to disembark at Troy will be the first to die.	(5)
5	For a long time the Greeks did nothing. Among them was a soldier called Protesilaus. Because he was not afraid of death, he shouted, 'Watch me, companions! I am brave. I am bold. I shall be the first to disembark on Trojan soil. In this way I shall be famous.'	(30)
6	a) i) is, eos, eis;	(1)
	ii) vulnera, miles;	(1)
	iii) statim, ubi, tandem.	(1)
	b) **vulnera** = wounds. Vulnerable means in danger of being wounded.	(2)
	c) i) accusative (plural)	(1)
	ii) It is after the preposition **contra** (+ acc.)	(1)
	d) i) Perfect	(1)
	ii) accipio.	(1)
	e) clari	(1)

Total: 55

Exercise 12.13

1	deos non timeo.	(4)
2	puer murum magnum aedificabat.	(5)
3	servi Romanos semper necant.	(5)
4	viri boni cum domino/magistro ambulabant.	(6)

Total: 20

Exercise 12.14

1	contra <u>Romanos</u> cras ruemus.	(1)
2	<u>oppidum</u> armis oppugnabimus.	(1)
3	mors seni <u>mox</u> veniet.	(1)
4	vulnera regis mala <u>sunt</u>.	(2)
5	<u>nautae</u> propter moram hodie aberant.	(1)

Total: 6

Exercise 12.15

1	the noble king	(2)
2	the noble kings	(2)
3	a difficult death	(2)
4	difficult women	(2)
5	the brave soldier	(2)
6	the brave soldiers	(2)
7	all the girls	(2)
8	the sad men	(2)
9	the brave freedman	(2)
10	the cruel wounds	(2)
11	the fortunate son	(2)
12	the difficult journey	(2)
13	the cruel husbands	(2)
14	the sad mistress	(2)
15	of the huge temple	(2)
16	with the noble prisoners	(3)
17	in the huge forum	(3)
18	out of the beautiful garden	(3)
19	with the fortunate prisoners	(3)
20	without the wise companions	(3)

Total: 45

Exercise 12.16

1	all the rivers	(2)
2	all the spears	(2)
3	the brave leader	(2)
4	the brave leaders	(2)
5	the cruel women	(2)
6	the brave enemy	(2)
7	the easy word	(2)
8	the difficult book	(2)
9	the noble men	(2)
10	the difficult way	(2)
11	the cruel words	(2)
12	the cruel word	(2)
13	the sad freedmen	(2)
14	the noble name	(2)
15	the sad mistress	(2)
16	to the noble queen	(3)
17	in the huge garden	(3)
18	with the wise husband	(3)
19	near the huge forum	(3)
20	without the bold forces	(3)

Total: 45

Exercise 12.17

1	accusative (singular), masculine. You had a cruel master.	(2 + 4)
2	accusative (singular), neuter. You love the easy word.	(2 + 4)
3	accusative (plural), neuter. They praise all the wines.	(2 + 4)
4	accusative (plural), masculine. I read all the books.	(2 + 4)
5	accusative (plural), feminine. I was looking at all the parts.	(2 + 4)
6	accusative (plural), neuter. I am not carrying everything.	(2 + 4)
7	accusative (singular), feminine. We were entering the huge wood.	(2 + 4)
8	accusative (singular), masculine. They had praised the brave leader.	(2 + 4)
9	accusative (plural), masculine. He sees the sad freedmen.	(2 + 4)
10	accusative (plural), feminine. I praise all the woods.	(2 + 4)

Total: 60

Exercise 12.18

1	pluperfect. The fortunate master had freed the brave slave.	(1 + 6)
2	present. You love all the girls.	(1 + 4)
3	present. I do not love everyone.	(1 + 4)
4	perfect. The teacher praised the difficult books.	(1 + 6)
5	perfect. They killed the cruel master with a huge sword.	(1 + 6)
6	future. We shall always fear the cruel soldiers.	(1 + 6)
7	pluperfect. The brave soldiers had praised the bold citizen.	(1 + 7)
8	imperfect. The boy was brave.	(1 + 4)
9	future. He will give all the weapons to you.	(1 + 5)
10	perfect. You heard the cruel words of the wise mistress, didn't you?	(1 + 7)

Total: 65

Exercise 12.19

1	adjective. Your master is brave and strong.	(1 + 7)
2	noun. Those soldiers are brave and strong.	(1 + 7)
3	(demonstrative) pronoun. That girl is noble.	(1 + 5)
4	adjective. That book is difficult.	(1 + 5)
5	verb. My master is cruel but bold.	(1 + 7)
6	conjunction. However all the boys are working.	(1 + 5)
7	(interrogative) adverb. Why are you sad, boy?	(1 + 5)
8	conjunction. I am sad because the master is cruel.	(1 + 8)
9	adjective. All the words are difficult.	(1 + 5)
10	verb. The king of the city is not noble, is he?	(1 + 6)

Total: 70

Exercise 12.20

1	nominative (singular). The cruel master punishes all the boys.	(1 + 6)
2	ablative (singular). We are reading an easy book with the master.	(1 + 6)
3	accusative (singular). I did not like that noble woman.	(1 + 6)
4	ablative (plural). They were all playing in the woods.	(1 + 5)
5	nominative (plural). Not all the masters are cruel.	(1 + 6)
6	accusative (singular). The sad slaves fear the cruel master.	(1 + 6)
7	nominative (singular). The noble master praises the citizens.	(1 + 5)
8	accusative (plural). My brother prepares everything.	(1 + 5)
9	accusative (plural). We often make difficult journeys.	(1 + 5)
10	nominative (singular). The slaves are sad because (their) master is often cruel.	(1 + 10)

Total: 70

Exercise 12.21

1	silva <u>magna</u>	(1)
2	<u>libri</u> difficiles	(1)
3	in <u>saevo</u> bello	(1)
4	cum puella <u>laeta</u>	(1)
5	<u>dominos/magistros</u> crudeles	(1)
6	propter milites <u>claros</u>	(1)
7	in silva <u>magna</u>	(1)
8	milites <u>miseri/tristes</u>	(1)
9	cives <u>malos</u>	(1)
10	cum comitibus <u>saevis</u>	(1)

Total: 10

Exercise 12.22

1	<u>via</u> facili	(1)
2	cum <u>puero</u> crudeli	(1)
3	<u>cum</u> militibus fortibus	(1)
4	omnes <u>puellae</u>	(1)
5	<u>hasta</u> crudeli	(1)
6	ad <u>dominum/magistrum</u> nobilem	(1)
7	<u>hastis</u> omnibus	(1)
8	pueri fortis, <u>tamen</u>	(1)
9	<u>cum</u> puella nobili	(1)
10	<u>libro</u> tristi	(1)

Total: 10

Exercise 12.23

1	regina nobilis tristis <u>erat</u>.	(2)
2	omnes pueri sapientes vinum <u>amant</u>.	(2)
3	rex crudelis militem <u>miserum</u> punivit.	(1)
4	omnia bella crudelia <u>sunt</u>.	(2)
5	murus <u>clarus</u> et ingens erat.	(1)
6	<u>viri</u> audaces bene pugnaverant.	(1)
7	omnes hostes <u>saevos</u> superabimus.	(1)
8	omnes cives regem nobilem <u>timebant</u>.	(2)
9	<u>dominum/magistrum</u> crudelem non amamus.	(1)
10	is rex nobilis <u>est</u>.	(2)
11	villae omnium civium <u>magnae</u> sunt.	(1)
12	omnes agricolae <u>in</u> silva ingenti bene laborabant.	(1)
13	laborare cum <u>ancilla</u> crudeli facile non est.	(1)
14	civis fortis <u>prope</u> forum ingens pugnabat.	(1)
15	<u>ad</u> urbem itinere facili advenimus.	(1)

Total: 20

Exercise 12.24

1	Because Hector had killed Patroclus.	(2)
2	He wanted to kill Hector.	(2)
3	Near the city of Troy.	(1)
4	**fortiter**; bravely.	(1 + 1)
5	**subito**; suddenly.	(1 + 1)
6	He shouted, 'Listen to me, Hector!'	(2)
7	He said he was very brave, whereas Hector was a cruel man.	(2)
8	He threatened to kill him.	(2)
9	When Hector heard Achilles's words, he replied to him, 'Listen to my words, Achilles! I am happy because I killed your friend Patroclus. I am not afraid of you. You do not frighten me. You are not brave. You are not bold. Come! Fight! Victory will be easy for me. I will soon defeat you.	(30)
10 a)	occiderat.	(1)
b)	audi, veni, pugna.	(1)
c)	me, ego, tu.	(1)
d)	occidam, vincam, erit.	(1)
11	accusative (singular), because it follows **prope** (+ acc.).	(2)
12	perfect; **conspicio**.	(2)
13	**clamavit** means he shouted. An exclamation is when one shouts.	(1)
14	neuter.	(1)

Total: 55

Chapter 13

Exercise 13.1

1	The more famous master	(2)
2	The wiser woman	(2)
3	The more savage god	(2)
4	The bolder Roman	(2)
5	The braver leader	(2)
6	The more wretched citizens	(2)
7	The angrier farmers	(2)
8	The wiser freedmen	(2)
9	The higher mountains	(2)
10	The fiercer battles	(2)

Total: 20

Exercise 13.2

1	Into the deeper river	(3)
2	Near the bigger temples	(3)
3	With the more beautiful wives	(3)
4	Without the better forces	(3)
5	Over the bigger walls	(3)
6	Among the smaller boys	(3)
7	After the longer battles	(3)
8	In the deeper sea	(3)
9	With the worse masters	(3)
10	On account of the more miserable parents	(3)

Total: 30

Exercise 13.3

1	The boldest/very bold enemy	(2)
2	The deepest/very deep river	(2)
3	The cruelest/very cruel woman	(2)
4	The bravest/very brave soldier	(2)
5	The bravest/very brave soldiers	(2)
6	The most beautiful/very beautiful wife	(2)
7	The longest/very long book	(2)
8	The longest/very long rivers	(2)
9	The largest/very large crowd	(2)
10	The most difficult/very difficult journey	(2)

Total: 20

Exercise 13.4

1	All the Roman soldiers were bolder.	(6)
2	The girl's sister is more fortunate.	(5)
3	All the masters are wiser.	(5)
4	That girl has a more famous brother.	(6)
5	The soldiers always loved the luckier leader.	(6)
6	The poets are afraid of the very cruel woman.	(5)
7	All the farmers were working well.	(5)
8	We love the wise father of the more beautiful girl.	(6)
9	We come/came to the city by an easier route (journey).	(6)
10	We shall soon capture more prisoners.	(5)

Total: 55

Exercise 13.5

1	My friend is brave; your friend is braver.	(10)
2	That soldier is braver than the leader.	(7)
3	That river is long; the deepest river is longer.	(10)
4	Your body is longer than mine.	(7)
5	That girl is wiser than my brother.	(8)
6	The masters are wiser than the boys.	(7)
7	Greek masters are often very wise.	(6)
8	The Roman temple is higher than my villa.	(8)
9	My book is not easy, but is very difficult.	(8)
10	The Roman soldiers were braver than the Greek soldiers.	(9)

Total: 80

Exercise 13.6

1 The soldiers are bolder than the Trojan citizens. (7)
2 That girl is very beautiful; I have never seen a more beautiful girl. (10)
3 That Roman master was very angry; I have never seen an angrier master. (11)
4 The Roman soldier was very bold; I have never seen a bolder soldier. (10)
5 That woman was very sad; I have never seen a sadder woman. (10)
6 Achilles was a very brave but very cruel soldier. (7)
7 The Romans were often bolder than the Greeks. (8)
8 The Greek cities were more beautiful than the Roman ciites. (8)
9 All the women were wiser than the men. (8)
10 The Romans were famous, but the Greeks were more famous than the Romans. (11)

Total: 90

Exercise 13.7

1 Brutus <u>vir</u> sapientissimus erat. (1)
2 murum altissimum <u>aedificabas</u>. (2)
3 hostes milites audacissimos <u>habebant</u>. (2)
4 regem felicissimum <u>monemus</u>. (2)
5 dominum crudelissimum <u>timet</u>. (2)
6 <u>equi</u> fessi itinera longissima faciebant. (1)
7 regina cives fortissimos <u>laudat</u>. (2)
8 uxorem carissimam <u>amat</u>. (2)
9 templum sacrissimum <u>aedificabatis</u>. (2)
10 cenas optimas <u>parat</u>. (2)

Total: 18

Exercise 13.8

1 verbis laetissimis <u>clamat</u>. (2)
2 murum altiorem <u>spectabamus</u>. (2)
3 magistrum iratissimum <u>vocabas</u>. (2)
4 cum pueris felicissimis non <u>pugnabam</u>. (2)
5 nomen viri sapientioris <u>habet</u>. (2)
6 cum <u>puella</u> pulchriore saepe ambulant. (1)
7 donum regi clarissimo <u>est</u>. (2)
8 iram dominorum crudelissimorum <u>timet</u>. (2)
9 <u>pecuniam</u> eis post bellum longissimum dedit. (1)
10 <u>libros</u> ad urbem itinere faciliore portabat. (1)

Total: 17

Exercise 13.9

1 <u>filius</u> meus altissimus clarissimusque est. (1)
2 Marcus sapientior quam Flavia <u>est</u>. (2)
3 nonne pueri sapientiores quam <u>puellae</u> sunt? (1)
4 templum altius quam muri urbis <u>non</u> est. (1)
5 <u>puellas</u> pulcherrimas spectabant. (1)

Total: 6

Exercise 13.10

1 Achilles was watching Hector. Hector was watching Achilles. Hector was a very brave and very bold man. However Achilles was braver and bolder than Hector. Suddenly Hector threw his spear. The spear flew towards Achilles. However it stuck in Achilles's shield. When Achilles saw the Trojan's spear, he laughed. Then he spoke cruel words to Hector as follows: 'You have not killed me, Hector,' he said. 'I am braver than you. I am the bravest of all the Greeks. Now I shall kill you.' With these words (thus he spoke and) he threw his spear at Hector. The spear stuck in Hector's body. Hector fell to the ground, dead. Achilles was very happy. He laughed. (30)

2 a) me = me; te = you; (1 + 1)
   b) fortior = braver; audacior = bolder; (1 + 1)
   c) fortissimus = bravest; audacissimus = boldest; laetissimus = very happy. (1 + 1)

3 a) Subject = Hector; object = hastam; (2)
   b) 3rd person singular, perfect; (3)
   c) iacio. (1)

4 accusative (singular); because it follows ad (+ acc.) (2)
5 audacior means bolder. Audacious is another word for bold. (2)
6 ablative (singular); because it follows in (+ abl.) (2)
7 accusative (singular); because it follows ad (+ acc.) (2)

Total: 50

Exercise 13.11

1 dux clarus audacissimus erat. (1)
2 amicum felicissimum habeo. (1)
3 dux multas hastas in templum iecit. (1)
4 viri sapientissimi mortem saepe timent. (2)
5 multae hastae ducem fortissimum vulnerabant. (1)
6 gladii hostium longiores quam sagittae erant. (2)
7 muri oppidi ingentes erant. (1)
8 urbem multis hastis oppugnamus. (1)
9 virtus civis boni regem sapientissimum semper terrebat. (1)
10 gladii militum longissimi erant. (1)

Total: 12

Exercise 13.12

1 I am a good freedman, but you are better. (10)
2 Sextus is a very bad boy, isn't he? (6)
3 Julius Caesar was a very good (the best) leader. (6)
4 Our temple is bigger than the walls of the town. (8)
5 Alexander was a better soldier than Julius Caesar. (8)
6 Your mother's food was very good. (6)
7 The very big ships were approaching the very small island. (7)
8 I have more money than you. (7)
9 Italy is bigger than Britain. (6)
10 Britain is smaller than Italy. (6)

Total: 70

Exercise 13.13

1 That wood is very small. (5)
2 The boy is bigger than the girl. (6)
3 Very many bold soldiers seized the town. (6)
4 The master was the worst of all the masters. (6)
5 The Romans are better than the Greeks. (6)
6 The Trojans are worse than the Greeks. (6)
7 The Roman soldiers were the best/very good. (5)
8 The Romans had better soldiers than the Greeks. (7)
9 The Greeks had worse soliders than the Romans. (7)
10 Very many citizens were defending the very big town. (6)

Total: 60

Exercise 13.14

1 My wound is very bad. (5)
2 I have never had (received) a worse wound. (5)
3 The mountains of Italy are bigger than the mountains of Britain. (9)
4 The walls of Troy were once very big. (6)
5 The soldiers were in very great danger. (6)
6 The farmer has very many very big fields. (7)
7 There are very many horses in the woods. (6)
8 I have never sailed in a bigger ship than that (one). (8)
9 The Greeks had built bigger and better temples than the Romans. (9)
10 The temples of the Romans were smaller and worse than those of the Greeks. (9)

Total: 70

Exercise 13.15

1 <u>puer</u> pessimus erat. (1)
2 <u>puellae</u> optimae erant. (1)
3 dux plurimos milites <u>habebat</u>. (2)
4 <u>Romani</u> plurimas naves habebant. (1)
5 duces optimos <u>semper</u> cupimus. (1)
6 <u>templum</u> maius aedificabatis. (1)
7 in <u>villa</u> minima habitant. (1)
8 bellum ferocissimum omnes <u>timemus</u>. (2)
9 puellae minores feminam crudelem <u>non</u> <u>timent</u>. (3)
10 mater mea magistrum optimum <u>laudat</u>. (2)

Total: 15

Exercise 13.16

1	accusative (singular). The freedman loves his very beautiful wife.	(1 + 5)
2	accusative (plural). We never listened to the very wise words.	(1 + 5)
3	accusative (plural). They quickly prepared very big ships.	(1 + 5)
4	accusative (plural). The very savage Greeks had terrified the citizens.	(1 + 5)
5	accusative (plural). Very beautiful women do not praise the men.	(1 + 6)
6	nominative (plural). The Roman soldiers have very big bodies.	(1 + 6)
7	genitive (singular). They built very big temples near the walls of the city.	(1 + 7)
8	accusative (singular). The bold leader led (his) soldiers into the very big forum.	(1 + 8)
9	accusative (singular). You don't have a very big shield, do you?	(1 + 5)
10	ablative (plural). Why were the nine very big boys reading in the woods?	(1 + 8)

Total: 70

Exercise 13.17

1	accusative (plural). Very many women loved (their) noble husbands.	(1 + 6)
2	ablative (singular). The sailor hurried out of the very deep water.	(1 + 6)
3	dative (plural). The boy gave many gifts to his parents.	(1 + 6)
4	nominative (singular). The very savage mistress was punishing the slaves.	(1 + 5)
5	accusative (singular). The Romans had led their greatest forces into the battle.	(1 + 7)
6	ablative (singular). We made a journey to Rome by a very long road.	(1 + 6)
7	nominative (plural). They were all looking at the very bright light.	(1 + 5)
8	accusative (singular). The farmer praised the very beautiful sky.	(1 + 6)
9	accusative (plural). Horses always like the biggest fields.	(1 + 6)
10	nominative (singular). The very angry master terrified the boys and girls.	(1 + 7)

Total: 70

Exercise 13.18

1	preposition. Very many citizens feared the enemy and fled from the city.	(1 + 10)
2	comparative adjective. The Romans waged more savage wars than the Greeks.	(1 + 7)
3	noun. Although the leader had conquered many enemies, nobody praised him.	(1 + 10)
4	preposition. All soldiers fear death in war.	(1 + 7)
5	verb. Greek citizens were wiser than Roman citizens.	(1 + 9)
6	conjunction. The Roman soldiers had seized many towns and conquered many enemies.	(1 + 11)
7	noun. Yesterday in the city I caught sight of very many very beautiful girls.	(1 + 8)
8	adverb. Roman soldiers always fought bravely for Roman citizens.	(1 + 9)
9	demonstrative pronoun. Those slaves had a very cruel master. They did not like him.	(1 + 10)
10	preposition. The citizens were defending the walls of the town against the enemy with very great courage.	(1 + 9)

Total: 100

Exercise 13.19

1	preposition. **ad murum maiorem curro.**	(1 + 1)
2	noun. **pecuniam in via minore inveni.**	(1 + 1)
3	noun. **servi felicissimi e villa effugerunt.**	(1 + 1)
4	verb. **rex plus pecuniae quam ego habebat.**	(1 + 2)
5	adjective. **dux saevus oppidum maximum occupaverat.**	(1 + 1)
6	noun. **murus maximus templum servabat.**	(1 + 1)
7	noun. **Romani Graecos hastis longissimis vicerunt.**	(1 + 1)
8	preposition. **agricola equum minimum in viam duxit.**	(1 + 1)
9	noun. **filii ducis fortissimi hostes timebant.**	(1 + 1)
10	verb. **miles fortis amicum optimum gladio necat.**	(1 + 2)

Total: 22

Exercise 13.20

1   Very cruel. (2)
2   He tied his body to his chariot by his feet. (3)
3   He dragged it around the walls of Troy. (4)
4   When they saw his body they were very sad. (6)
5   Paris was the son of Priam. Therefore he was the brother of Hector. He was very angry because Achilles had killed Hector. He took his weapons, ran out of the city and rushed into battle. He soon found Achilles. He said cruel words to him, saying 'Achilles, you are a very bad man. No one is worse than you. You have killed Hector, my brother. However I am a better soldier than you. You will never escape. No one will save you. I shall now kill you.' (30)
6   a) crudelissimus, tristissimi, iratissimus, pessimus; (1)
    b) peior, melior; (1)
    c) circum, ex, in, ad; (1)
    d) occiderat. (1)
7   subject = Paris; object = hastam. (2)
8   accusative; because it follows ad (+ acc.). (2)
9   masculine; Achilles. (2)

Total: 55

Chapter 14

Exercise 14.1

1	He is able.	(1)	11	I am able.	(1)
2	You are able.	(1)	12	We were able.	(1)
3	He was able.	(1)	13	He has been able.	(1)
4	He had been able.	(1)	14	They have been able.	(1)
5	He will be able.	(1)	15	We had been able.	(1)
6	We have been able.	(1)	16	They are able.	(1)
7	To be able.	(1)	17	They will be able.	(1)
8	You had been able.	(1)	18	We are able.	(1)
9	You were able.	(1)	19	You have been able.	(1)
10	You are able.	(1)	20	I shall be able.	(1)

Total: 20

Exercise 14.2

1	I am not able to work.	(3)
2	He is able to flee.	(2)
3	We are able to conquer.	(2)
4	I was not able to sing.	(3)
5	They were able to flee.	(2)
6	I am able to wander.	(2)
7	We were not able to run.	(3)
8	They were (have been) able to attack.	(2)
9	I am not able to sleep.	(3)
10	You were not able to fight.	(3)

Total: 25

Exercise 14.3

1	The companions were able to sail to the island.	(6)
2	We shall never be able to conquer the enemy.	(5)
3	The soldiers were not able to seize the city.	(6)
4	The freedmen were not able to escape from the town.	(7)
5	The soldiers will be able to capture the famous town.	(6)
6	The Romans were not able to throw (their) spears.	(6)
7	That king is not able to rule well.	(7)
8	The citizens were not able to defend the city well.	(7)
9	The lucky Roman is not able to drink bad wine.	(8)
10	We have not been able to come into the forum today.	(7)

Total: 65

Exercise 14.4

1	accusative (singular). Who will be able to come to the forum tomorrow?	(1 + 7)
2	accusative (singular). We won't be able to make the long journey today, will we?	(1 + 7)
3	accusative (singular). The soldiers are not able to defend the deep river.	(1 + 7)
4	accusative (singular). The master was not able to free that slave.	(1 + 7)
5	nominative (plural). The companions were not able to run quickly.	(1 + 6)
6	accusative (plural). Masters are not able to do everything.	(1 + 6)
7	ablative (singular). The Greeks were unable to overcome the Romans in the cruel battle.	(1 + 9)
8	nominative (singular). The tired man will not be able to write the long book.	(1 + 8)
9	dative (singular). I was not able to give my son much money.	(1 + 8)
10	accusative (plural). The tired soldiers were unable to fight well against the bold enemy.	(1 + 10)

Total: 85

Exercise 14.5

1 <u>librum</u> legere possum. (1)
2 <u>ex</u> oppido effugere non poteramus. (1)
3 <u>mox</u> ambulare non potero. (1)
4 ambulare <u>non</u> potes. (1)
5 <u>muros</u> oppidi delere non poterant. (1)
6 cum <u>nautis</u> laetis navigare possum. (1)
7 cum <u>amicis</u> cantare poterat. (1)
8 <u>statim</u> venire poterunt. (1)
9 <u>pecuniam</u> videre non poterant. (1)
10 e <u>villa</u> discedere potestis. (1)

Total: 10

Exercise 14.6

1 puer <u>vinum</u> bibere non potest. (1)
2 cives <u>oppidum</u> defendere non poterunt. (1)
3 cives regem superare <u>non</u> potuerunt. (1)
4 hostes <u>pecuniam</u> civium invenire non poterant. (1)
5 dux <u>multas</u> copias parare non poterat. (1)
6 nonne <u>villam</u> videre potestis? (1)
7 cur eum <u>librum</u> legere non potes? (1)
8 amici mei <u>murum</u> delere possunt. (1)
9 <u>servus</u> tristis matrem videre poterat. (1)
10 <u>cenam</u> dominae parare non possumus. (1)

Total: 10

Exercise 14.7

1 ablative (singular). I shall soon escape from the city. (1 + 5)
2 ablative (singular). The noble king is present in the forum. (1 + 6)
3 nominative (plural). The Roman companions were able to defend the city. (1 + 6)
4 accusative (singular). Who can see the prisoner? (1 + 5)
5 accusative (singular). Because he was waiting for his friend, Marcus was unable to depart. (1 + 9)
6 ablative (singular). Because they could see the master, the citizens ran out of the villa. (1 + 10)
7 nominative (plural). The citizens were (present) in the forum because they couldn't depart. (1 + 10)
8 accusative (plural). We cannot overcome the enemy. (1 + 5)
9 accusative (plural). We were greeting the soldiers because they had overcome the enemy in battle. (1 + 9)
10 genitive (plural). The leader of the enemy can't lead the tired soldiers back to the mountains, can he? (1 + 10)

Total: 85

Exercise 14.8

1 3rd person singular, imperfect, **possum**. He was able. (4 + 2)
2 3rd person singular, perfect, **sum**. He was/has been. (4 + 2)
3 3rd person plural, perfect, **reduco**. They led back. (4 + 2)
4 1st person plural, imperfect, **sum**. We were. (4 + 2)
5 2nd person singular, perfect, **advenio**. You have arrived. (4 + 2)

Total: 30

Exercise 14.9

1	The Greeks had been attacking Troy for a long time.	(2)
2	They were fighting bravely but were unable to capture the city.	(3)
3	Because the walls were very high and strong.	(3)
4	He was a very bold soldier. He was angry with them.	(4)
5	Don't be stupid.	(1)
6	They were wiser than them.	(2)
7	a) audacissimus, optimum, maximum;	(1)
	b) sapientiores;	(1)
	c) audite, nolite, aedificate.	(1)
8	accusative (singular), because it is the object.	(2)
9	future.	(1)
10	masculine.	(1)
11	**maximum** means very big or biggest, and the English word *maximum* means the biggest.	(2)
12	3rd.	(1)

Total: 25

Exercise 14.10

1	templum magnum erat.	(4)
2	hastas saevas timemus.	(4)
3	oppidum gladiis oppugnabant.	(4)
4	Romani miseri erant.	(4)
5	cum amico ambulat.	(4)

Total: 20

Exercise 14.11

1	regina ad villam ambulabat.	(5)
2	dominus/magister templum non intrabat.	(5)
3	multos equos semper habent.	(5)
4	nautae virum saevum timebant.	(5)

Total: 20

Exercise 14.12

1	That boy loves himself.	(5)
2	The Romans decided to free themselves.	(5)
3	The Trojans prepared to defend themselves.	(5)
4	The very beautiful girl is always looking at herself.	(6)
5	The leader ordered (his) soldiers to make the journey with him.	(7)
6	The wise freedmen never praise themselves.	(6)
7	The Trojan citizens were defending themselves bravely.	(6)
8	That soldier wounded himself with his (own) sword.	(7)
9	The sad citizens handed themselves over to the enemy.	(6)
10	After the battle many prisoners freed themselves.	(7)

Total: 60

Exercise 14.13

1	The old man isn't dead, is he?	(5)
2	Many remained, a few escaped.	(6)
3	Don't leave me here, companions!	(5)
4	We heard the shouts of many old men.	(5)
5	The brave soldiers want to save themselves.	(6)
6	Fight well for your country, citizens!	(5)
7	The Greeks are not braver than us.	(7)
8	The Greek soldiers were very lucky, weren't they?	(6)
9	You are safe, (but) we are in great danger.	(10)
10	Who will be able to conquer us?	(5)

Total: 60

Exercise 14.14

1	nominative (singular). The old man was both brave and bold.	(1 + 7)
2	ablative (singular). The unhappy boy is not standing in the middle of the street, is he?	(1 + 8)
3	nominative (plural). Not all the citizens were brave.	(1 + 6)
4	accusative (singular). The leader will soon be able to seize that town, won't he?	(1 + 8)
5	nominative (plural). Our men were not able to conquer the Greeks.	(1 + 6)
6	accusative (singular). Soldiers always love a lucky leader.	(1 + 6)
7	ablative (singular). My father wounded himself with a sword.	(1 + 6)
8	accusative (singular). When the Greeks seized Troy, they led/brought Helen back to Greece.	(1 + 10)
9	accusative (singular). The Trojans were defending their city well, weren't they?	(1 + 7)
10	genitive (plural). The shouts of those women were loud (large).	(1 + 6)
		Total: 80

Exercise 14.15

Note that in a temporal clause, where **ubi** is followed by a perfect tense in Latin, in English this is often translated with a pluperfect.

1	perfect. The gods and goddesses were very angry when they saw the goddess Discordia.	(1 + 10)
2	perfect. When Paris (had) captured Helen, Menelaus sent messengers to all (his) companions.	(1 + 12)
3	perfect. When they heard about Helen the Greeks sent forces to Menelaus.	(1 + 11)
4	perfect. When they (had) sailed across the sea the Greeks' forces attacked Troy.	(1 + 10)
5	imperfect. Achilles was happy when he (had) killed Hector.	(1 + 8)
6	perfect. When the Greeks (had) built the big horse they left it near the city.	(1 + 11)
7	perfect. When the Greeks (had) left the horse near the city they departed.	(1 + 9)
8	imperfect. When the Trojans saw the very big horse, they were afraid.	(1 + 8)
9	perfect. Many Trojans fled when they saw the Greeks in the middle of the city.	(1 + 11)
10	perfect. When the Greeks (had) destroyed the city of Troy, they sailed to Greece.	(1 + 10)
		Total: 110

Exercise 14.16

1	**nobilissimus**; Although he is very noble, the sailor fears the water.	(1 + 8)
2	**audax**; Although he was a bold soldier, Achilles did not want to fight.	(1 + 10)
3	**clarissimam**; Although the Greeks attacked the very famous city, they were not able to capture it with weapons.	(1 + 12)
4	**meliores**; Although they had better soldiers, the enemy did not fight well.	(1 + 10)
5	**sapientior, multi, multam**; Although I am wiser than many men, I do not have much money.	(3 + 13)
6	**suam**; Although the Trojans defended their city, they were unable to save it.	(1 + 11)
7	**fessus**; Although he was tired, the soldier fought for a long time.	(1 + 8)
8	**sapientissimus**; Although (their) master was very wise, the freedmen did not like him.	(1 + 10)
9	**magna**; Although the old man's voice was loud (big), we could not hear it.	(1 + 11)
10	**validi**; Although they were afraid of the enemy, the strong citizens fought against them.	(1 + 10)
		Total: 115

Exercise 14.17

1	**aedificamus**.	(1 + 2)
2	**habebant**.	(1 + 2)
3	**parabat**.	(1 + 2)
4	**spectat**.	(1 + 2)
5	**estis**.	(1 + 2)
		Total: 15

Exercise 14.18

1 3rd person singular, perfect, **pono**; he has placed. (4 + 2)
2 3rd person singular, perfect, **possum**; he was/has been able. (4 + 2)
3 3rd person plural, perfect, **reduco**; they led back. (4 + 2)
4 2nd person singular, perfect, **effugio**; you have escaped. (4 + 2)
5 1st person plural, future, **relinquo**; we shall leave. (4 + 2)

Total: 30

Exercise 14.19

1 (viri) boni deos non timent. (6)
2 pueri cenam laudabant. (4)
3 Romani feminas claras amant. (5)
4 cum amico bono ambulabam. (5)

Total: 20

Note: Words in brackets may be omitted.

Exercise 14.20

1 (viri) mali et (feminae) malae templa delent. (7)
2 multae (feminae) pecuniam non habent. (6)
3 vir filium laetum amabat. (5)
4 equi prope muros ambulabant. (5)
5 domini saevi viros miseros saepe necant. (7)

Total: 30

Note: Words in brackets may be omitted.

Exercise 14.21

1 servabat. He was saving. (1 + 2)
2 videbant. They were seeing. (1 + 2)
3 superabam. I was overcoming. (1 + 2)
4 aedificabamus. We were building. (1 + 2)
5 stabant. They were standing. (1 + 2)
6 timebant. They were afraid. (1 + 2)
7 delebatis. You were destroying. (1 + 2)
8 spectabat. He was watching. (1 + 2)
9 respondebant. They were replying. (1 + 2)
10 amabat. He was loving. (1 + 2)

Total: 30

Exercise 14.22

1 Built a very big wooden horse. (2)
2 Put lots of soldiers inside the horse and left it on the shore near the city. (2 + 2)
3 Hurried out of the gates. (1)
4 They were astonished. They looked at the horse for a long time. (2)
5 That the Greeks had departed and that they had defeated them. (1 + 2)
6 It was a gift and they should drag it into the middle of the city. (1 + 2)
7 A second Trojan however shouted in a loud voice, 'The horse is not a gift, is it? The Greeks never give gifts. The Greeks are deceitful people. Don't drag the horse into the city, citizens! We ought to destroy it!' At last however the Trojans decided to drag the horse into the city. (30)
8 a) tamen, autem; (1)
   b) diu, sic, num, tandem; (1)
   c) in, e. (1)
9 a) perfect; (1)
   b) discedo; (1)
   c) discedebant. (1)
10 dative (plural) (1)
11 a) equum means *horse*, and equestrian means to do with horses. (2)
   b) equos (1)

Total: 55

Exercise 14.23

1 They dragged it into the city. (1)
2 The Greeks had left. They had defeated the Greeks. (2 + 2)
3 With a lot of food and wine. (2)
4 They went to sleep. (2)
5 The Greeks came silently out of the horse. (4)
6 Rushed through the streets of the city shouting loudly. (2)
7 The Trojans were unable to defend themselves. The savage Greeks killed many Trojans with their swords. Among the dead was the old man Priam, the king of Troy. The Greeks left few Trojans alive. Thus after ten years the Greeks captured the city of Troy by means of trickery. They destroyed the greatest part of the city. Now they were able to take Helen back to Greece. (30)
8 a) discesserant, vicerant; (1)
   b) in, per, inter, post, ad; (1)
   c) laetissimi, maximam. (1)
9 mortuos means *dead*. A mortuary is a room where dead bodies are stored. (2)
10 Genitive (singular), because it means 'of'. (2)
11 possum. (1)
12 Subject = Graeci; object = urbem Troiam. (2)

Total: 55

Chapter 15

Exercise 15.1

1	noun; shout	(2)
2	noun; companion	(2)
3	noun; body	(2)
4	noun; leader	(2)
5	noun; river	(2)
6	noun; man/person	(2)
7	noun; journey	(2)
8	noun; light	(2)
9	noun; soldier	(2)
10	noun; woman	(2)
11	noun; name	(2)
12	noun; parent	(2)
13	noun; king	(2)
14	noun; wife	(2)
	Total: 28	

Exercise 15.2

1	adjective; dear	(2)
2	adjective; others/remaining	(2)
3	adjective; long	(2)
4	adjective; middle	(2)
5	noun; citizen	(2)
6	noun; enemy	(2)
7	noun; young man	(2)
8	noun; sea	(2)
9	noun; mountain	(2)
10	noun; ship	(2)
11	noun; old man	(2)
12	noun; city	(2)
13	verb: approach	(2)
14	verb: wander	(2)
	Total: 28	

Exercise 15.3

1	verb: wait for	(2)
2	verb: free	(2)
3	verb: tell	(2)
4	adjective; dead	(2)
5	adjective; few	(2)
6	adjective; alone	(2)
7	adjective; alive	(2)
8	adverb: surely?	(2)
9	adverb: surely not?	(2)
10	noun: no one	(2)
11	noun: nothing	(2)
12	noun; courage	(2)
13	noun; voice	(2)
14	noun; wound	(2)
	Total: 28	

Exercise 15.4

1	numeral: twelve	(2)
2	numeral: eighteen	(2)
3	numeral: fourteen	(2)
4	numeral: fifteen	(2)
5	numeral: sixteen	(2)
6	numeral: seventeen	(2)
7	numeral: thirteen	(2)
8	numeral: eleven	(2)
9	numeral: nineteen	(2)
10	numeral: twenty	(2)
11	verb: receive	(2)
12	verb: catch sight of	(2)
13	verb: escape	(2)
14	verb: flee	(2)
	Total: 28	

Exercise 15.5

1	verb: arrive	(2)
2	verb: find	(2)
3	verb: punish	(2)
4	verb: hand over	(2)
5	verb: conquer	(2)
6	adverb: however	(2)
7	conjunction: both ... and	(2)
8	noun; weapons	(2)
9	noun; forces	(2)
10	noun; gift	(2)
11	noun; brother	(2)
12	noun; children	(2)
13	noun; mother	(2)
14	noun; delay	(2)
	Total: 28	

Exercise 15.6

1	noun; death	(2)
2	noun; part	(2)
3	noun; father	(2)
4	noun; sister	(2)
5	demonstrative pronoun: that/he	(2)
6	preposition: before	(2)
7	preposition: around	(2)
8	preposition: among	(2)
9	preposition: after	(2)
10	preposition: on behalf of	(2)
11	preposition: on account of	(2)
12	preposition: without	(2)
13	preposition: under	(2)
14	preposition: over	(2)
	Total: 28	

Exercise 15.7

1	verb: collect	(2)
2	verb: ought/owe	(2)
3	verb: defend	(2)
4	verb: carry on	(2)
5	verb: save	(2)
6	verb: wound	(2)
7	adjective; bold	(2)
8	adjective; cruel	(2)
9	adjective; difficult	(2)
10	adjective; easy	(2)
11	adjective; lucky	(2)
12	adjective; brave	(2)
13	adjective; huge	(2)
14	adjective; noble	(2)
		Total: 28

Exercise 15.8

1	adjective; all	(2)
2	adjective; wise	(2)
3	adjective; sad	(2)
4	adverb: quickly	(2)
5	adverb: for	(2)
6	adverb: now	(2)
7	adverb: how!	(2)
8	adverb: then	(2)
9	conjunction: after	(2)
10	reflexive pronoun: him/her/itself	(2)
11	adverb: tomorrow	(2)
12	adverb: by chance	(2)
13	adverb: in vain	(2)
14	adverb: yesterday	(2)
		Total: 28

Exercise 15.9

1	adverb: today	(2)	8	verb: announce	(2)
2	adverb: afterwards	(2)	9	verb: kill	(2)
3	adverb: also	(2)	10	verb: seize	(2)
4	conjunction: before	(2)	11	verb: am able	(2)
5	conjunction: although	(2)	12	verb: lead back	(2)
6	verb: he says	(2)	13	verb: rush	(2)
7	verb: don't!	(2)	14	verb: greet	(2)
					Total: 28

Exercise 15.10

1	genitive singular, of the king	(3)	6	ablative singular, from the mountain	(3)
2	genitive plural, of the companions	(3)	7	accusative singular, old man	(3)
3	genitive singular, of the woman	(3)	8	genitive plural, of the young men	(3)
4	genitive singular, of the name	(3)	9	genitive singular, of the journey	(3)
5	accusative singular, wife	(3)	10	ablative singular, by the soldier	(3)
					Total: 30

Exercise 15.11

1	**amabit**, he will love	(1 + 1)
2	**monebunt**, they will advise	(1 + 1)
3	**regam**, I shall rule	(1 + 1)
4	**audiemus**, we shall hear	(1 + 1)
5	**eris**, you will be	(1 + 1)
		Total: 10

Exercise 15.12

1	**amaverat**, he had loved	(1 + 1)
2	**monuerant**, they had warned	(1 + 1)
3	**rexeram**, I had ruled	(1 + 1)
4	**audiveramus**, we had heard	(1 + 1)
5	**fueras**, you had been	(1 + 1)
		Total: 10

Exercise 15.13

1	of that master	(2)
2	to that girl	(3)
3	with those kings	(3)
4	of those mothers	(2)
5	without those parts	(3)
6	those wars	(2)
		Total: 15

Exercise 15.14

1	the huge mountains	(2)
2	of the huge temples	(2)
3	with the sad mother	(3)
4	without the bold companions	(3)
5	after the cruel war	(3)
6	of the lucky soldier	(2)
		Total: 15

Exercise 15.15

1	of the bolder king	(2)
2	on account of the crueler mistresses	(3)
3	the angrier freedman	(2)
4	with the very brave leaders	(3)
5	over the higher mountains	(3)
6	the best parents	(2)
		Total: 15

Exercise 15.16

1	he can/is able	(2)
2	they could/were able	(2)
3	you can/are able	(2)
4	to be able	(2)
5	they can/are able	(2)
6	you can/are able	(2)
		Total: 12

Exercise 15.17

1	A famous king, king of Argos.	(2)
2	His only daughter.	(2)
3	Your daughter will have a son who will kill you.	(2 + 2)
4	It terrified him.	(1)
5	He built a tower and put Danae in it, and ordered the slaves to guard her.	(4)
6	The wretched king however was not safe.	(2)
7	Jupiter was the king of the gods. Juno, the queen of the gods, was his wife. Although Jupiter loved his wife, he also loved very many women. After he saw the beautiful Danae, he decided to love her too. He therefore went into the tower where the girl was. Afterwards Danae gave birth to a small son. The boy's name was Perseus.	(30)
8 a)	-que, et	(1)
b)	punire	(1)
c)	perterritus, iratus.	(1)
9 a)	video	(1)
b)	perfect	(1)
c)	vidit means he saw. A vision is something that has been seen.	(2)
10 a)	genitive	(1)
b)	because it means *of*	(1)
c)	puerorum.	(1)
		Total: 55

Exercise 15.18

1	He shut Danae and Perseus in a big chest.	(3)
2	He ordered his slaves to carry the chest to the shore and throw it in the sea.	(2 + 3)
3	They were afraid of the waves.	(2)
4	The waves drove it to an island.	(3)
5	He found them and saved them.	(2)
6	Danae and Perseus lived happily on the island for a long time. Perseus was now a young man and his mother was still a beautiful woman. When the king of the island, called Polydectes, caught sight of Danae, he immediately fell in love with her and wanted to marry her. However Perseus did not like Polydectes. He shouted at him, 'You will never marry my mother.'	(30)
7	a) sed, et;	(1)
	b) fortis.	(1)
8	a) dative (singular).	(1)
	b) because it means *to the king*.	(1)
9	nominative (singular)	(1)
10	a) respondeo;	(1)
	b) perfect;	(1)
	c) respondit means he answered. A response is something you give in answer.	(2)
11	feminine	(1)

Total: 55

Exercise 15.19

1	They terrified Perseus.	(1)
2	Although he was a brave young man, she frightened him.	(2)
3	The gods and goddesses helped him.	(2)
4	A new sword and a polished shield.	(3)
5	He was happy.	(2)
6	He no longer feared her.	(1)
7	He sailed away from the island and set off to find Medusa.	(2 + 2)
8	It was a long journey. However after many dangers Perseus at last came to the land where Medusa lived. 'Medusa is here, isn't she?' the boy asked. 'Where is she? I want to see her.' Suddenly Medusa approached. Perseus fought bravely with Medusa and with the help of the gods he killed her. Then he cut off her head and made the journey to his own island.	(30)
9	a) imperfect;	(1)
	b) 3rd;	(1)
	c) faciebat means he made. A factory is a building where one makes things.	(2)
10	ablative (singular), because it follows the preposition in (+ abl.).	(2)
11	magnus = big.	(2)
12	a) feminine;	(1)
	b) is.	(1)

Total: 55

Exercise 15.20

When Perseus had saved Andromeda, he sailed to Greece. When Polydectes saw Perseus, he was angry. 'Why are you here?' he shouted at Perseus. 'You couldn't capture Medusa's head, could you?' Perseus replied, 'I have killed Medusa and I have her head here. Look!' Perseus showed Medusa's head. Polydectes looked at the head and was immediately turned into stone.

Perseus had killed Polydectes. Danae, Perseus's beautiful mother, was now safe. For a long time Perseus and Danae lived happily. Once Perseus made a journey to the city of Larissa. There the citizens were watching some games. Perseus threw a discus. By chance the discus struck a spectator and killed him. The spectator was Acrisius. The gods had said true words: Perseus had killed his grandfather.

Total: 30

Exercise 15.21

1 magister Romanus pueros laudabat. (5)
2 cum regina pulchra ambulabamus. (5)
3 Marcus amicus bonus erat. (4)
4 dominus clarus ancillas gladio monet. (6)

Total: 20

Level 3
Chapter 16

Exercise 16.1

1	this citizen	(2)
2	this city	(2)
3	this river	(2)
4	this leader	(2)
5	these ships	(2)
6	this freedman	(2)
7	this mother	(2)
8	these companions	(2)
9	these woods	(2)
10	this gift	(2)
11	these bodies	(2)
12	these years	(2)
13	these brothers	(2)
14	this war	(2)
15	this young man	(2)
16	this wife	(2)
17	these men	(2)
18	this sea	(2)
19	these wounds	(2)
20	this part	(2)

Total: 40

Exercise 16.2

1	of this queen	(2)
2	of this soldier	(2)
3	of these soldiers	(2)
4	of these ships	(2)
5	by this king	(2)
6	in this war	(2)
7	on account of this light	(2)
8	of this freedman	(2)
9	of these slaves	(2)
10	by/with these words	(2)
11	in this river	(2)
12	to/for this mistress	(2)
13	of these wives	(2)
14	by this wound	(2)
15	by this young man	(2)
16	after these battles	(2)
17	before this dinner	(2)
18	to/for this young man	(2)
19	to these mountains	(2)
20	of this king	(2)

Total: 40

Exercise 16.3

1	The name of this boy is Brutus.	(6)
2	This river is deep.	(5)
3	These boys are small.	(5)
4	These girls are sad.	(5)
5	I praised this woman.	(4)
6	He gave water to this old man.	(5)
7	This young man fought bravely for (his) country.	(7)
8	The angry freedman led this horse out of the wood.	(8)
9	Who fears these shouts?	(5)
10	The prisoner was unable to escape from the town with these men.	(10)

Total: 60

Exercise 16.4

1	hic miles librum <u>magistro</u> ostendebat.	(1)
2	hi milites cenam optimam <u>consumpserunt</u>.	(2)
3	muros in hac urbe <u>aedificavimus</u>.	(2)
4	has <u>urbes</u> delere non poteramus.	(1)
5	hanc feminam tristem <u>numquam</u> laudat.	(1)
6	ad hanc insulam <u>venerunt/veniebant</u> et flumina spectaverunt/spectabant.	(2)
7	custodes hoc <u>gladio</u> superare poterat.	(1)
8	copiae <u>regis</u> clari hostes superare poterant.	(1)
9	hi iuvenes lucem claram <u>spectabant</u>.	(2)
10	iter trans hos montes numquam <u>fecimus</u>.	(2)

Total: 15

Exam Practice Answers

Exercise 16.5

1 The prisoners killed all the guards with these weapons. All the prisoners killed the guards with these weapons. (7)
2 The leader of these soldiers has never fought in a big battle. (9)
3 The guard killed the wretched prisoner in his sleep with this sword. (9)
4 The chief led all the ships to the small island because of the storm. (10)
5 These citizens were very much afraid of that savage king. (8)
6 The mistress had led this slave-girl into that very big villa. (9)
7 We remained in the small forum for a long time because of these battles. (9)
8 The Romans built a very famous city on these seven mountains, didn't they? (10)
9 Why are you always punishing this old man? (6)
10 We were waging this war for a long time after the death of the king. (8)

Total: 85

Exercise 16.6

1 hunc. All the masters were praising this very famous poet. (1 + 7)
2 hae. These very sad women had always feared the enemy chief. (1 + 8)
3 eo. The Romans overcame our allies in that battle. (1 + 8)
4 hanc. Give this letter to my mistress! (1 + 6)
5 his. O allies, you won't be able to conquer the enemy with these weapons, will you? (1 + 8)
6 eos. The very famous leader had led (his) soldiers back across those mountains. (1 + 8)
7 his. The master praised (his) sons and daughters with these words. (1 + 7)
8 hoc. Nine old men were sleeping in this temple. (1 + 7)
9 eos. The women praised those very noble citizens. (1 + 6)
10 eius. The woman loved (her) husband but she killed his parents with a sword. (1 + 10)

Total: 85

Exercise 16.7

1 nominative singular, masculine. This sailor was sailing to the small island. (3 + 7)
2 accusative singular, feminine. I saw that very beautiful girl yesterday. (3 + 6)
3 accusative singular, feminine. The messenger will soon arrive at this city. (3 + 7)
4 accusative singular, neuter. We can not carry this body out of the town. (3 + 8)
5 accusative plural, neuter. The soldiers collected all these weapons. (3 + 6)
6 genitive singular, feminine. This beautiful woman's name is Helena. (3 + 7)
7 genitive singular, feminine. The walls of that city are very high. (3 + 6)
8 ablative singular, masculine. The soldier fought well with this sword. (3 + 6)
9 dative plural, masculine. The master will give a present to these young men. (3 + 6)
10 genitive plural, masculine. The women loved the wine of these young men. (3 + 6)

Total: 95

Exercise 16.8

1 haec femina fortis ad insulam <u>navigavit</u>. (2)
2 hanc puellam pulcherrimam heri <u>vidi</u>. (2)
3 nuntius eam epistulam <u>reginae</u> dedit. (1)
4 hoc <u>corpus</u> ex oppido portabam. (1)
5 milites omnia haec arma mihi <u>ostenderunt</u>. (2)

Total: 8

Exercise 16.9

1 Because Paris had led his wife Helen to Troy. (2)
2 Punish Paris and destroy the city of Troy. (2 + 2)
3 He sent messengers to all the cities of Greece. (3)
4 He had captured Helen and fled to Troy. (3)
5 He was angry and wanted to destroy this city. (3)
6 'Prepare your weapons! Collect your ships and soldiers! We shall sail to Troy and punish the Trojans!' When the Greeks heard these words, they prepared many forces. The forces of the Greeks came to a port called Aulis. When Menelaus saw these ships and soldiers, he was very happy. He greeted them all and immediately prepared to sail to Troy. (For) he wanted to wage war against the Trojans and to free Helen. (30)
7 a) punire, delere, navigare, gerere, liberare (1)
   b) hi (1)
   c) audite, parate, colligite (1)
   d) navigabimus, puniemus (1)
8 Accusative, because it is the object. (2)
9 a) Perfect. (1)
   b) audio. (1)
   c) audiverunt means *they heard*. At an audition, the judges hear the actor play the part. (2)

Total: 55

Exercise 16.10

1 that freedman (2)
2 that ship (2)
3 that war (2)
4 those companions (2)
5 those cities (2)
6 those wars (2)
7 that woman (2)
8 those weapons (2)
9 those bodies (2)
10 that river (2)
11 those horses (2)
12 that chief (2)
13 that wood (2)
14 those forces (2)
15 those words (2)
16 that town (2)
17 that young man (2)
18 those men (2)
19 that friend (2)
20 those soldiers (2)

Total: 40

Exercise 16.11

1 of that guard (2)
2 with those friends (2)
3 of those old men (2)
4 to/for that woman (2)
5 in that city (2)
6 of those girls (2)
7 to/for that god (2)
8 of those young men (2)
9 on that journey (2)
10 by/with those weapons (2)
11 by those soldiers (2)
12 to/for that king (2)
13 of those dangers (2)
14 by that light (2)
15 by/with those arrows (2)
16 of those men (2)
17 of that friend (2)
18 of those women (2)
19 of that city (2)
20 those shouts (2)

Total: 40

Exercise 16.12

1	That old man is fortunate.	(5)
2	That girl is cruel.	(5)
3	Those soldiers are tired.	(5)
4	That ship is huge.	(5)
5	That temple is big and beautiful.	(7)
6	Those words are cruel.	(5)
7	I have not praised that king.	(5)
8	The chief often punishes those citizens.	(6)
9	The leader does not like those women.	(6)
10	The name of that leader is Marcus.	(6)

Total: 55

Exercise 16.13

1	This master is good, that one is bad.	(7)
2	This island is big, that one is small.	(7)
3	That companion feared this master.	(6)
4	This master terrified that old man.	(6)
5	Those soldiers attacked this city.	(6)
6	Those young men were watching these girls.	(6)
7	This woman sailed to that island.	(7)
8	Those soldiers fled from this town.	(7)
9	I saw this girl in that street.	(7)
10	That master had punished these citizens.	(6)

Total: 65

Exercise 16.14

1	urbem magnam cepi.	(4)
2	patrem gladio necavit.	(4)
3	epistulas ad dominum mittemus.	(5)
4	hastam iaciebam.	(3)
5	vinum consumite, cives!	(4)

Total: 20

Exercise 16.15

1	vinum prope flumen magnum ponebamus/posuimus.	(6)
2	milites contra Romanos pugnabant.	(5)
3	dux militum pecuniam ad urbem numquam mittebat/misit.	(8)
4	cras omnes in oppidum curremus.	(6)
5	o miserae ancillae, cenam parate!	(5)

Total: 30

Exercise 16.16

1	nautae fortes multas naves parabant/paraverunt.	(6)
2	corpora civium in templum portabatis.	(6)
3	hodie iter in montes faciemus.	(6)
4	olim puer et puella patrem amabant.	(7)
5	multam pecuniam duci tradidimus.	(5)

Total: 30

Exercise 16.17

1	I shall go back.	(2)
2	They have died.	(2)
3	You were going.	(2)
4	They go in.	(2)
5	I have gone.	(2)
6	You will go.	(2)
7	He has died.	(2)
8	He goes out.	(2)
9	They were going.	(2)
10	They will go across.	(2)
11	You go.	(2)
12	He has returned.	(2)
13	I shall go out.	(2)
14	They have gone.	(2)
15	They have approached.	(2)

Total: 30

Exercise 16.18

1	I die.	(2)
2	You will go.	(2)
3	We were going out.	(2)
4	He goes across.	(2)
5	I have returned.	(2)
6	They will go out.	(2)
7	We were going.	(2)
8	He has died.	(2)
9	He will return.	(2)
10	He was going.	(2)
11	He is approaching.	(2)
12	We have returned.	(2)
13	He goes.	(2)
14	I have gone out.	(2)
15	He has gone.	(2)

Total: 30

Exercise 16.19

1	They have gone across.	(1)
2	He will go.	(1)
3	We are going.	(1)
4	We shall go across.	(1)
5	They go.	(1)
6	You are dying.	(1)
7	He was going out.	(1)
8	They have gone back.	(1)
9	They will approach.	(1)
10	He will go out.	(1)
11	They go across.	(1)
12	They will return.	(1)
13	We shall return.	(1)
14	They die.	(1)
15	You were going.	(1)

Total: 15

Exercise 16.20

1	Yesterday we crossed the river.	(4)
2	Today we are crossing the sea.	(4)
3	I am going to the city.	(4)
4	Go, boy!	(3)
5	Tomorrow we shall go to the city.	(5)
6	We were going along the road.	(4)
7	Many young men perished.	(4)
8	The boys soon returned.	(4)
9	Will you return to the city tomorrow?	(5)
10	He went out quickly.	(3)

Total: 40

Exercise 16.21

1 The Greeks sent many soldiers and many ships to Aulis. And when Menelaus saw those men and those ships, he was very happy. He did not like Troy. He wanted to destroy that city without delay. However the ships could not sail. The ships could not sail because the winds were contrary. The Greeks waited near the ships for a long time. They did nothing. They waited for favourable winds for a long time. No one was happy. But at last the winds became (were) favourable.

Menelaus shouted to his companions: 'Friends 'he said,' those winds are now favourable. Prepare the ships! Prepare your weapons! We ought to cross the sea!'

When the Greeks heard these words they quickly prepared the ships and left Aulis. (30)

2   a) illos, illas, illam, illi, haec (1)

    b) parate (1)

    c) miserunt, conspexit, clamavit, audiverunt, paraverunt, abierunt (1)

3   a) accusative (plural); (1)

    b) naves means *ships*. A naval officer serves on a ship. (2)

4 neuter (1)

5   a) 3rd person plural; (2)

    b) abeo. (1)

Total: 40

Chapter 17

Exercise 17.1

1	We are loved.	(2)
2	He is praised.	(2)
3	They are wounded.	(2)
4	You are called.	(2)
5	I am carried.	(2)
6	We are freed.	(2)
7	It is reported.	(2)
8	You are praised.	(2)
9	They are killed.	(2)
10	You are being watched.	(2)

Total: 20

Exercise 17.2

1	He is warned.	(2)
2	You are seen.	(2)
3	It is moved.	(2)
4	It is held.	(2)
5	You are terrified.	(2)
6	They are destroyed.	(2)
7	They are seen.	(2)
8	We are moved.	(2)
9	You are warned.	(2)
10	We are ordered.	(2)

Total: 20

Exercise 17.3

1	We are ruled.	(2)
2	It is placed.	(2)
3	You are captured.	(2)
4	It is defended.	(2)
5	They are loved.	(2)
6	You are sent.	(2)
7	They are handed over.	(2)
8	You are being killed.	(2)
9	They are conquered.	(2)
10	It is thrown.	(2)

Total: 20

Exercise 17.4

1	He is heard.	(2)
2	They are found.	(2)
3	I am compelled.	(2)
4	He is killed.	(2)
5	We are helped.	(2)
6	They are driven.	(2)
7	He is left.	(2)
8	He is captured.	(2)
9	They are led.	(2)
10	We are driven.	(2)

Total: 20

Exercise 17.5

1	The old man wounds the soldier.	(4)
2	The soldier is wounded by the old man.	(5)
3	The young man reads the book.	(4)
4	The book is read by the young man.	(5)
5	The boys prepare the food.	(4)
6	The food is prepared by the boys.	(5)
7	The master praises the boys.	(4)
8	The boys are praised by the master.	(5)
9	The enemy seize the city.	(4)
10	The city is seized by the enemy.	(5)

Total: 45

Exercise 17.6

1	I love the girl.	(4)
2	The girl is loved by me.	(5)
3	The old men drink the wine.	(4)
4	The wine is drunk by the old men.	(5)
5	The Romans capture the town.	(4)
6	The town is captured by the Romans.	(5)
7	The king rules the land.	(4)
8	The land is ruled by the king.	(5)
9	The Greeks conquer the Romans.	(4)
10	The Romans are conquered by the Greeks.	(5)

Total: 45

Exercise 17.7

1 The Romans always conquer the Greeks.	(5)
2 The Greeks are always conquered by the Romans.	(6)
3 The master often punishes the farmers.	(5)
4 The farmers are often punished by the master.	(6)
5 The poet always reads books.	(5)
6 Books are always read by the poet.	(6)
7 The wife of the chief loves his (the chief's) father.	(6)
8 The old man is loved by the wife of the chief.	(6)
9 Many soldiers defend the city.	(5)
10 The city is defended by soldiers.	(5)
Total: 55	

Exercise 17.8

1 The storm destroys the ships.	(4)
2 The ships are destroyed by the storm.	(4)
3 The enemy do not like us.	(5)
4 We are not liked by the enemy.	(5)
5 The boys like the master.	(4)
6 The master is liked by the boys.	(5)
7 The citizens wound the king.	(4)
8 The kind is wounded by the citizens.	(5)
9 The boy sees the city.	(4)
10 The city is seen by the boy.	(5)
Total: 45	

Exercise 17.9

1 We are watched by the cruel enemy.	(5)
2 Many of the enemy are killed by swords.	(5)
3 I am sent by the master to the mistress.	(6)
4 I am loved by my father.	(5)
5 You are never praised by the master.	(5)
6 The soldiers are wounded by arrows and spears.	(5)
7 The water is carried into the villa by the soldier.	(6)
8 The lucky slaves are freed by the master.	(6)
9 You are captured by the cruel soldiers.	(6)
10 We are defended by the king, aren't we?	(6)
Total: 55	

Exercise 17.10

1 Those freedmen are praised by this mistress.	(7)
2 This book is read by that old man.	(7)
3 On account of the long battles, the old men are defended in the city by the guards.	(10)
4 This poet is greeted by that young man.	(7)
5 Wise men are always listened to by everyone.	(7)
6 The body of that wretched woman is carried into the temple by (her) son.	(10)
7 Bad leaders are often killed by (their) soldiers.	(7)
8 Who is terrified by the gods?	(5)
9 Who is feared by the citizens?	(5)
10 Although we are feared by the citizens, we all build very big country-houses.	(10)
Total: 75	

Exercise 17.11

1 superari. The Roman soldiers do not want to be overcome by the enemy.   (1 + 8)
2 capi. The citizens did not want to be captured by the savage guards.   (1 + 8)
3 regi. The Romans did not want to be ruled by kings.   (1 + 7)
4 audiri. The small girl was not able to be heard by (her) mother.   (1 + 8)
5 moneri. The boys ought to be warned by the wise master.   (1 + 7)
6 videri. The very high mountains can't be seen by the old men, can they?   (1 + 7)
7 defendi. Why do you want to be defended by the cruel chief?   (1 + 7)
8 regi. Everyone wanted to be ruled by the wise queen.   (1 + 7)
9 aedificari. Very many temples can be built near the big river.   (1 + 8)
10 interfici. The woman does not want to be killed by her famous husband.   (1 + 8)

Total: 85

Exercise 17.12

1 Many very brave men are killed in war.   (7)
2 Patroclus is killed by Hector.   (5)
3 Hector is killed by Achilles.   (5)
4 Hector's body is seen by the Trojans.   (6)
5 The walls of Troy are not destroyed.   (5)
6 This city is not captured by the Greeks.   (7)
7 At last a very big horse is built by the Greeks.   (7)
8 The horse is placed near the city.   (5)
9 This soldier is left by the Greeks.   (6)
10 The city of Troy is at last captured by
   the Greeks.   (7)

Total: 60

Exercise 17.13

1 corpora civium, milites, in urbem portate!   (7)
2 o miles, civi forti pecuniam trade!   (6)
3 fortiter pugnate, o amici, contra Romanos!   (6)
4 multos libros magistro ostendi.   (5)
5 in flumen cum equis cucurristis.   (6)
6 videte, o pueri! magister e templo venit.   (8)
7 omnes filios reginae timemus.   (5)
8 nautae mali naves bonas numquam
   aedificant.   (7)
9 librum in flumen iecit.   (5)
10 olim ad oppidum venerunt.   (5)

Total: 60

Exercise 17.14

1 amici miseri dominum laetum spectant.   (6)
2 puellam tristem in via invenimus.   (6)
3 ad villam domini, pueri, lente ambulate.   (7)
4 pueri matrem amici semper amaverunt.   (6)
5 ad templum sine amico venit.   (6)
6 mox montes pluchros vident.   (5)
7 videte, puellae! multos amicos habet.   (7)
8 rex de montibus venit.   (5)
9 omnes gladios magnos et hastas (magnas) habent.   (7)
10 cives laeti oppidum intrant.   (5)

Total: 60

Exercise 17.15

1 Destroying the city of Troy. (2)
2 In the middle of the city. They were killing many Trojan soldiers. (2 + 2)
3 Setting fire to the temples, and capturing many citizens. (2 + 2)
4 A Trojan prince; in the city. (1 + 1)
5 He called his friends together and spoke to them. (1 + 2)
6 'O friends,' he said, 'our city is being seized by the Greeks. We are in very great danger. Our soldiers are being killed. Our temples are being set on fire. I do not want to be captured. We ought to escape. Take up your weapons! Leave your homes! Prepare your ships! Leave immediately!' After this Aeneas and his companions hurried through the streets of the city and quickly went out of the gates. (30)
7   a) delebant, aderant, necabant, incendebant, capiebant, etc. (1)
    b) vidit, convocavit, dixit, festinaverunt, exierunt; (1)
    c) maximo. (1)
8   a) 3rd person. (1)
    b) dico. (1)
9 Vocative (plural). (1)
10   a) Accusative (plural). (1)
    b) It is the object. (1)
11 celeriter means *quickly*. When you accelerate, you go more quickly. (2)

Total: 55

Exercise 17.16

1 The Roman leader had 100 soldiers. (6)
2 The Greeks collected 1000 ships. (5)
3 The cruel king killed 90 prisoners. (6)
4 The inhabitants had built 80 temples. (5)
5 The young man found 40 bodies in the wood. (7)
6 The chief led 50 soldiers into the forum. (7)
7 You don't have 70 ships, do you? (5)
8 After 60 years the famous queen died. (7)
9 They went into the forum with 30 citizens. (5)
10 20 men remained in the mountains for a long time. (7)

Total: 60

Exercise 17.17

1 The leader collected the prisoners and killed the tenth one. (8)
2 The poet was reading the ninth book quickly. (6)
3 The old man loved his eighth wife very much. (6)
4 The first king of the Roman city was Romulus. (7)
5 The fourth king of Rome collected many ships near the sea. (9)
6 The fifth king, called Tarquinius Priscus, praised the little slave very much. (10)
7 The second king of the city, called Numa Pompilius, built a very great temple. (10)
8 The citizens drove the seventh king out of the city. (7)
9 The sixth king of Rome had been a slave. (6)
10 The third king overcame many inhabitants. (6)

Total: 75

Chapter 18

Exercise 18.1

1	They were (being) carried.	(2)
2	They will be sent.	(2)
3	I shall be heard.	(2)
4	I shall be wounded.	(2)
5	We were (being) ruled.	(2)
6	They were being killed.	(2)
7	I shall be feared.	(2)
8	I shall be punished.	(2)
9	They are spotted.	(2)
10	They will be killed.	(2)
11	We shall be captured.	(2)
12	I shall not be conquered.	(2)
13	We were being ordered.	(2)
14	We shall be warned.	(2)
15	You were being led.	(2)
16	You are sent.	(2)
17	They were (being) sent.	(2)
18	It is placed.	(2)
19	You will be overcome.	(2)
20	You will be killed.	(2)
	Total: 40	

Exercise 18.2

1	It was read/he was chosen.	(2)
2	They were praised.	(2)
3	I shall be called.	(2)
4	They were led back.	(2)
5	I am praised.	(2)
6	It will be destroyed.	(2)
7	They will be killed.	(2)
8	They were being prepared.	(2)
9	We shall be moved.	(2)
10	We are being moved.	(2)
11	They are attacked.	(2)
12	It will be given.	(2)
13	It is reported.	(2)
14	They will be seen.	(2)
15	He will be ruled.	(2)
16	They were punished.	(2)
17	You will be conquered.	(2)
18	They are heard.	(2)
19	We shall be punished.	(2)
20	We are praised.	(2)
	Total: 40	

Exercise 18.3

1	Who will be praised by the master tomorrow?	(6)
2	Many will be praised by the master tomorrow.	(6)
3	Many horses were being led out of the fields.	(6)
4	We shall never be overcome by the Romans.	(5)
5	Messengers were being sent to the city.	(5)
6	The boys are often punished by that master.	(7)
7	A thousand ships were being prepared by the Greeks.	(6)
8	This book will soon be read by me.	(7)
9	Many weapons were being given to the soldiers by the leader.	(7)
10	You are praised because you are brave.	(5)
	Total: 60	

Exercise 18.4

1	After ten years the Greeks seized the city of Troy.	(8)
2	Long words are not often said by little boys.	(9)
3	Greeks are not often seen in Britain.	(7)
4	Many prisoners were being guarded by the guards.	(6)
5	The cruel master was not praised by the slaves.	(7)
6	Many fields were being destroyed by the enemy.	(6)
7	That horse will be wounded by a soldier with a spear.	(7)
8	Many tribes will be overcome by the Romans.	(6)
9	The Greeks will at last be conquered by the Romans.	(6)
10	Many spears will be carried into the forum by the soldiers.	(8)
	Total: 70	

Exercise 18.5

1 viri laeti prope flumen cantabant. (6)
2 patrem clarum et villam magnam habeo. (7)
3 hostes sine hastis pugnabant. (5)
4 dominus malus omnes viros fortes laudavit. (7)
5 ancilla reginae pecuniam amat. (5)

Total: 30

Exercise 18.6

1 omnes milites in viis pugnabant. (6)
2 multos amicos et villas magnas habes. (7)
3 cenam cum puellis pulchris consumebamus. (6)
4 o pueri, librum magistro ostendite! (5)
5 dux vinum civium numquam consumet. (6)

Total: 30

Exercise 18.7

1 At the island of the Lotus Eaters. (2)
2 His sailors. Astonished. (2 + 1)
3 Half asleep. They were unable to move. (3)
4 What they were doing and what they had done. (2)
5   a) They told him not to be angry. (1)
    b) They had eaten it. (1)
    c) They wanted to stay there and sleep. They did not want to go home. (3)
6   a) pellebantur, vinciebantur; (1)
    b) autem, et; (1)
    c) ite, capite, vincite, ducite. (1)
7 comes. (1)
8 accusative (plural). (1)
9 is. (1)
10 iratissimi (line 15)
    a) superlative of **iratus**. (1 + 1)
    b) **iratissimi** means *very angry*. If someone is irate they are very angry. (2)

Total: 25

Exercise 18.8

1 I shall come in a few days. (4)
2 I have slept for the whole day. (4)
3 I was running for many hours; now I am tired. (8)
4 I shall return within a few years. (4)
5 We worked for seven days. (4)
6 We arrived in the fourth year. (4)
7 We shall depart in a few hours. (4)
8 I saw him in the third hour. (5)
9 He slept for many hours. (4)
10 I shall work for many days. (4)

Total: 45

Exercise 18.9

1	The city was ruled by kings for many years.	(7)
2	The children of the cruel mistress slept for a few hours.	(7)
3	The city was attacked by the Greeks for many years.	(7)
4	The soldiers remained in the horse for a few hours.	(7)
5	The young men worked in the villa for five hours.	(7)
6	You were making a journey across the mountains for the whole day.	(7)
7	The freedmen remained in the(ir) mistress's villa for many days.	(8)
8	The sad slave-girls were preparing the dinner for the young men for two hours.	(8)
9	The old man remained near the very deep river for three days.	(8)
10	The Roman citizens were ruled for six years by the cruel king.	(9)

Total: 75

Exercise 18.10

1	The city will be captured within a few hours.	(5)
2	The old man died on the third day.	(5)
3	The prisoners were freed by the guards in the tenth hour.	(7)
4	At that time we were ruled by kings.	(6)
5	The enemy overcame our forces on the fourth day.	(7)
6	The cruel king will be killed on that day.	(6)
7	The Romans will give help to our soldiers within eight days.	(8)
8	The mother and father will see their children within a few days.	(7)
9	The best citizens had built the temple within four years.	(7)
10	We shall lead the chief to the city in the sixth year.	(7)

Total: 65

Exercise 18.11

1	**auditis**. You hear.	(1 + 2)
2	**discesserunt**. They have departed.	(1 + 2)
3	**fui**. I have been.	(1 + 2)
4	**erat**. He was.	(1 + 2)
5	**tradebantur**. They were handed over.	(1 + 2)
6	**vulneramur**. We are wounded.	(1 + 2)
7	**puniebatur**. He was being punished.	(1 + 2)
8	**colligebantur**. They were being collected.	(1 + 2)
9	**mitteris**. You will be sent.	(1 + 2)
10	**occidentur**. They will be killed.	(1 + 2)

Total: 30

Exercise 18.12

1   accusative, referring to time 'how long'. (2)
    I watched that girl for five hours. I am afraid of her. (9)
2   accusative, referring to time 'how long'. (2)
    This old man loved (his) dear wife for 70 years. (8)
3   ablative, referring to time 'within which'. (2)
    That storm destroyed many ships within a few hours. (8)
4   nominative. Agreeing with the subject. (2)
    Flavia is the most beautiful of all the girls, isn't she? (7)
5   vocative, addressing the citizens. (2)
    Don't be afraid, citizens! Help will arrive. (7)
6   accusative, referring to time 'how long'. (2)
    We were terrified by that master for seven years. (7)
7   ablative, referring to time 'when'. (2)
    Food and wine were being carried into the villa on the second day. (8)
8   accusative, referring to time 'how long'. (2)
    The beautiful girls are watched by the young men for many hours. (8)
9   accusative, referring to time 'how long'. (2)
    The big ships were being driven towards the island by the storm for many days. (9)
10 ablative, agreeing with domino. (2)
    The prisoners will be killed by the cruel master on the second day, won't they? (9)

Total: 100

Exercise 18.13

1   The sailors were tired because they had eaten the lotus fruit. They were being dragged to the ships by Ulysses's companions and were very angry. Ulysses shouted to his friends, 'These sailors were compelled to remain in this land by the Lotus Eaters. They have eaten the lotus fruit. Throw them into the ships! Leave quickly!' When the Greeks had thrown the sailors into the ships, they quickly prepared everything. Then with many shouts they crossed the sea. (30)
2   a) pluperfect. (1)
    b) **consumo**. (1)
    c) **consumpserant** means *they had consumed*. Consumption refers to what one has consumed or used. (2)
3   passive. (1)
4   a) superlative. (1)
    b) **iratus**. (1)
    c) **iratissimi** means *very angry*. Irate means angry. (2)
5   feminine. (1)

Total: 40

Chapter 19

Exercise 19.1

1	He has been/was killed.	(2)
2	She has been/was killed.	(2)
3	You have been/were killed.	(2)
4	They have been/were killed.	(2)
5	You have been/were wounded.	(2)
6	I have been/was sent.	(2)
7	She has been/was captured.	(2)
8	You have been/were captured.	(2)
9	We have been/were punished.	(2)
10	They have been/were heard.	(2)
11	He has been/was seen.	(2)
12	She has been/was seen.	(2)
13	They have been/were seen.	(2)
14	We have been/were carried.	(2)
15	They have been/were conquered.	(2)
16	He has been/was driven.	(2)
17	She has been/was left.	(2)
18	She has been/was led.	(2)
19	It has been/was said.	(2)
20	You have been/were warned.	(2)

Total: 40

Exercise 19.2

1	The boy was punished.	(3)
2	The boys were punished.	(3)
3	The girl was seen.	(3)
4	The girls were seen.	(3)
5	The temple was built.	(3)
6	The temples were built.	(3)
7	The Romans were conquered.	(3)
8	The soldier was wounded.	(3)
9	The spears were thrown.	(3)
10	The old man was killed.	(3)
11	The town was attacked.	(3)
12	The towns were attacked.	(3)
13	The citizens were warned.	(3)
14	The citizen was warned.	(3)
15	The father was loved.	(3)
16	The mother was loved.	(3)
17	The words were heard.	(3)
18	The voices were heard.	(3)
19	The city was destroyed.	(3)
20	The light was seen.	(3)

Total: 60

Note: Verbs may be translated with a perfect or simple past, as above.

Exercise 19.3

1	The king said many words.	(5)
2	Many words were said by the king.	(6)
3	The girls heard the soldiers' voices.	(5)
4	The soldiers' voices were heard by the girls.	(6)
5	The friends soon prepared the food.	(5)
6	The food was soon prepared by the Romans.	(6)
7	At last the Romans conquered the Greeks.	(5)
8	At last the Greeks were conquered by the Romans.	(6)
9	The boy loved the girl greatly.	(5)
10	The girl was loved greatly by the boy.	(6)

Total: 55

Exercise 19.4

1	The Romans were seen by the enemy.	(5)
2	I was punished by the master.	(4)
3	The girl was seen by the boy.	(5)
4	The girls were seen by the boys.	(5)
5	The temple was built by the citizens.	(5)
6	The walls were destroyed by the enemy.	(5)
7	Many words were said by the old men.	(6)
8	The arrow was thrown by the soldier.	(5)
9	The slave was freed by the master.	(5)
10	The gift was sent by the mother.	(5)

Total: 50

Exercise 19.5

1	Many spears were thrown by the soldiers in the battle.	(8)
2	The town had already been destroyed by the enemy.	(7)
3	Our messengers have been captured by the enemy.	(7)
4	Money was given to the soldiers by the leader.	(7)
5	The money was received by the happy soldiers.	(7)
6	The good king's wine was given to the old man.	(7)
7	Many lands had been conquered by the queen.	(6)
8	Many citizens had been led through the streets.	(7)
9	The city's temples will soon be destroyed by the enemy.	(7)
10	That leader has been praised by the soldiers.	(7)

Total: 70

Exercise 19.6

1	The master is not loved by the boys.	(6)
2	The soldier has been wounded by a sword.	(5)
3	Much food is thrown into the river by the friends.	(8)
4	We are being overcome by the enemy!	(4)
5	Many wounds had been received by the soldiers.	(7)
6	This slave will be punished by the master tomorrow.	(7)
7	Many words had been said by the leader.	(7)
8	Money was given to the citizens by the king.	(7)
9	The enemy's weapons were captured by the Romans.	(7)
10	The beautiful woman had been seen by the boy.	(7)

Total: 65

Exercise 19.7

1	When Helen was seen by the young man she was led to the city of Troy.	(12)
2	Many ships were prepared and sent to Menelaus.	(10)
3	Troy was defended by the citizens for a long time.	(6)
4	A huge horse had been left near the sea.	(7)
5	The horse was seen by the Trojans.	(6)
6	The horse can't be dragged into the city, can it?	(7)
7	We do not want the city of Troy to be seized.	(6)
8	At last the city was captured.	(5)
9	Because they had been wounded by the enemy, many citizens fled from the city.	(12)
10	Because the city had been destroyed, the Trojans never returned.	(9)

Total: 80

Exercise 19.8

1	venite, cives! hostes urbem capiunt.	(6)
2	currite, viri! milites muros deleverunt.	(6)
3	patrem domini saevi non amamus.	(6)
4	ad villam regis saepe ambulabant.	(6)
5	templa magna oppidi vidi.	(5)
6	amici tristes filium feminae monebant.	(6)
7	nautae pueris laetis clamabant.	(5)
8	di de montibus numquam veniunt.	(6)
9	(ego) sine gladio magno numquam pugno.	(6)
10	o cives fortes, circum muros urbis saepe ambulatis.	(8)

Total: 60

Exercise 19.9

1	We had been seen.	(2)
2	It had been moved.	(2)
3	She had been praised.	(2)
4	They had been killed.	(2)
5	We had been led.	(2)
6	You had been captured.	(2)
7	I had been sent.	(2)
8	He had been compelled.	(2)
9	She had been defended.	(2)
10	We had been wounded.	(2)
11	It had been given.	(2)
12	It had been written.	(2)
13	It had been destroyed.	(2)
14	You had been asked.	(2)
15	He had been led.	(2)
16	You had been punished.	(2)
17	We had been ordered.	(2)
18	She had been seen.	(2)
19	It had been reported.	(2)
20	He had been killed.	(2)

Total: 40

Exercise 19.10

1	At last the forces had been prepared.	(4)
2	He had been wounded by the spears.	(3)
3	She had been wounded by the spears.	(3)
4	We had been praised by the master.	(4)
5	All the walls had been destroyed by the enemy.	(6)
6	I had been left by (my) friends.	(4)
7	You had been overcome by the Romans.	(4)
8	We had been heard by the master.	(4)
9	They had been conquered by the Greeks.	(4)
10	You had been freed by the master.	(4)

Total: 40

Exercise 19.11

1	Helen had been captured by a brave young man.	(6)
2	Helen had been quickly led to the city of Troy.	(6)
3	Forces had been prepared by the Greeks.	(5)
4	Ships had soon been sent to the city of Troy.	(6)
5	Troy had been attacked by the Greeks.	(5)
6	Many men had been killed.	(4)
7	A very large horse had been built by the Greeks.	(6)
8	The horse had been placed in the middle of the city by the Trojans.	(7)
9	Many Trojans had been killed by the Greeks.	(6)
10	At last the city had been captured.	(4)

Total: 55

Exercise 19.12

1 Because the city of Troy had been captured by the Greeks. (2)
2 He had ordered the Greeks to build the wooden horse. (2)
3 Because they were loved by the gods. (2)
4 Troy had been captured; (1)
  the walls had been destroyed; (1)
  the temples had been destroyed; (1)
  almost all the chiefs had been killed; (1)
  much money had been captured; (1)
  we had many rewards; (1)
  Helen was being taken back to Greece. (1)
5 Everyone will soon go back to Greece. (2)
6 We will soon see our wives, sons and daughters. (2)
7 No. He did not see his wife Penelope nor his son Telemachus for a long time. (4)
8 He wandered over the seas with his companions for many years and underwent very many dangers. (4)

Total: 25

Exercise 19.13

1 monitus sum, I have been warned. (2)
2 rectus sum, I have been ruled. (2)
3 auditus sum, I have been heard. (2)
4 portatus sum, I have been carried. (2)
5 interfectus sum, I have been killed. (2)
6 ductus sum, I have been led. (2)
7 deletus sum, I have been destroyed. (2)
8 captus sum, I have been captured. (2)
9 vulneratus sum, I have been wounded. (2)
10 missus sum, I have been sent. (2)
11 visus sum, I have been seen. (2)
12 victus sum, I have been conquered. (2)
13 iactus sum, I have been thrown. (2)
14 amatus sum, I have been loved. (2)
15 punitus sum, I have been punished. (2)

Total: 30

Exercise 19.14

1 punitae eramus, we had been punished. (2)
2 petitae eramus, we had been sought. (2)
3 custoditae eramus, we had been guarded. (2)
4 liberatae eramus, we had been freed. (2)
5 portatae eramus, we had been carried. (2)
6 salutatae eramus, we had been greeted. (2)
7 collectae eramus, we had been collected. (2)
8 traditae eramus, we had been handed over. (2)
9 vulneratae eramus, we had been wounded. (2)
10 missae eramus, we had been sent. (2)
11 visae eramus, we had been seen. (2)
12 victae eramus, we had been conquered. (2)
13 iactae eramus, we had been thrown. (2)
14 ductae eramus, we had been led. (2)
15 coactae eramus, we had been compelled. (2)

Total: 30

Exercise 19.15

1 liber a viro sapienti scriptus est. (1)
2 dona ancillae bonae data sunt. (1)
3 senex hasta occisus est. (1)
4 pueri fortes a parentibus amantur. (1)
5 templa prope muros urbis aedificabantur. (1)
6 celeriter venite, puellae! villa vestra deleta est. (2)
7 navis ingens a nautis sapientibus aedificata erat. (1)
8 puella a regina fugere iussa est. (1)
9 ceteros cives in montes misimus. (2)
10 nauta prope forum occisus est. (1)

Total: 12

Exam Practice Answers

Exercise 19.16

1. 3rd person plural, present, passive. (3)
   Women are not praised by (their) cruel husbands. (8)
2. 3rd person plural, future passive. (3)
   The swift ships will be driven from the very small island tomorrow. (8)
3. 3rd person plural, imperfect, active. (3)
   All the swift soldiers were running into battle. (7)
4. 1st person plural, perfect, passive. (3)
   We have often been punished by the cruel master. (6)
5. 3rd person singular, future, active. (3)
   This girl won't be swift, will she? (6)
6. 3rd person plural, present, active. (3)
   Storms often destroy the swift ships. (6)
7. 3rd person plural, present, active. (3)
   Wise citizens never trust the worst/very bad kings. (7)
8. 3rd person plural, perfect, active. (3)
   The Romans persuaded many tribes. (6)
9. 3rd person plural, pluperfect, passive. (3)
   Many animals had already been killed by the cruel men. (8)
10. 3rd person plural, pluperfect, active. (3)
    Many swift citizens had already fled from the town. (8)

Total: 100

Exercise 19.17

1. dative; it follows **credo** (+ dat.) (2)
   Do not trust that soldier, o master! (6)
2. ablative; it means 'by' (2)
   The swift ships won't all be destroyed by that storm, will they? (9)
3. accusative; it is the object. (2)
   The wisest old men will never be able to do this. (7)
4. nominative; it is the subject. (2)
   Great rewards have often been given to these young men. (7)
5. accusative; it is the object. (2)
   The Romans therefore destroyed this whole city. (7)
6. genitive; it means 'of'. (2)
   The leader praised the courage of all the citizens. (6)
7. dative; it follows **credo** (+ dat.). (2)
   The very happy woman has trusted the wise girls. (6)
8. nominative; it is the subject. (2)
   That swift woman will be warned by this master tomorrow. (9)
9. nominative; it is the complement, agreeing with **senes**. (2)
   Few old men have been swift. (5)
10. accusative; referring to/being compared with the object, **tempestatem**. (2)
    The sailors had never seen a storm more savage than that (one). (8)

Total: 90

Exercise 19.18

1	10 years.	(2)
2	The walls had been destroyed and the temples set fire to.	(2)
3	They had not been able to escape.	(2)
4	They had left Troy and gone back to Greece in swift ships.	(4)
5	Many days.	(1)
6	The ships were driven there by a storm.	(2)
7	They always wanted to sleep and to stay in that land.	(2)

Total: 15

Exercise 19.19

Ulysses sent three sailors to the town of the Lotus Eaters. He ordered these sailors to look for food and water and to return to the ships within a few hours. He himself meanwhile remained with (his) other companions near the ships. They remained there for many hours. After seven hours however the three sailors had not returned. They were being held by the Lotus Eaters. The affair terrified Ulysses. He was worried. At last the worried leader decided to look for the sailors. He said these words to his companions: 'I am worried. Our friends have not returned. They have been absent for a long time. Perhaps they have been captured by the Lotus Eaters. I will look for them. Who can come with me?'

Total: 30

Exercise 19.20

1	a)	superati erant.	(1)
	b)	custodite.	(1)
	c)	liberabuntur.	(1)
2	neuter.		(1)
3	a)	perfect.	(1)
	b)	relinquo.	(1)
4	a)	ablative.	(1)
	b)	Because it describes time 'within which'	(1)
5	a)	inveniunt.	(1)
	b)	An invention is something that has been found out or discovered.	(1)

Total: 10

Exercise 19.21

1	milites fortiter semper ducis.	(5)
2	villam omnibus civibus ostendebamus.	(5)
3	currite, feminae! viri saevi veniunt.	(7)
4	dis clamabunt.	(3)

Total: 20

Chapter 20

Exercise 20.1

1   The boy, who is working in the villa, is tired. (9)
2   The girl, who was walking in the forum, was angry. (9)
3   The soldiers, who were conquered in the battle, marched into the mountains. (10)
4   The girls, who were playing in the wood, did not trust the master. (10)
5   You will praise the leader, who was fighting well, won't you? (8)
6   The woman, who loves her husband, is singing with her children. (9)
7   The bad boys caught sight of the master, who was reading a book. (9)
8   The guards freed the prisoners, who had been captured in the war. (9)
9   The sailors feared the sea, which was/because it was very deep. (8 + 1)
10 The wars, which were very long, always terrified the bold citizens. (10)

Total: 90 + 1

Exercise 20.2

1   The king led the citizens, whom he had punished, into the town. (9)
2   The girl, whom everyone likes, was singing in the temple with (her) friends. (11)
3   Everyone praises the wine which the master was drinking. (8)
4   We suddenly caught sight of the very deep river, which we will not be able to cross. (10)
5   The famous man, whom you saw in the forum, is dead. (9)
6   We do not like the work which is/because it is difficult. (8 + 1)
7   The women, whom the cruel king had punished, went out of the city. (10)
8   That is not the leader whom you wounded in the battle, is it? (10)
9   These are the slave-girls whom the master freed yesterday, aren't they? (10)
10 Everyone praised the very big temples which the famous king had built. (10)

Total: 95 + 1

Exercise 20.3

1   This is the good schoolmaster to whom I gave the money. (8)
2   These are the friends to whom you will give the wine. (7)
3   This is the girl whose father is famous and noble. (10)
4   These are the citizens whose master is cruel. (8)
5   The villa in which I live is very small. (7)
6   These are the boys with whom I often play. (7)
7   The boy with whom I am playing is my friend. (8)
8   The words which the master said were bad. (8)
9   There is the villa from which many slaves escaped. (9)
10 The noble woman whom you see is very bold. (8)

Total: 80

Exercise 20.4

1 cuius; genitive singular. (3)
   Menelaus, whose wife was Helen, was very famous. (9)
2 qui; nominative singular. (3)
   Paris, who was a Trojan prince, came to Menelaus. (10)
3 quae; nominative singular. (3)
   Paris immediately decided to capture Helen, who was very beautiful. (10)
4 quae; nominative singular. (3)
   Paris led Helen to the city of Troy in a ship which was very swift. (13)
5 qui; nominative singular. (3)
   Menelaus, who was very angry, sent many messengers to all the cities of Greece. (13)
6 quas; accusative plural. (3)
   The forces which Menalaus collected were large. (8)
7 cuius; genitive singular. (3)
   Troy was a town whose walls were very strong. (8)
8 quae; nominative singular. (3)
   Menelaus wanted to destroy Troy, which was a big city. (10)
9 quose; accusative plural. (3)
   The soldiers whom Menelaus praised were very brave. (8)
10 quam; accusative singular. (3)
   Helen, whom Menelaus loved greatly, was at last taken back to Greece. (11)

Total: 130

Exercise 20.5

1 virum qui in foro <u>ambulat</u> amo. (2)
2 cives qui prope muros <u>stant</u> spectamus. (2)
3 pater pecuniam <u>filiae</u>, quam amabat, dedit. (1)
4 ad forum <u>sine</u> amicis quos amat ambulat. (1)
5 <u>omnes</u> reginam quae urbem diu regebat amabant. (1)
6 Marce, cibum quem mihi paraveras <u>consumebam</u>. (1)
7 <u>hodie</u> magister (meus) librum quem mihi dedisti leget. (1)
8 multi senes <u>miseri/tristes</u> in templo quod aedificaveras sedebant. (1)
9 a <u>magistro</u> quem amas, Marce, laudatus sum. (1)
10 a <u>civibus</u> qui urbem custodiunt moniti sumus. (1)

Total: 12

Exercise 20.6

1 Eaten the lotus fruit. (1)
2 They were led out of the town of the Lotus Eaters to the ships by their companions. (3)
3 When they saw them they were very happy. (2)
4 Shouted to the guards in a loud voice. (3)
5 They were being compelled to stay by the Lotus Eaters. (2)
6 They did not want to return to their own land which they loved. (4)
7 a) quam;
   b) manere, redire, discedere;
   c) iacite, discedite. (3)
8 a) Perfect. (1)
   b) 3rd person plural. (2)
   c) iacio. (1)
9 a) Ablative. (1)
   b) It follows in (+ abl.) (1)
   10 possum. (1)

Total: 25

Exercise 20.7

1 Romani saepe milites boni sunt. (6)
2 ad villam currebant. (4)
3 cives corpora ex urbe portaverunt. (6)
4 lente ambulate, pueri. (4)

Total: 20

Exercise 20.8

1 ablative; it follows **ex** (+ abl.) (1 + 1)
Paris left the city of Troy and went to Menelaus.
2 accusative; it is the object of **duxit**. (1 + 1)
Paris captured Helen and led her to the city of Troy.
3 genitive; it means *of the friends*. (1 + 1)
Menelaus asked for the help of his friends and collected many forces.
4 accusative. It is the object of **collegit**. (1 + 1)
Menelaus collected great forces because he wanted to attack Troy.
5 nominative. it is the subject of **erat**. (1 + 1)
The Greeks attacked Troy and punished Paris, who was the son of the king.
6 accusative; it is the object of **defendebant**. (1 + 1)
The Greeks, with many weapons and bold forces, seized the city which the Trojans were defending.
7 accusative; it is the object of **servaverunt**. (1 + 1)
The Trojans fought bravely but did not save the city.
8 nominative; it is the subject of **oppugnabant**. (1 + 1)
The Trojans greatly feared the Greeks who were attacking the city.
9 accusative; it follows **prope** (+ acc.). (1 + 1)
At last the Greeks built a huge horse and left it near the sea.
10 ablative; it follows **ex** (+ abl.) (1 + 1)
Many soldiers ran out of the horse and destroyed the temples.

Total: 20

Exercise 20.9

1 insomnia; **somno** means *by sleep* and insomnia is an inabilty to sleep. (1 + 1)
On account of the difficult work you have been overcome with sleep.
2 feminine; **feminarum** means *of the women*, and feminine means to do with females. (1 + 1)
We saw a big crowd of women who were shouting in the street.
3 library; **libros** means *books*, and a library is where one keeps books. (1 + 1)
Because I want to be wise, I always read books.
4 audacious; **audaci** means *bold*, and audacious is another word for bold. (1 + 1)
Yesterday I gave a lot of money to the bold soldier.
5 virile; **viri** means *men*, and virile means manly. (1 + 1)
Many men are often killed in savage battles.
6 civilian, civic; **cives** means *civilians*, and civic affairs are those that affect civilians. (1 + 1)
On the fifth day the chief drove the citizens out of the town.
7 custody, custodian; **custodes** means *guards*, and custodians are guards who guard things, or
keep them in custody. (1 + 1)
The guards held the miserable prisoners in their villas.
8 convention; **convenerunt** means *they came together*, and a convention is when people come together. (1 + 1)
All the inhabitants came together in(to) the forum.
9 laudable; **laudabas** means *you praised*, and laudable means praiseworthy. (1 + 1)
No one trusted the faith of the leader whom you were praising.
10 senile, senility; **senis** means *of the old man*, and in old age, people can go senile or suffer from senility. (1 + 1)
The proud chief always punished the sons of the old man.

Total: 20

Exercise 20.10

1 nominative; it is the subject of **amabant**. (2)
   Many tribes who did not like the Romans asked for help. (10)
2 nominative; it is being compared with the subject of **habet**, and goes in the same case. (2)
   This farmer, who has more horses than he (has), is very happy. (12)
3 ablative; it follows **ab** (+ abl.) (2)
   That city, which was being attacked by the enemy for a long time, was at last seized. (11)
4 ablative; referring to time 'when'. (2)
   The city of Troy, which the Greeks were attacking for a long time, was captured in the tenth year. (11)
5 dative; it means to whom. (2)
   The sailors, to whom we gave very swift ships, will sail from the island today. (11)

Total: 65

Exercise 20.11

1 pluperfect. The farmers, who had worked in the fields for a long time, were forced to flee. (1 + 10)
2 imperfect. The animals which were (present) in the woods, were looking for food in vain. (1 + 10)
3 perfect passive. Many ships which the Romans had driven towards the island were destroyed
   by a storm. (1 + 11)
4 imperfect. The master wanted to punish that boy, didn't he? (1 + 7)
5 present. The old man, who wants to see (his) daughter, was walking through the mountains for
   many days. (1 + 12)

Total: 55

Exercise 20.12

1 **quam**, accusative. (2)
   The water was being brought by the slave into the villa which the famous queen had built. (12)
2 **qui**, nominative. (2)
   Masters do not often trust the unhappy citizens who like rewards. (11)
3 **quos**, accusative. (2)
   The small city was being attacked for many years by the enemy, whom we fear. (11)
4 **quorum**, genitive. (2)
   The old men, whose children were fighting in the war, were praised by the leader. (11)
5 **quem**, accusative. (2)
   Why did you give wine to the angry farmer whom we all fear? (10)

Total: 65

Exercise 20.13

1 celeriter. The soldiers quickly killed many animals with the arrows which we had. (1 + 9)
2 tandem. Many animals were killed at last by the soldiers with (their) spears. (1 + 8)
3 cur. Why were the Greeks attacking the the city of Troy for many years? (1 + 8)
4 iterum. Don't do this again, young man! (1 + 6)
5 fortiter. The soldiers, whose bodies we found, had fought bravely for (their) country. (1 + 9)

Total: 45

Chapter 21

Exercise 21.1

1	You carry.	(1)
2	It will be carried.	(1)
3	He has carried.	(1)
4	To carry.	(1)
5	I have carried.	(1)
6	They have carried.	(1)
7	They have been carried.	(1)
8	He has been carried.	(1)
9	He carries.	(1)
10	We shall carry.	(1)
11	He was carrying.	(1)
12	He was (being) carried.	(1)
13	They will carry.	(1)
14	They carry.	(1)
15	We had carried.	(1)
		Total: 15

Exercise 21.2

1	The man had carried much food.	(5)
2	Tomorrow I shall carry much money.	(5)
3	What are you carrying?	(3)
4	The soldiers bear arms.	(4)
5	Weapons were borne by the soldiers.	(5)
6	What will be carried by the soldiers tomorrow?	(6)
7	Food will be carried into the villa by the young men tomorrow.	(8)
8	The swords were carried by the soldiers.	(5)
9	What was the bold soldier carrying?	(5)
10	The old man was carrying a body.	(4)
		Total: 50

Exercise 21.3

1	Tomorrow we shall carry the best wine into the master's villa.	(8)
2	Our forces had seized another city.	(6)
3	The chief wanted to lead other soldiers into the battle.	(8)
4	The leader himself led (his) forces bravely into the battle.	(8)
5	The master always praised the same boys.	(6)
6	After the war some remained in the city, others returned across the mountains.	(12)
7	The king was guarding the guards themselves in the forum.	(7)
8	The king himself was guarding the guards in the forum.	(7)
9	We often listened to the same poet.	(5)
10	The woman always gave the same presents to her very dear husband.	(8)
		Total: 75

Exercise 21.4

1   accusative; it agrees with **regem**. (2)
     No one wanted to praise the same king. (6)
2   nominative; it agrees with **princeps**. (2)
     The chief himself won't kill the wretched inhabitants, will he? (7)
3   accusative; it agrees with **reginam**. (2)
     Who will lead the queen herself into the temple? (7)
4   accusative; it agrees with **corpora**. (2)
     We all carried other bodies from the battle. (8)
5   nominative; it agrees with **cives**. (2)
     On account of the long delay the dead citizens had been carried into the town. (9)
6   nominative; it agrees with **milites**. (2)
     The same soldiers were always fighting without the best weapons. (8)
7   ablative; it agrees with **silva**. (2)
     Those young men were waiting for the other friends in the same wood. (9)
8   ablative; it agrees with **gladiis**. (2)
     These men had wounded those animals with the same swords. (8)
9   genitive; it means *of him* or *his*. (2)
     The wife of the king herself will rule after his death, won't she? (9)
10 genitive; it agrees with **regis**. (2)
     The wife of the king himself won't rule after her (own) death, will she? (9)

Total: 100

Exercise 21.5

1   Ulysses and his companions had escaped from the Lotus Eaters. (2)
2   They sailed for many days and nights across the sea. (4)
3   They were driven by the wind and waves. (2)
4   At another land. (2)
5   A tribe of giants lived there. (2)
6   They prepared food on the shore. (2)
7   All night. (1)

Total: 15

Exercise 21.6

At first light they rose from (their) sleep. Ulysses himself and 12 friends, when they had collected (their) swords and spears, they left the shore and looked for food and water. Soon they came to a cave in which there was a lot of food. When the Greeks saw the food they were very happy. (And) because they did not want to die of hunger, they decided to carry the food to the ships. Ulysses ordered his friends to hurry. However, while they were carrying the food to the ships, the Greeks saw a huge giant.

Total: 30

Exercise 21.7

1   puellae parvae Romanos non timebant. (6)
2   feminae corpora militum in templum portabant/portaverunt. (7)
3   regem clarum numquam vidi. (5)
4   dominus/magister saevus puellam gladio terret. (6)
5   vir corpus ex oppido portat. (6)

Total: 30

Exam Practice Answers

Exercise 21.8

1. multi pueri et puellae in via saepe currunt. (9)
2. Romanus tristis reginam spectabat. (5)
3. corpus in templo invenerunt. (5)
4. pecuniam nautae tradidi. (4)
5. filius domini/magistri in montes iter fecit. (7)

Total: 30

Exercise 21.9

1. vinum bonum omnes amamus. (5)
2. magistri libros et vinum in naves semper portant. (9)
3. viri iter difficile non amant. (6)
4. filium ducis cepi. (4)
5. currite, pueri! magister venit. (6)

Total: 30

Exercise 21.10

Any suitable translation of **volo**, *i.e. 'wish,' 'want' or 'am willing', will be acceptable.*

1. We wish. (1)
2. He does not wish. (1)
3. He was willing. (1)
4. They were willing. (1)
5. He did not want. (1)
6. They did not want. (1)
7. You do not want. (1)
8. He wished. (1)
9. They wished. (1)
10. You want. (1)
11. You will not want. (1)
12. To be willing. (1)
13. They will want. (1)
14. He did not want. (1)
15. You were willing. (1)
16. You do not want. (1)
17. To be unwilling. (1)
18. They do not want. (1)
19. He will wish. (1)
20. They did not want. (1)

Total: 20

Exercise 21.11

1. accusative singular. (2)
   The Greeks wanted to attack Troy itself. (6)
2. nominative plural. (2)
   The other Greeks never want to work. (6)
3. nominative singular. (2)
   Ulysses himself wanted to return to Greece. (7)
4. nominative singular. (2)
   This boy does not want to sing. (6)
5. accusative singular. (2)
   The soldiers, however, did not want to do this. (6)
6. accusative singular. (2)
   The boy did not want to listen to another master. (6)
7. nominative singular. (2)
   Helen herself did not want to go to the city of Troy. (8)
8. nominative plural. (2)
   All citizens want to be wise. (6)
9. accusative plural. (2)
   The Romans wanted to conquer many other tribes. (7)
10. accusative plural. (2)
    The master does not want to frighten the same boys. (7)

Total: 85

Exercise 21.12

1. He says that the boy is running. (4)
2. He says that the boys are shouting. (4)
3. They say that the builder is working. (4)
4. They say that the soldiers are fighting. (4)
5. I hear that the bird is singing. (4)
6. I hear that the old men are sleeping. (4)
7. I believe that (my) mother is unhappy. (4)
8. We believe that (our) father is tired. (4)
9. I hear that the soldiers are coming. (4)
10. He hears that (his) son-in-law is dead. (4)

Total: 40

Exercise 21.13

1. The guard says that this prisoner is escaping. (6)
2. The guard said that these inhabitants were escaping. (6)
3. The master hears that this poet is approaching. (6)
4. He heard that these young men were approaching. (5)
5. I saw that all the farmers were working. (5)
6. I see that all the slave-girls are working. (5)
7. The master does not believe that the boy is working. (6)
8. The chief did not believe that the citizens were good. (7)
9. The father says that his son loves money. (7)
10. The girls said that this master was good. (7)

Total: 60

Exercise 21.14

1 We believe that all the teachers are wise.	(6)
2 I see that you are working well at last.	(6)
3 I hear that the girl is coming.	(4)
4 They say that the Romans are attacking the town.	(5)
5 The sailors said that a very big storm-cloud was approaching.	(6)
6 The leader shouted that he was a brave soldier.	(6)
7 The masters believe that the girls are working well.	(6)
8 We hear that that man has a loud voice.	(7)
9 I hear that the king himself is escaping with the plunder.	(7)
10 Marcus says that (his) mother prepares good dinners.	(7)

Total: 60

Exercise 21.15

1 He was very afraid.	(2)
2 He believed they were in great danger.	(3)
3 He believed he himself was also in great danger.	(2)
4 That the giant was approaching.	(2)
5 It was savage and had one eye in the middle of its head.	(4)
6 Hurry, go back into the cave!	(2)
7 a) se.	(1)
b) magnopere, iam, quoque, facile, mox.	(1)
c) iratissimum.	(1)
8 a) dative.	(1)
b) It follows **persuasit** which takes the dative.	(1)
9 Present infinitive.	(1)
10 a) Perfect.	(1)
b) credo.	(1)
11 a) exspectant.	(1)
b) An expectation is something that one waits for.	(1)

Total: 25

Exercise 21.16

1 prope equos magnos ambulabamus.	(5)
2 Romani multas naves aedificaverunt.	(5)
3 hostes cives hastis necaverunt.	(5)
4 currite, agricolae! venit.	(5)

Total: 20

Exercise 21.17

All the Greeks were very much afraid. They had already seen that Polypphemus was a very cruel animal. Ulysses, who was the boldest of the Greeks, decided to overcome Polyphemus with trickery. He took a cup full of wine and approached the giant. 'Drink this wine, Polyphemus,' he said. 'It is very sweet.' The giant took the wine and immediately drunk it. Then he shouted to Ulysses, 'This wine is very good. Give me more wine!' Ulysses gave him another cup, then a third, then a fourth. Polyphemus was soon drunk. He suddenly fell to the ground and fell asleep. When the Greeks saw that Polyphemus was asleep, they took a stake and thrust it into the giant's eye. He immediately got up and shouted in a loud voice, 'Who are you? Who is harming me?' He was blind and very angry. The Greeks wanted to escape from the cave.

Total: 100

Chapter 22

Exercise 22.1

1	adjective; proud	(2)
2	verb; I go	(2)
3	verb; I go out	(2)
4	(demonstrative) pronoun; this	(2)
5	(demonstrative) pronoun; that	(2)
6	verb; I go in	(2)
7	verb; I perish	(2)
8	verb; I go back	(2)
9	verb; I go across	(2)
10	noun; citizen	(2)
11	noun; body	(2)
12	noun; leader	(2)
13	noun; river	(2)
14	noun; enemy	(2)

Total: 28

Exercise 22.2

1	noun; journey	(2)
2	noun; soldier	(2)
3	noun; mountain	(2)
4	noun; ship	(2)
5	noun; father	(2)
6	noun; king	(2)
7	noun; city	(2)
8	numeral; one hundred	(2)
9	ordinal; tenth	(2)
10	numeral; one thousand	(2)
11	numeral; ninety	(2)
12	ordinal; ninth	(2)
13	ordinal; tenth	(2)
14	numeral; thirty	(2)

Total: 28

Exercise 22.3

1	noun; year	(2)
2	verb: I guard	(2)
3	noun; guard	(2)
4	noun; day	(2)
5	noun; faith	(2)
6	noun; hour	(2)
7	verb; I order	(2)
8	verb; I persuade	(2)
9	numeral; eighty	(2)
10	ordinal; second	(2)
11	verb; I seek	(2)
12	noun; thing, matter	(2)
13	noun; hope	(2)
14	noun; storm	(2)

Total: 28

Exercise 22.4

1	preposition; around	(2)
2	preposition; against	(2)
3	preposition; down from	(2)
4	preposition; on behalf of, in front of	(2)
5	preposition; without	(2)
6	noun; animal	(2)
7	adjective; swift	(2)
8	verb; I compel	(2)
9	verb; I wish	(2)
10	verb; I kill	(2)
11	noun; work	(2)
12	conjunction; and not	(2)
13	noun; night	(2)
14	noun; work	(2)

Total: 28

Exercise 22.5

1	verb; I drive	(2)
2	noun; chief	(2)
3	verb; I leave	(2)
4	adjective; difficult	(2)
5	adjective; brave	(2)
6	adjective; easy	(2)
7	adjective; all, every	(2)
8	adjective; sad	(2)
9	verb; I march, hurry	(2)
10	verb; I trust, believe	(2)
11	noun; race, tribe	(2)
12	adverb; meanwhile	(2)
13	adverb; slowly	(2)
14	adverb; almost	(2)

Total: 28

Exercise 22.6

1	(relative) pronoun; who	(2)
2	noun; sleep	(2)
3	verb; I find	(2)
4	verb; I send	(2)
5	verb; I show	(2)
6	verb; I place	(2)
7	verb; I hand over	(2)
8	verb; I come	(2)
9	verb; I carry, bear	(2)
10	adjective; other	(2)
11	(definitive) pronoun; the same	(2)
12	(intensive) pronoun; self	(2)
13	verb; I help	(2)
14	verb; I do not wish, am unwilling	(2)

Total: 28

Exercise 22.7

1 3rd singular, perfect passive, **cogo**. He was compelled. (6)
2 1st plural, present passive, **fero**. We are carried. (6)
3 1st singular, perfect passive, **mitto**. I have been sent. (6)
4 3rd plural, perfect active, **pono**. They have placed. (6)
5 3rd plural, perfect active, **rego**. They have ruled. (6)
6 3rd plural, perfect active, **possum**. They have been able. (6)
7 1st plural, pluperfect active, **laudo**. We had praised. (6)
8 1st plural, future passive, **video**. We shall be seen. (6)
9 3rd plural, perfect active, **volo**. They have wished/been willing. (6)
10 3rd plural, imperfect active, **curro**. They were running. (6)

Total: 60

Exercise 22.8

1 The horses are loved by the girls. (5)
2 They are often praised by the master. (5)
3 The old man is watched in the forum. (5)
4 The land is ruled by the queen. (5)
5 The prisoners are warned by the guards. (5)
6 No one is loved by the mistress. (5)
7 The citizens are guarded in the town. (5)
8 The animals are killed in the woods. (5)
9 The soldiers are overcome in the war. (5)
10 The ship is built by the sailors. (5)

Total: 50

Exercise 22.9

1 He ruled for many years. (4)
2 He stayed for five days. (4)
3 He departed in the sixth year. (4)
4 He will die within six days. (4)
5 They were present in the seventh hour. (4)

Total: 20

Exercise 22.10

1 They will be led into the city. (4)
2 They will be driven out of the town. (4)
3 He will be killed by the guards. (4)
4 The book was not being read. (4)
5 The dinner was being eaten slowly. (4)

Total: 20

Exercise 22.11

1 The young men were guarded for five days. (5)
2 The soldiers were killed on the second day. (5)
3 The inhabitants were driven against the walls. (5)
4 The difficult work was done at last. (5)
5 The swift ships had already been built. (5)

Total: 25

Exercise 22.12

1	The mother who did not love (her) children was present in the villa.	(10)
2	The chiefs who led their forces into battle were the best.	(10)
3	The old man who was found in the mountains soon died.	(9)
4	You praised the women whom everyone loved.	(7)
5	The king to whom you gave the money is the best, isn't he?	(9)
		Total: 45

Exercise 22.13

1	He says that the food is good.	(5)
2	We hear that the enemy are coming to the city.	(6)
3	They said that the leader was seizing the town.	(5)
4	He shouted that he wanted/was willing to fight.	(5)
5	I hear that the woman is singing.	(4)
		Total: 25

Exercise 22.14

1	filiam feminae tristis vocabas.	(5)
2	vinum prope murum posuit.	(5)
3	amici pecuniam hostibus numquam tradunt.	(6)
4	epistulam in flumen iecerunt.	(5)
5	pueri, ambulate lente!	(4)
		Total: 25

Exercise 22.15

1	amici boni pecuniam in templo semper inveniunt.	(8)
2	milites magistrum miserum e villa duxerunt.	(7)
3	currite, Romani! dominus viros malos in urbem misit.	(10)
4	nautas semper vocabam.	(4)
5	cives fortes contra hostes pugnabant.	(6)
		Total: 35

Exercise 22.16

1	Other giants, friends of Polyphemus.	(2)
2	Polyphemus's voice. They quickly hurried to his cave.	(1 + 2)
3	Why are you shouting? Who is harming you?	(2)
4	No body is harming me.	(1)
5	Ulysses had said his name was Nobody.	(2)
6	They were astonished and didn't stay there any longer.	(3)
7	They thought he was drunk.	(2)
		Total: 15

Exercise 22.17

Although Polyphemus had been wounded, the Greeks were afraid. Polyphemus himself was very angry. He believed that the Greeks wanted to escape from the cave. He therefore put a huge rock in front of the way in. On account of this, no one was able to go out. Then the savage giant fell asleep. In the cave with Polyphemus there were some sheep. These used to remain there for the whole night, and were unable to escape.

Total: 30

Exercise 22.18

1	accusative.	(1)
2	reflexive pronoun; himself.	(1 + 1)
3	ablative, because it refers to time 'when'.	(1 + 1)
4	liberat.	(1)
5	sub, ex.	(1)
6	a) perfect.	(1)
	b) exeo.	(1)
	c) exeo means *I go out*, and an exit is where one goes out.	(1)

Total: 10

Exercise 22.19

1	viri semper lente ambulabant.	(5)
2	tandem cives de montibus venerunt.	(6)
3	pecuniam patri dedi.	(4)
4	omnes cives deos timent.	(5)

Total: 20